POSSESSED VICTORIANS

*To my wonderful parents Charles and Pansylea
and to my brother, Charles, in memory*

for giving me a love of learning

Possessed Victorians

Extra Spheres in Nineteenth-Century Mystical Writings

SARAH A. WILLBURN
Trinity College, Hartford, CT, USA

ASHGATE

Published by
Ashgate Publishing Limited
Gower House
Croft Road
Aldershot
Hants GU11 3HR
England

Ashgate Publishing Company
Suite 420
101 Cherry Street
Burlington, VT 05401-4405
USA

Ashgate website: http://www.ashgate.com

British Library Cataloguing in Publication Data
Willburn, Sarah A.
   Possessed Victorians : extra spheres in nineteenth-century
   mystical writings. – (The nineteenth century series)
   1. Eliot, George, 1819–1880. Daniel Deronda 2. English
   fiction – 19th century – History and criticism 3. Spirit
   possession in literature 4. Identity (Psychology) in
   literature
   I. Title
   823.8'0937

Library of Congress Cataloging-in-Publication Data
Willburn, Sarah A., 1969–
   Possessed Victorians : extra spheres in nineteenth-century mystical
writings / Sarah A. Willburn.
      p. cm.—(The nineteenth century series)
   Includes bibliographical references and index.
   ISBN 0-7546-5540-7 (alk. paper)
   1. English prose literature—19th century—History and criticism. 2. Mysticism in
literature. I. Title. II. Series: Nineteenth century (Aldershot, England)

   PR788.M95W55 2006
   828'.808093824822—dc22

                                                                                    2005033640

ISBN-13: 978-0-7546-5540-4
ISBN-10: 0-7546-5540-7

Printed and bound in Great Britain

Contents

SECTION THREE: SUBJECTIVITY RECONFIGURED

List of Figures

The Nineteenth Century Series
General Editors' Preface

The aim of the series is to reflect, develop and extend the great burgeoning of interest in the nineteenth century that has been an inevitable feature of recent years, as that former epoch has come more sharply into focus as a locus for our understanding not only of the past but of the contours of our modernity. It centres primarily upon major authors and subjects within Romantic and Victorian literature. It also includes studies of other British writers and issues, where these are matters of current debate: for example, biography and autobiography, journalism, periodical literature, travel writing, book production, gender, non-canonical writing. We are dedicated principally to publishing original monographs and symposia; our policy is to embrace a broad scope in chronology, approach and range of concern, and both to recognize and cut innovatively across such parameters as those suggested by the designations 'Romantic' and 'Victorian'. We welcome new ideas and theories, while valuing traditional scholarship. It is hoped that the world which predates yet so forcibly predicts and engages our own will emerge in parts, in the wider sweep, and in the lively streams of disputation and change that are so manifest an aspect of its intellectual, artistic and social landscape.

Vincent Newey
Joanne Shattock
University of Leicester

Acknowledgments

Having begun research for this book in the last millennium, I have generated a long list of people I want to acknowledge for their help along the way. First of all, I'd like to thank Eve Kosofsky Sedgwick for smart reading tips, encouragement, and lending an ear to hear about the progress of *Possessed Victorians* from its earliest incarnation to its completion. I also thank Thomas Pfau for crucial comments and conversation throughout the writing of this project. Other kind readers from the twentieth century who have enriched this book include Michael Moon, Irene Tucker, Marianna Torgovnick, and Jennifer Thorn. After this work was first drafted, it was unwritten before being rewritten. During the stages of unwriting and rewriting, Michael Tratner has been an incredibly generous reader and interlocutor. Furthermore, I am building a small altar in my home to honor the sophisticated responses Justin Crumbaugh has given to this book during its completion. For their profusion of enthusiasm for this work and various forms of support over the long haul, I thank Marja Lutsep, Ross Forman, Craig Dworkin, Jon Rossini, Julia Kazaks, Rebecca Merrill, Elaine Morena, Peter Daniolos, Sasha Welland, and Mark McConnel. My parents, Pansy and Charles, and my beloved, Michael Penn, have each heard, read, and considered more about possessed Victorians than perhaps the Victorians themselves did; their perseverance and patience with me are astonishing. I am most thankful for them.

Several people have influenced this project more diffusely by being the types of readers I want this work to attract. These include Greg Tomso, Riche Richardson, Melissa Solomon, Paula Reiter, Natalie Houston, Jennifer Snead, Marc Brudzinski, James Tweedie, Jonathan Kahana, Bethany Schneider, Jean Fox O'Barr, Suzanne Daly, Susanne Mrozik, and Amy Martin. To this list I would also add two teachers who were among the first to kindle my interest in the intersection of nineteenth-century mystical culture and literature: Joss Marsh and Alex Chasin.

Feedback from participants at "Nineteenth-Century Sex," "Religion and the Fragmentation of Nineteenth-Century Culture," and "Nineteenth-Century Worlds," three INCS conferences in recent years, has improved this work.

For space and time to concentrate on this book, I am grateful to Amrita Basu and E.B. Lehman for a research year, 2002–2003, at Five College Women's Studies Research Center in South Hadley, Massachusetts. Fellow associates, Lynn Comella, Isis Nusair, Barbara Woshinsky, Natasha Pravaz, and Maureen Shanihan, provided much food for thought and helpful comments. For camaraderie I also thank my colleagues at Bryn Mawr, Mount Holyoke, Hampshire, and Trinity Colleges. For their combined intelligence and exciting conversation about matters of identity and subjectivity, I especially appreciate the organizers, Amy Martin and Michelle Stephens, and other members of the "Identities" faculty seminar in 2003–2004 at

Mount Holyoke. Special recognition also goes to Duke University, Mount Holyoke College, and Trinity College for providing research support.

Conversing about spirit possession with my students at Trinity in 2005, especially Jessica Kuskey, Kristin Allukian, Deana David, Caroline Blonski, Jennifer Tate, and Abby Cooper, has helped me to better articulate in this work the significance of mystical themes in nineteenth-century literature. For coaxing this project into its final form, I am grateful to Ann Donahue at Ashgate, as well as Laura Poole and Pat FitzGerald. Technical magic for the figures in this book has been provided by Sally Dickinson at the Watkinson Library of Trinity College and by Aime DeGreenier and Manisha Pradhananga of Information Technology at Mount Holyoke. More broadly, I would like to thank Eric Pumroy of Special Collections at Bryn Mawr College as well as the librarians at the British Library, at Perkins Library of Duke University, at the Mount Holyoke Library, at the Stanislaus County Public Library, and at the Watkinson Library of Trinity College, for fielding a great diversity of questions about locating various primary sources during the research and writing of this project.

Finally, to each reader who comes to this book, I thank you for sharing an interest in possessed Victorians.

Introduction

[Harris and a female follower] told me about the fays while I was up at Fountain Grove; how at first a little "Two-in-one" would move into a person's breast as soon as they could find entrance, and then clearing a space would begin to build their house; soon they would have a garden and plant fruit-trees; and then little baby fays would be born. The fays have many babies, and so they keep and keep on enlarging the spaces and filling them full of beautiful houses, gardens, and groves, till at last the whole being, to the very extremities of fingers and toes, is all a fairy universe, a world of loveliness. Just think of having lovely little fays bathing in the veins.

A sister in the New Life, Santa Rosa, California, 9 June 1881.[1]

The above journal entry, written by a member of a Swedenborgian cult, the New Life, imagines the body as a place for divine colonization by fairies. The sister's body becomes an extra sphere, "a fairy universe." Because of her mystical ontology, the sister records a civilization planted and growing in her body in several of her journal entries. To put it quite simply, she is possessed, and, as such, she defines civilization in a new way.

The New Life provides an example of nonautonomous personal identity in the nineteenth century that in turn suggests the way that the divide between visible and invisible was traversed by some Victorians, revealing places for communal life in extra spheres apart from the public and private spheres of the real world. Besides being a particularly intriguing cult documented by a number of primary sources (see Chapters 1 and 4 for further discussion), the New Life also provides an emblem for the central inquiries of this volume. What happens to identity in the nineteenth century when people are possessed, and how does spiritual possession refigure models for civilization and community? Filled with fairies, New Life subjectivity is very dynamic, transitory, recordable, and yet invisible: It's spectral.

Engels and Marx in the widely cited first words of the *Communist Manifesto* wrote that a "spectre is haunting Europe," in reference to the specter of communism menacing capitalist society.[2] A specter, by its very nature, can permeate without being visible. Marx and Engels, concerned with the material, economic conditions of life and labor, chose this metaphorical use of the *spectre* at the precise cultural moment when other specters were starting to haunt Europe and America. In 1848, spiritualism became an international phenomenon, originating in upstate New York and quickly sweeping the United States and Europe, bringing specters to the homes of all levels of society. Unlike Marx and Engels, spiritualists were not focused on the material,

---

1   A sister in the New Life, quoted in Herbert Wallace Schneider and George Lawton, *A Prophet and a Pilgrim* (New York: Columbia University Press, 1942), 525.

2   Friedrich Engels and Karl Marx, *The Communist Manifesto* [1848] (New York: Penguin Putman, 1998), 49.

economic conditions of life, symbolized by their possessions, but on the mystical and invisible conditions of spiritual life, enabled by spirit possession.

The double meaning of *possession*, something one owns, and *possession*, to be spiritually possessed by another, creates a bridge between the psychic economy of being possessed and the material possessions of liberal economy. Both economies value interiority and expression, but mystical economy, unlike liberalism, is not predicated on ownership of private property or on imagining self-possession (social atomism). Although I do not provide a causal analysis in this book, it seems that a deep cultural dissatisfaction with the liberal state is correlated with a social obsession with mysticism and spirit possession. Spiritualism arises at the height of the Industrial Revolution (and the related explosion of commodity culture) and at the time that the idealization of the bourgeois family is well under way. Spiritualism relies on the modeling of liberalism through embracing an opposite meaning of possession. Mysticism counters liberalism by assuming, procedurally, that interiority need not be predicated on privacy. My book examines how popular mystical culture answers liberal theory by negotiating between discrete and yet related systems of possession. Mystical visions provide a highly subjective and pervasive cultural technology of envisioning the state through imaginative creation and exploration of "extra spheres" visible to the inner eye. Through these visions, community can reside in the imaginary rather than only in the public sphere or the family circle. Mysticism responds to liberalism and, in a sense, I think it is illogical to try to think fully about either of them in the nineteenth century without thinking of the other. Just because scholarship of the last generation emphasized liberalism in defining the Victorian individual does not mean that mysticism did not also centrally define that individual. As this book will illustrate, many influential Victorians were possessed. This spirit possession, in turn, revises the definition of the liberal individual.

Possessed accounts characterize the most radical and conceptually political *uses* of the human body (and its individual) rather than the individual's most politically radical *expressions*. In nineteenth-century possessed accounts, the roles that radical body uses take include mediumship, clairvoyance, astral travel, and the transmigration of souls. These radical roles, or body uses, often work toward achieving such values as love, equality, beauty, pleasure, natural order, domination, subordination, promiscuity, and collectivity within a single body. The least common-denominator of the goals of nineteenth-century possessed accounts is not one of imagining the varieties of unfettered expression but rather of claiming that mystical personal expression can contribute to aligning society with imaginary spiritual harmony or confronting society with an exiled other.

Spiritualism claimed that spirits from "beyond the vale," could interact with the living within the context of a séance.[3] Certain people, with the ability to see or channel

---

[3]   See Richard Noakes, "Spiritualism, Science and the Supernatural in Mid-Victorian Britain," in *The Victorian Supernatural*, ed. by Nicola Bown, Carolyn Burdett, and Pamela Thurschwell (Cambridge: Cambridge University Press, 2004), 23–43, for a concise introduction to spiritualism. Noakes writes, "Most Spiritualists insisted that

spirits, were called mediums or spirit controls. Within spiritualist beliefs, the dead and disembodied could materialize at a séance, or their words and deeds could be channeled through the mouth and body of a medium. By the late 1850s, there were millions of spiritualists in England and America—involved with spiritualist practices that allowed a great widening of their imagined community memberships. Through valuing the unseen more than the visible, notions of personal identity and political economy changed for mystical practitioners. These changes in identity and political economy are, in turn, documented in many Victorian fictional and nonfictional accounts that serve as the source materials this volume analyzes.[4]

---

manifestations furnished proof of one or more of the following claims: the independence of spirit and matter, the survival and immortality of the spirit following bodily death, the eternal progress of all in the other world, and the possibility that under certain conditions spirits of the dead could manifest themselves to the living" (27).

[4] Humanities scholarship in the past 15 years has shown a critical interest in spiritualism, mysticism, the occult, and mesmerism. Spiritualism has been the focus of the works of some historians whose interest affiliates with women and political organization in terms of reform and suffrage as well as with spiritualist-based working-class labor organizations. See, for instance, Anne Braude's *Radical Spirits: Spiritualism and Women's Rights in Nineteenth-Century America* (Boston: Beacon Press, 1989) and Logie Barrow's *Independent Spirits: Spiritualism and English Plebeians, 1850–1910* (London: Routledge and Kegan Paul, 1986). Alex Owen's *The Darkened Room: Women, Power and Spiritualism in Late Victorian England* (Philadelphia: University of Pennsylvania Press, 1990) has explored spiritualism in terms of medical discourse surrounding women and hysteria. Additionally, Pamela Thurschwell's *Literature, Technology and Magical Thinking, 1880–1920* (Cambridge: Cambridge University Press, 2001) considers mediumship and *fin-de-siècle* literature against the backdrop of technology and psychoanalysis. More generally, some historians have explored spiritualism in terms of a faith-to-pseudo-science continuum. For instance, see Janet Oppenheim, *The Other World: Spiritualism and Psychical Research in England, 1850–1914* (Cambridge: Cambridge University Press, 1985). A few recent works, such as Daniel Cottom's *Abyss of Reason* (Oxford: Oxford University Press, 1991) and Bette London's *Writing Double: Women's Literary Partnerships* (Ithaca: Cornell University Press, 1999), have started to examine spiritualist practices (including mediumship and table-turning) in terms of discourse of what is considered rational and also in terms of mediumship as an example of collaborative authorship. Furthermore, Gauri Viswanathan's scholarship in *Outside the Fold: Conversion, Modernity and Belief* (Princeton: Princeton University Press, 1998) treats the occult practices of Theosophy through presenting the interface of Eastern mysticism and postcolonial theory. Other works, such as Alison Winter's *Mesmerized: The Powers of Mind in Victorian Britain* (Chicago: University of Chicago Press, 1998), have focused on cultural practices, such as mesmerism, which result in an altered state of consciousness. More generally, in the past few years there has been a revival of interest in Victorian religious and mystical practices marked by periodical essays such as *Victorian Literature and Culture*'s special topics issue in 2003 on Victorian religion. These works with diverse approaches rarely cover the same authors or historical personages because spiritualists and other popular mystical groups, unlike members of an organized religion, do not have a centralized institutional organization and history.

Many studies of Victorian religion concentrate on strongly routinized and centrally controlled religious communities, such as the Anglican Church, Catholicism, or the Anglo-Catholic revival in the 1840s. The study of mystical practices, though, better allows for the consideration of broad representational concepts like genre, trope, and characterization because the lack of a set religious form creates a wider array of representations. I study the representational and theoretical common features of mystical accounts. A recognition that millions of Victorian individuals participated in decentralized and somewhat nonhierarchical forms of mystical communities—through various types of spiritualism, Kabbalism, and Eastern practices—expands our understanding of Victorian culture and literature in a way that research on religions defined by their integral tie to the organizational units of church and state fails to address. Though studies of religion usually focus on one tradition, I address people and literary characters who did not make exclusive religious commitments. Understanding the complexity of individuals who held multiple mystical and religious affiliations at once, as is the case for someone who is both Anglican and a militant millenarian visionary (see Chapter 2), for example, pushes beyond a narrow understanding of what the phrase *Victorian religion* means.

Mystical accounts, furthermore, contain many depictions of how possession and imagined community affect subjectivity. Often scholars consider identity and agency in the nineteenth-century novel through the political and cultural context of the bourgeois individual. Instead, I consider how communities of readers and writers are influenced by the invisible beyond the bourgeois networks of family, property, commerce, and state. I analyze the ways in which mystical literature uniquely describes subjectivity, and I explain how literary representations of mysticism uniquely portray the individual.

A prevalent concept of an entitled and propertied Victorian citizen is described by C.B. Macpherson's phrase "possessive individual."[5] Macpherson defines nineteenth- and twentieth-century liberal-democratic theory in terms of its seventeenth-century roots in Hobbes and Locke. He claims that modern individualism, like that of the seventeenth century, has at its base a possessive quality:

> Its possessive quality is found in its conception of the individual as essentially the proprietor of his own person or capacities, owing nothing to society for them. The individual was seen neither as a moral whole, nor as part of a larger social whole, but as an owner of himself. The relation of ownership, having become for more and more men the critically important relation determining their actual freedom and actual prospect of realizing their full potentialities, was read back into the nature of the individual. The individual, it was thought, is free inasmuch as he is proprietor of his person and capacities. The human essence is freedom from dependence on the wills of others, and freedom is a function of possession

---

5   See C.B. Macpherson, *The Political Theory of Possessive Individualism: Hobbes to Locke* (Oxford: Clarendon Press, 1962). Although Macpherson is certainly not the most recent critical voice on the topic of Victorian political economy, he has set up the terms that subsequent scholars have addressed.

... Society consists of relations of exchange between proprietors. Political society becomes a calculated device for the protection of this property and for the maintenance of an orderly relation of exchange.[6]

Macpherson goes on to note that nineteenth- and twentieth-century political theorists, such as John Stuart Mill, have "reject[ed] those assumptions [that an individual's freedom is a function of possession and the protection of property is the primary goal of society] ... on the ground that the assumptions are morally offensive."[7]

The name "possessive" suits such characters as Henleigh Grandcourt in *Daniel Deronda*, Sir Willoughby in Meredith's *The Egoist*, or Mr Rochester in *Jane Eyre*. Although these characters might succeed in real life, because of their wealth and property, they rarely do so in Victorian fiction. Instead, they are killed, mocked, or punished. The power of narrative agency is transferred to those characters who are "possessed." For example, Jane Eyre has a skill from beyond the vale that allows her to hear Rochester call out her name from over two hundred miles away. More than a gothic convention, this extrasensory capacity creates a happy ending by replacing economic capital with spiritual capital. Victorian fiction frequently presents an effective identity as relying on an imaginary collective ethos (such as Daniel Deronda who, after undergoing a transmigration of souls, has a medieval Jewish scholar within, see Chapter 1) rather than on a privatized political entitlement.

Narratives of possessed individualism, in turn, have consequences for our notion of separate spheres. I conclude that the phrase *extra spheres* should be added to public and private spheres to adequately understand Victorian polity. Because of an absence of civic parity in the nineteenth century, a number of individuals envisioned their political participation to take place in a realm we would consider the imaginary. With this idea of possessed individualism, I reconsider the connection of property to rights and identity and show how extra spheres place stress on the public sphere.

Nancy Armstrong's influential work *Desire and Domestic Fiction* argues for the construct of the Victorian domestic woman who lives in a separate sphere as the prototype of the modern self with psychological interiority.[8] As Armstrong aptly notes, the female domestic (private) sphere is a construction that clearly can be found in many Victorian novels. In such works, this concept, which Armstrong calls female domestic dominance, appears over and over again as a trope. At home, women rule, and their political power comes indirectly through the influence they exert on the men in their lives and through the education of children, as well as through acts of household management and philanthropy (consider Lady Fawn in *The Eustace Diamonds* or Mrs Thorton in *North and South*). The paradigm of Victorian domestic dominance is a useful one because of its descriptive force, particularly in the way that it pertains to many period novels.

---

[6] Macpherson, *Political Theory of Possessive Individualism*, 3.

[7] *Ibid.*, 275.

[8] See Nancy Armstrong, *Desire and Domestic Fiction* (Oxford: Oxford University Press, 1987).

Nonetheless, this model does not tell the whole story because it does not address the way that Victorian mystical practices critique liberalism. There are ways to understand interiority in the novel beyond separate spheres and domesticity. The reliance of voting and other rights on the ownership of private property to nineteenth-century political theorists was recognized to be a dominant mode of social organization and also considered an offensive notion by many, such as John Stuart Mill, because of its opposition to a concept of natural, presocial, inherent human rights. Gillian Brown shows the role that domesticity takes in literary representations of a system of possessive individualism in nineteenth-century America. In her study of the domestic novel, she writes that "nineteenth-century American individualism takes on its peculiarly 'individualistic' properties as domesticity inflects it with values of interiority, privacy and psychology."[9]

I argue, however, that the values of interiority, privacy and psychology do not apply solely to *possessive* individualism. *Interiority* and *psychology*, but not *privacy* in its conventional usage often are represented in literary and nonliterary mystical accounts as existing outside of liberalism's claims that the ownership of private property allows for the fullest expression of individual identity and agency in the nineteenth century. In accounts of spirit possession, a mystical subjectivity, which I describe as possessed individualism, entails a nonautonomous and yet discrete psychology and interiority. Instead of having the ownership of private property as the necessary authorization for individual identity, a particular physical (not merely psychic) ability to become possessed is what authorizes individual expression and civic participation according to nineteenth-century writers of mystical accounts, including George Eliot, Charlotte Brontë, Samuel Guppy, Laurence Oliphant, Camilla and Newton Crosland, and Marie Corelli.

Another mid-Victorian writer, Elizabeth Barrett Browning, defines one type of spirit possession through her discussion of mediumship. In a letter to her friend Mary Hunter on New Year's Eve 1859 she writes, "Now let me write down my creed that you may see it with your two eyes clearly ... My theology is simply physical, and has to do with ordinary nature. I understand by a medium a peculiar physical adaptitude."[10] As Browning describes it, mediumship is a "physical adaptitude." Some people have inner vision and the ability to channel the dead and the disembodied, others do not have the physicality that would allow for such a thing. Browning introduces the simple theory that a medium *is* a physical aptitude and, furthermore, that theology can be simply physical. Becoming possessed is a certain physical ability that leads to cultural power, just as money and property are possessions that enable political power. By analogy, I argue that spirit possession is the authorizing principle of the possessed

---

[9] Gillian Brown, *Domestic Individualism: Imagining Self in Nineteenth-Century America* (Berkeley: University of California Press, 1990), 1.

[10] Elizabeth Barrett Browning, *A Note on William Wordsworth with a Statement of Her Views on Spiritualism* (London: Richard Clay and Sons, 1919), letter to Mary Hunter, 31 December 1859.

individual just as the ownership of private property is the authorizing principle of the liberal individual.

Mysticism, like liberalism, takes an interest in the individual and provides a model of political economy. As I have mentioned, even with the intense interest that nineteenth-century mystics of all stripes (spiritualists, pantheists, Buddhists, Kabbalists, etc.) take in the *individual* and his or her *interiority and expression,* a similar passionate interest in the conventional maintenance of privacy and private property does not follow. The mystics treated herein sometimes take an interest in the domesticity of privately owned residences in terms of how one might manage a house if one were perpetually in a trance state or what it might mean if the furniture at home walks and talks. Domestic space in these accounts is primarily a setting for becoming possessed rather than for showing the ownership of one's possessions.[11] Possessed accounts always grapple with what social organization looks like beyond the heuristic of liberalism in the nineteenth century. In nineteenth-century mystically inflected accounts—fiction and nonfiction, canonical and noncanonical—social organization often functions outside the paradigm that there is a dichotomy between the public and private spheres and outside the default that the real world matters most. Sometimes interiority, such as the interiority of a character in a novel, does not imply that a character is an individual personality moving through a landscape of privacy.

In hundreds of accounts that I have read, individualism is not possessive, is not domestic, is not privatized: It is possessed instead. Understanding possessed individualism as a heuristic explains more fully nineteenth-century social organization and conceptual political goals regarding the idea of community in literary and nonliterary accounts. Mystical accounts often provide insight into how to understand widening notions of free individual expression. Often, a discourse around nineteenth-century free expression adhered to the political goal of universal franchise. Mystical accounts, whether they were spiritualist, Kabbalist, fiction, or nonfiction, are also sometimes in favor of democratic principles. The goal of the movement toward universal franchise in Britain and the United States in the nineteenth century is for the political representation of every individual and that individual's free civic expression. In looking at the broader trends of mystical accounts, however, free expression is sometimes a means (rather than the end) to achieving a harmonious social whole (which is defined quite variously by distinct authors: from Heaven as a big Britain to living in a California orange grove that happens to be in an ur-Mother/Father's body). At other times, free expression is not a means for achieving social unification in mystical accounts but is a means to achieve greater particularity outside of the concept of a nation through anarchism or exile.

In her study of British liberalism from 1862 to 1891, Julia Stapleton writes about Cobden and Bright, two important "icons of middle-class Dissent," who sought to open the franchise beyond land owners. She notes their:

---

[11]   Displaying property ownership is evident in many Victorian novels, of course, including some works by Dickens, Trollope, Thackeray, and Hardy.

political force lying in the denunciation of the stranglehold on hereditary aristocracy over Church and State to the detriment of that sense of personal worth which they insisted belonged to all members of society. Their chief hope lay in the extension of the franchise …[12]

This concept of the personal worth of all members of society is also discussed by M.W. Taylor, who writes:

> Before the 1880s, "individualism" had been a pejorative term used to describe the allegedly egotistical and atomistic social theory of liberalism … . However, when the older generation of Radicals began to describe themselves as Individualists, they attempted to reverse its initially pejorative connotations by the sense in which it was used by these political thinkers "Individualism … referred to 'that condition in which a man is free to make the most and best of his individual talents, energies, and opportunities, without being checked or fettered by the State in those directions where he does not interfere with the liberty and possessions of other people.'" [G. Brooks, *Industry and Property*, London 1895, 236–7] … The advance of democracy brought about by the extensions of the franchise in 1867 and 1884 gave rise to the expectation that the new century would be characterized by a new type of politics aimed at securing the welfare of the mass of the population.[13]

This idea of liberalism, or individualism, as a person being free to make the most of individual opportunities without state interference as long as one's actions do not interfere with the liberty and possessions of others goes back to Locke and Hobbes. What Stapleton's and Taylor's historical accounts of liberalism in late-nineteenth-century Britain share is the nineteenth-century concept that individuals can have their fullest free expression through voting and thus the extension of the franchise. The right to vote, however, is not the only aspect of individualism considered important in the nineteenth-century.

Accounts of possessed individualism also focus on free expression unfettered by the state. The difference between possessed individuals and other individualists is the reason for their individualist love of free expression. Possessed individuals' accounts desire the creation of extra spheres that contain the concept of an extraterrestrial social whole rather than an earthly state, such as Britain (regardless of its moving toward universal franchise). The possessed characters, possessed authors, and possessed individuals (who are always writers or written about, and sometimes both) discussed in this work all desire an imaginary social unification regardless of the specific political objectives they may desire for the real world, such as franchise or no universal franchise, democracy, anarchy, monarchy, intentional community, or tribalism. I have developed the phrase *possessed individualism* because it helps

---

[12]   Julia Stapleton, ed., *Liberalism, Democracy and the State in Britain: Five Essays 1862–1891* (Bristol: Thoemmes Press, 1997), 7.

[13]   M.W. Taylor, *Men versus the State: Herbert Spencer and Late Victorian Individualism* (Oxford: Clarendon Press, 1992), 2–3.

explore the many character types in nineteenth-century literature that do not fit into the possessive individualism paradigm delineated by such scholars as C.B. Macpherson, Nancy Armstrong, and Gillian Brown.

Once the veil of liberal theory is lifted off Victorian literature, a blind spot of liberalism, which is possessed individualism, comes into focus. Encountering possessed individualism as a heuristic for reading nineteenth-century literature allows the reader to notice all sorts of possessed characters who are not circumscribed by a lack of property but are rather developed because of their physical aptitude for possession. My aim in this work is to explore these concepts of possessed characterization in several striking examples, fiction and nonfiction, to describe more completely the types of subjectivity and characterization represented in nineteenth-century literature. Reading canonical and noncanonical literature's references to mystical practices allows a rethinking of the project of social realism in the nineteenth-century novel. At the same time, interpreting nonfictional Victorian texts in terms of their literary elements, such as characterization, provides a fuller description of Victorian subjectivity.

This book is organized into three sections to accommodate the diversity of accounts of spirit possession that I address. The first section, "Possessed Individualism," sets out a definition of the central term. I address the philosophical structure of possessed individualism through a consideration of George Eliot's final novel, *Daniel Deronda*. Eliot explores what happens when, through mysticism, ideology physically inhabits the individual and identity becomes corporate rather than singular. The second section, "Extra Spheres," analyzes a number of accounts in terms of the assumptions and claims made about mystical practices. This involves threading through an analysis of spiritual vision, as a physical and metaphorical construct, as well as thinking about the influence of mysticism on the life of the individual. These possessed individuals who explore extra spheres collectively stand as a type of mystical hero/ine in accounts that share similar generic features. This serves as the broad topic of the final section of the book, "Subjectivity Reconfigured." In the two chapters of the third section, I incorporate Marxist theory about commodities and an analysis of gender constructs to explain how the concept of possessed individualism refigures an analysis of Victorian identity in the novel. I begin with an analysis of a walking and talking séance table named Mary Jane. Mary Jane, who behaves as a subject, provides an interesting inversion of the theory of commodity fetishism: Rather than being a commodity with an exchange value, she is a commodity who values exchanges. Mary Jane *inverts* commodity fetishism in the sense of transforming it through a reversal, rather than by opposing it. Finally, I take the mid-to-late Victorian genre of novels about trance states as a case to consider how possessed individualism disrupts society and how it rethinks the social body.

Nineteenth-century accounts of popular mystical practices offer a rich topography for considering alternative views, embraced by many Victorians, of identity, historical narrative, and social space. The concepts of possessed individualism and extra spheres link life in the realm of the real world to that in other realms, making common the interests and communications between the animate and the inanimate, the living and the dead, the material and the immaterial. Spirit possession leads to a new type of polity, making the century of mystical accounts a liminal and transitory space marked by playfully shifting boundaries. Viewing Victorian mystical culture helps rethink scholarly concepts of social institutions, political economy, and gender constructions. The concepts of possessed individualism and extra spheres can help us reconsider our own assumptions about how the nineteenth century constructed political selves and how definitions of an individual were formulated in mystical ways. When mysticism takes its rightful place beside liberalism in a description of Victorian political economy, we can see both the ontological structuring of the human body and the category of property centrally defining the individual in the nineteenth century.

SECTION ONE

POSSESSED INDIVIDUALISM

Chapter 1

Possessed Individualism in George Eliot's *Daniel Deronda*

"Just think of having lovely little fays bathing in the veins," ponders a sister in the New Life in 1881.[1] Daniel Deronda, the title character of Eliot's final novel, makes some similar observations.[2] Granted, he does not have fairies living in his body; all the same, he is possessed after Mordecai, on his deathbed, gives him a kiss that also provides transmigration. Daniel's individualism is not possessive but comes through being possessed—a point that anchors this chapter. Here I look at the important intervention that a study of popular religion makes in terms of understanding Victorian identity. *Daniel Deronda* serves as a prime example of how mysticism may reshape the concept of personal identity—a trope that occurs very frequently within Victorian fiction.

From the point of view of plot, the interweaving of narratives, and a sense of the day-to-day lives of many characters, *Daniel Deronda* is stylistically realist and epic not unlike *Middlemarch*.[3] However, Eliot's novel is different from her earlier work and from other coeval realist novels. Mystical concepts, such as "spiritual intermediators between the Divine fullness of light and the dim world—the pre-existence of the soul—the transmigration of souls—the magical operation of human actions on the higher world," ideas that Eliot includes in the notebooks she kept in preparation for the writing of *Daniel Deronda*, are embodied in the plot of this novel.[4] Character becomes

---

[1]   A sister in the New Life quoted in Herbert Wallace Schneider and George Lawton, *A Prophet and a Pilgrim* (New York: Columbia University Press, 1942), 525.

[2]   George Eliot's final novel, *Daniel Deronda* (1876), charts three years (1865–1867) in the lives of two central characters, Daniel Deronda and Gwendolen Harleth. Their stories only partially overlap. By the end of the novel, Gwendolen, who thought she would be happy marrying for money, has discovered the degree to which her husband is a sadist, has possibly drowned him, and ends being somewhat estranged from Daniel with whom she is in (a sort of) love. Daniel, in the same course of time, has decided not to court Gwendolen; is married to the Jewish, English-born Mirah; has discovered that he himself is Jewish as well as English; and has taken on the proto-Zionist mission of Mirah's elder, scholarly brother, Ezra Mordecai Cohen, who dies of consumption.

[3]   For a discussion that delineates genres in *Daniel Deronda* by gender, placing the Gwendolen plot in the genre of tragic romance and the Daniel plot in epic, see Sarah Gates, "'A Difference of Native Language': Gender, Genre, and Realism in *Daniel Deronda*," *English Literary History* 68.3 (2001): 699–724.

[4]   Eliot quoted in Jane Irwin, *George Eliot's Daniel Deronda Notebooks* (Cambridge and New York: Cambridge University Press, 1996), 175.

not a question of development on the model of a *bildungsroman* but a question of the ways in which ideology can inhabit/move in/move through a physical body. This novel, then, is a striking exploration of identity because it uses mystical concepts to refigure an effective, whole identity as a plural and collective one within a single body. This in turn reimagines the concept of colonization as a personal, not a global act.

By exploring what happens when ideology is considered as a force that can physically embody an individual, Eliot presents a model of subjectivity based on neither birth nor the possession of property but on being possessed by a collective spirit: what I call *possessed individualism*. This leads Eliot to describe a proto-Zionist movement in a most unusual way, a way that also might retheorize the operations of political culture at large. After Daniel comes to contain Mordecai, a medieval scholar and the spirit of Israel, it is as if the nation exists within Daniel as opposed to the other way around. The idea emerges that a community may rely on a model of possessed individualism. In Lockean terms, the nation itself takes the physical body of its citizen as its first property and proof of its viability and identity. Eliot is imagining what it would mean for a communal body to reside in the physical body of an individual: If people can become literally possessed with others, this, in turn, refigures civil polity.

Gwendolen Harleth and Daniel Deronda begin as characters who appear similar.[5] Because of their birth, both have uncertain futures. Gwendolen, because of her gender and her family's financial straits, must consider marrying for money; the opening scene of the novel shows her engaged in gambling, foreshadowing this destiny. Daniel has an uncertain future because he does not know who his parents are; therefore, he, too, is not in a direct line of inheritance. Insofar as their pasts have not set up their futures, Gwendolen and Daniel serve as two characters with whom Eliot can play out what identity may come to mean outside of fixed systems of inheritance, patrilineal descent, and marriage. Although they are seemingly alike at the beginning of the novel, Eliot portrays them making radically different economic decisions that in turn lead to their divergent fates in the novel.

Gwendolen as Possessive Individual

Gwendolen Harleth is presented in the first book of *Daniel Deronda* as a spoiled child. Early in the novel, Gwendolen is told by the artist Klesmer that she is unsuited to the stage—lacking the talent of a true artist. She feels angry and hurt in being judged by someone without preference given for her beauty and birth: "At that moment she wished that she had not sent for him: this first experience of being taken on some

---

5　　James Caron identifies an important part of this similarity: Gwendolen and Daniel are both rather passive in the novel and open to the powerful will of Grandcourt and of Mordecai, respectively. See James Caron, "The Rhetoric of Magic in *Daniel Deronda*," *Studies in the Novel* 15:1 (Spring 1983), 1–9, especially 2–6, 8.

other ground than that of her social rank and her beauty was becoming bitter to her."[6] Discovering that she cannot "achieve substantiality for herself and know gratified ambition without bondage" leads Gwendolen to agree to the sadistic Grandcourt's proposal of marriage (295; ch. 23, 348; ch. 27).

Gwendolen seeks identity through material possessions. Her father's firm, Grapnell, has failed. Having no wealth of her own, Gwendolen spends the first portion of the novel getting the wealthy and older Grandcourt to marry her. Daniel and his "uncle," Sir Hugo Mallinger, have just discussed the possibility of Grandcourt and Gwendolen marrying in the following exchange:

> "I suppose pedigree and land belong to a fine match," said Deronda, coldly.
>
> "The best horse will win in spite of pedigree, my boy. You remember Napoleon's *mot—Je suis un ancêtre*," said Sir Hugo, who habitually undervalued birth, as men after dining well often agree that the good of life is distributed with wonderful equality.
>
> "I am not sure that I want to be an ancestor," said Deronda. "It doesn't seem to me the rarest sort of origination."
>
> "You won't run after the pretty gambler, then?" said Sir Hugo, putting down his glasses.
>
> "Decidedly not."
>
> This answer was perfectly truthful; nevertheless it had passed through Deronda's mind that under other circumstances he should have given way to the interest this girl had raised in him, and tried to know more of her. But his history had given him a stronger bias in another direction. He felt himself in no sense free (201–2; ch.15).

In fact, Daniel comes to find that he is not free. His Jewish heritage, as it is revealed to him, infuses him with a larger social and religious identity. Gwendolen, in contrast, journeys through a quest for possessive individualism.

Gwendolen, a gambler through and through who "felt the possibility of winning empire," marries Grandcourt in spite of the revelation that he has a common-law wife, Lydia Glasher, and illegitimate children (95; ch. 6). Gwendolen wants the influence of his wealth and status and has decided through her marriage to be part of a system of possessive individualism. It should be noted that Victorian female and male characters could never operate *in the same way* within the dominant discourse of possessive individualism. Lacking suffrage and legal parity, a female subject, by definition, is dissimilar to a male subject in Victorian England. Yet, this does not preclude choice in the novel.[7] Not only does Gwendolen decide to marry Grandcourt, she later chooses to let him drown. It may not surprise the reader that she does not rescue him when he falls off the boat in the Mediterranean. In a somewhat traditional Eliot move, characters whom she judges or has finished exploring allegorically get knocked off the boat, so

---

6   George Eliot, *Daniel Deronda* (New York: Penguin Books, 1986), 300; ch. 23. Future references from this work will be cited by page number and chapter in the text.

7   Caron makes a version of the point I make, that Gwendolen has agency, when he writes of Grandcourt's temporary "abrogation" of Gwendolen's will in Eliot's novel: "Surely, this is no necessitarian world where human choice is futile" (6).

to speak—like the Tullivers in *Mill on the Floss*.[8] Grandcourt is not written out of the novel just because he is cruel and unsavory, though; he represents a system that is cruel and unsavory that Eliot does not like. It seems that his drowning makes a statement about undoing a specific system of English political economy: possessive individualism, as Macpherson termed it. Eliot seems at once in describing the person, property, and demise of Grandcourt and in describing Gwendolen's desire to be affiliated with his property to present an individualism that relies on a possessive quality and to show how this reliance is morally offensive.

Not even the death of Grandcourt, who is a possessive individual if ever there were one, improves matters for his widow. The fate of the youthful widow is at first perceived by her cousin Rex (who was her previous ardent suitor) as being particularly rosy. On hearing of the demise of Grandcourt from his aunt, (Gwendolen's mother) Mrs. Davilow, Rex asks his sister Anna to tell their father, the Rector, about it while Rex "stay[s] in the shrubbery for ten minutes" to think (776; ch. 58). His thoughts are narrated as follows:

> In Rex's nature the shame was immediate, and overspread like an ugly light all the hurrying images of what might come, which thrust themselves in with the idea that Gwendolen was again free—overspread them, perhaps, the more persistently because every phantasm of a hope was quickly nullified by a more substantial obstacle. Before the vision of "Gwendolen free" rose the impassable vision of "Gwendolen rich, exalted, courted;" and if in the former time, when both their lives were fresh, she had turned from his love with repugnance, what ground was there for supposing that her heart would be more open to him in the future? (776–7; ch. 58)

Rex immediately presumes that the influence and possessions of the dead Grandcourt will transfer to his widow—which in effect is exactly what Gwendolen had hoped to have from the marriage from the start. Furthermore, Rex subscribes to a logic of possessive individualism: A Gwendolen, "rich, exalted, courted," is in Rex's hypothetical thinking even more justified in rejecting his love because of the supposed transfer of Grandcourt's possessions—her freedom to choose is constituted or intensified by her becoming a woman with possessions. Grandcourt's will, however, is not what it is imagined by Rex to be.

The actual inheritance is not so kind to the widow. She has been disinherited in favor of Grandcourt's young, illegitimate son. She is given £2,000 a year and a home at the remote Gadsmere, the former residence of Lydia Glasher (782–3; ch. 59). The decision to marry Grandcourt has turned into Gwendolen's bondage, and the will of her dead husband is designed to be an extinguisher on her. Gwendolen, who is not with child, comes to have an interchangeable fate with Grandcourt's illegitimate son. Grandcourt's will does not delineate a unique fate for Gwendolen versus Lydia. One of them will be banished to Gadsmere, and he does not care who it is—because it is

---

8   George Eliot, *The Mill on the Floss* [1860] (New York: Washington Square Press, 1956).

only a son that he distinguishes with the possibility for proprietorship in his will. This constitutes a fine example of the exclusionary logic of possessive individualism.

Gwendolen seems rather to disappear in this novel—her character becomes regressively undeveloped, and her speech becomes fragmented. She becomes lost in her guilt in having married Grandcourt in the first place and in having wanted to kill him. She has made a giant mistake—she has married to gain possessions, perhaps feels wrong for denying Lydia's place in the process, and has discovered in the bargain that she hates Grandcourt. In effect, when she lets him drown, she puts a stop to a certain type of economic exchange that is morally offensive to her insofar as it has created "misery" (757; ch. 56).

This economy, though, is not separate from her; she falls away along with the system of possessive individualism in this novel. In her place, inheriting the possessions that she would have liked, is a young, illegitimate Henleigh, who is presented to the reader in the novel as a "boy ... seated on the carpet at some distance, bending his blond head over the animals from a Noah's ark, admonishing them separately in a voice of threatening command, and occasionally licking the spotted ones to see if the colours would hold" (390; ch. 30). He is a deified child who, by a chance and untimely drowning, has his illegitimacy legitimated—his possessive nature presumably will grow beyond admonishing the small animals and licking the spotted ones. He also, like Noah, is saved from the flood, while his father drowns. Grandcourt's possessions do not pass to Gwendolen through their marriage. Because Gwendolen is not allowed to be an independent proprietor, she is not allowed property, empire, or influence: Her father's company and Grandcourt have both failed her.

Daniel as Possessed Individual

While Gwendolen remains possessive in this novel, Daniel becomes increasingly possessed.[9] Gwendolen's story is truncated, solitary, and disconnected, but Daniel's

---

[9]   Several critics have noted the way Gwendolen is possessed by superstition or prophesy. I here warn of a potentially confusing equivocation in the term *possession* that I have previously discussed in the Introduction to this work: Some possession can be conscription, as it is at times for Gwendolen, whereas spiritual possession creates increased power for Daniel. Gwendolen is possessed by superstition and prophecy that often paralyze her with fear of Grandcourt and fear of her own agency. Superstition is a possession that is entirely outside of the guiding control of the possessed. See Nicolas Royle, *Telepathy and Literature: Essays on the Reading Mind* (Oxford: Basil Blackwell, 1991), especially 91–6, and Pamela Thurschwell, "George Eliot's Prophecies: Coercive Second Sight and Everyday Thought Reading," in *The Victorian Supernatural*, ed. Nicola Bown, Carolyn Burdett, and Pamela Thurschwell (Cambridge: Cambridge University Press, 2004), especially 90–91 and 98–100. In turn see James Caron, "The Rhetoric of Magic in *Daniel Deronda*," 6. Nicolas Royle writes of Gwendolen that "her feelings" are "as 'dim and alarming as a crowd of ghosts'" (Eliot quoted in Royle, 92).

story is more expansive, historical, and communal. Daniel's lack of real property does not become a limit on his agency in the novel, as it does for Gwendolen. Eliot presents him as operating under a different type of political economy through his full acceptance of the mystical elements of his religious and ethnic identity.

Eliot uses the character of Daniel as an allegorical figure who represents a new way of thinking about agency: possessed agency rather than autonomous agency. Unlike an *Exorcist*-esque plot in which possession equals torture for the host body, Daniel's possession equals greater agency and clarity of thought for him. To consider Eliot's characterization of the possessed is to widen an understanding of how subjectivity functions in Victorian literature and culture outside of liberalism. Possessed individualism is a way of describing the changing consciousness of the individual. The individual can no longer be imagined or hypothesized to exist exclusively as a single, autonomous entity. The transnationalism of the nineteenth century increasingly questions the rugged individual, the prepolitical individual, and the government-free individual. I argue that with these imaginings, possessive individualism by necessity must also disappear as a singularly viable political theory. A new political theory, mystical in its provenance, appears. Possessed individualism allows for the actual workings of polity, which are inherently corporate: The individual can only be part of the body politic and cannot successfully exist in isolation. This possessed model of the individual looks very different from how the Western individual is typically understood in the nineteenth century through possessive individualism. Reginia Gagnier writes of Marx's essay "On the Jewish Question" that:

> Marx understands equality in bourgeois society as the state of being equally regarded as a self-sufficient monad; liberty as liberty in isolation, determined by the extent of one's means, or property; security as the assurance of egoism; and property as that which belongs wholly to oneself alone, pertains solely to one's self-interest. In the liberal state, political man, or abstract man with formal rights, simply preserves established property rights. For Marx, the "Jewish Question," the question of the specificity and autonomy of Jews, dissolved in the face of the total occupation of modern life by market relations. Christians and Jews are indistinguishable in market society, where contract rather than community dominates social relations. Marx, in short, was so blinded by market relations that he could not see

---

Furthermore, as Thurschwell argues, "In Daniel Deronda, prophesy works splendidly for men, but disastrously for women" (100). She claims, "*Daniel Deronda* tells a story of two kinds of prophetic transmission which cannot be easily separated but which seem unable to coexist; that of the fearful English woman and the powerful Jewish mystic" (102). Mordecai, also English like Gwendolen, definitely garners his power from his inner mystical life. Thurschwell's point that Gwendolen and Mordecai are different types of prophetic figures that cannot coexist is important because being possessed by superstition rather than by social vision can be terrifying, as it is for Gwendolen. In this novel, as I will show in the remainder of this chapter, Gwendolen's marriage conscripts the individual in a possessive system while Daniel's embodiment expands an individual in a possessed system.

the communities—of Jews and Christians—that were not coextensive with them. Rather he saw social atomism.[10]

In describing Marx's views, Gagnier also elucidates the view that "property is the basis of human rights under capitalism—a theory that would later be elaborated as 'possessive individualism.'"[11] In *Daniel Deronda*, Eliot goes beyond a discourse linking property to rights in describing unconventional models for political selfhood at a time when social definitions and practices are in flux. This time of instability, as well as the relative merits of various competing political and social values (unity, autonomy, independence, interconnectedness), is reflected in the wobbly narrative of selfhood explored through the characterization of Daniel. He shows possessed individualism at work: He is an allegorical figure for a distinct type of political individual that Eliot explores in this novel.[12]

Daniel Deronda ends with Eliot describing a kiss that constitutes a transmigration of souls. In the novel's final scene, scholarly Jew Ezra Mordecai Cohen:

> took a hand of each [Deronda and Mirah] in his and said looking at Deronda, "Death is coming to me as the divine kiss which is both parting and reunion—which takes me from

---

[10] Regenia Gagnier, *The Insatiability of Human Wants: Economics and Aesthetics in Market Society* (Chicago: University of Chicago Press, 2000), 75.

[11] *Ibid.*, 75.

[12] An interesting look at the philosophical underpinnings of Eliot's idealism has been made by Sarah M. Putzell-Korab, "The Role of the Prophet: The Rationality of Daniel Deronda's Idealist Mission," *Nineteenth-Century Fiction* 37:2 (1982): 170–187. Putzell-Korab overviews the philosophical roots—German, classical, and medieval Jewish—of Eliot's take on idealism. She writes, "Like the Cabbalists, Mordecai and Deronda envision more than individual unity with an ideal; they envision what Heschel describes as a communal unity in which 'one's own bliss is subordinated to the redemption of all,' so that, according to his quotation of *The Zohar*, all may 'rise and attach [them]selves to the *En Sof* [idea],' and thus achieve the oneness of the upper and lower worlds" (175). Somewhat similarly, George Levine reads Eliot as under the influence of her partner, George Henry Lewes, finding her "realism" to be a subset of understanding the invisible unity of the cosmos. He writes, "Daniel must find an external reality that will allow him to recompose the self, free, however, of the conventions of personality" (22). See George Levine, "Eliot's Hypothesis of Reality," *Nineteenth-Century Fiction* 35:1 (1980): 1–28. He also notes, "Idealization and abstraction are, then, the tools of science and of the Jewish sections of *Daniel Deronda*. Daniel is almost literally abstracted from the contingencies of the sensible world, even from the contingencies of selfhood ... In the character of Daniel, George Eliot suggests that the very conditions of altruistic science depend upon alienation ... In her last novel she was taking the risk of knowledge in a Lewesian enterprise of projecting and testing a vision of the world that reaches beyond the fragments and discontinuities of ordinary perception to the continuous and perdurable cosmos ... George Eliot must strain the novel beyond the limits of realism to find an ideally illuminated space" (20, 16).

your bodily eyes and gives me full presence in your soul. Where thou goest, Daniel, I shall go. Is it not begun? Have I not breathed my soul into you? We shall live together." (882; ch. 70)

Ezra has no words for his sister but just for his brother-in-law, into whom he has breathed his soul.[13] Death is a "divine kiss" to Mordecai, and metaphorically he has breathed his soul into Daniel.[14]

Death is the kiss that removes Mordecai from Daniel's eyes and places him in his soul. The ending is no surprise; the reader sees it coming hundreds of pages in advance. Even before Daniel knows his mother and his ethnicity, we know of his future through the vision of Mordecai. Chapter 38 begins:

> "SECOND-SIGHT" is a flag over disputed ground. But it is a matter of knowledge that there are persons whose yearnings, conceptions—nay, travelled conclusions—continually take the form of images which have a foreshadowing power: the deed they would do starts up before them in complete shape, making a coercive type; the event they hunger for or dread rises into vision with a seed-like growth, feeding itself fast on unnumbered impressions. They are not always the less capable of the argumentative process, nor less sane than the commonplace calculators of the market: sometimes it may be that their natures have manifold openings, like the hundred-gated Thebes ... No doubt there are abject specimens of the visionary, as there is a minim mammal which you might imprison in the finger of your glove. That small relative of the elephant has no harm in him; but what great mental or social type is free from specimens whose insignificance is both ugly and noxious? (527–8; ch. 38)

In this narration of the visionary type, which is Eliot's first analysis of Mordecai in Book 5, Eliot forges a connection between physical and spiritual travel. Mordecai, as a visionary, "travels" to his conclusions. For him, to see a vision is to have a vision grow from a seed to a plant fed on the impressions of "second sight." That is, he travels through spiritual vision and the vision he has is internal to his own body, which is like the city of "hundred-gated Thebes." He is, then, part of the physical plant of the idea of Israel. He is a visionary tourist through his "second sight." This passage makes it unclear whether Mordecai will remain a "minim mammal" or grow into "a great mental

---

[13] Ezra Mordecai Cohen's name is symbolically rich. Ezra in the Hebrew Bible is the character who, after the Babylonian Exile, returns to Mount Zion to rebuild the temple, which had been destroyed by the Babylonians. Ezra Mordecai the character achieves his goal of having Daniel become his "executive self" by this transmigratory kiss on his deathbed. Through this kiss, he has colonized Daniel's body, making it his "second temple."

[14] Mordecai's history is narrated on pages 550–64, which is most of chapter 40. He, too, is of English birth and has learned Hebrew, which he has exclusively used for writing since he was a youthful student in Holland and Germany, and he has become a scholarly repository of Jewish history and theology.

or social type"—a visionary elephant.[15] (This is also a joking analogy that Eliot is making between Mordecai, the visionary elephant, and MP Laurence "the visionary" Oliphant—see next section.) The reader is asked to consider the possibility of Mordecai as an elephant visionary because this is the question that Daniel considers: "Mordecai['s] ... figure had bitten itself into Deronda's mind as a new question" (528). Mordecai at this point in the novel is a plant, a city, and someone who bites Daniel's mind.

Mordecai is a conceptual city-plant-elephant-Cabbalist-Israelite looking for a new body to replace his consumptive dying body. Eliot paves the way here for a strange and yet efficacious concept that an individual can become a collective self, a community in one body. Mordecai is similar to other visionaries in that "the deed they would do starts up before them in complete shape." Chapter 38, in fact, goes on to imply that the deed Mordecai would do is Daniel:

> Hence it was that his imagination had constructed another man who would be something more ample than the second soul bestowed, according to the notion of the Cabbalists, to help out the insufficient first—who would be a blooming human life, ready to incorporate all that was worthiest in an existence whose visible, palpable part was burning itself fast away ... And as the more beautiful, the stronger, the more executive self took shape in his mind, he loved it beforehand with an affection half identifying, half contemplative and grateful. (530; ch. 38)

The "more beautiful, the stronger, the more executive self," the one who will help out Mordecai, turns out to be Daniel. Mordecai's "half identifying" affection becomes a complete identification by the time Mordecai asks Daniel the rhetorical question: "Have I not breathed my soul into you?" (882; ch. 70). Daniel becomes the "something more ample than the second soul bestowed": Mordecai's vision ultimately transforms Daniel through a "seed-like growth" from a "minim mammal" (touched on like a finger on a tiny elephant in glove) to the "executive self": "The deed" in "complete shape" is Deronda. "[Mordecai's] imagination had constructed another man" (530; ch. 38).[16]

---

[15]   A recurrence of the image of the visionary as elephant also occurs in Hans Merrick's letter to Daniel Deronda about Mordecai that refers to Mordecai as allegorical: "I find him really a sort of philosophical-allegorical-mystical believer ... [Mordecai's] mind seems so broad that I find my own correct opinions lying in it quite commodiously, and how they are to be brought into agreement with the vast remainder is his affair, not mine. I leave it to him to settle our basis, never yet having seen a basis which is not a world-supporting elephant, more or less powerful and expensive to keep. My means will not allow me to keep a private elephant" (705; ch. 52). For Hans, elephant visionaries are too expensive to be privately kept.

[16]   Amanda Anderson constructs a somewhat different argument about Daniel and Mordecai, portraying Daniel as not fully subscribing to Mordecai's mystical vision. She describes Deronda as a thinking autonomous agent who subscribes to Mordecai's goal, while he remains not under the influence of Mordecai's mystical vision. Though I certainly think that Daniel is an effective agent in this novel, his efficacy does not stem from his rational decision to take on a proto-Zionist mission. Nonetheless, I agree with Anderson about

Mordecai becomes spiritually incorporated into Daniel's physical body by first being a figure who bites itself into Daniel's mind and then later by being a figure who kisses Daniel on the lips to transmigrate his soul into Daniel's body. When Mordecai makes Daniel his "executive self," they create a nationalist and ethnic Jewish community, but one located in a body, not a place (530). They therefore create a Jewish diaspora community. Mordecai is the only character who gets to the promised land when he breathes his vision into Deronda's body.

For Daniel, it is not "uncle" Sir Hugo who forms his path as an aristocrat, nor is it studying the law that gives him vocation. Likewise, it is not his fate to be with Gwendolen, and his reunion with his mother does not lead to much beyond anger and revolt, emotionally, although it does, of course, establish his Jewish descent. Instead, Mordecai's spiritual will leads to Daniel's individualism in much the same way that Grandcourt's testamentary will denies Gwendolen's individualism. Daniel becomes possessed. It is not a birth family, a guardian, or a marriage that is allowed to produce a heroic individual in this Eliot novel; it is, instead, religiously sanctioned imagination and imaginative possession that transmigrates Daniel into identity here. In fact, *Deronda* is an anagram for *adorned*, and Daniel does become the adorned nonautonomous "executive self" for the Jewish community in this novel.

Daniel agrees to take on Mordecai's mission of traveling to the East because he has no independent choice to make in the matter. Mordecai slips into first-person plural and then to third-person plural and finally back to a second person address that incorporates all of Israel into Daniel's veins:

> And you would have me hold it doubtful whether you were born a Jew! Have we not from the first touched each other with invisible fibres—have we not quivered together like the leaves from a common stem with stirrings from a common root? I know what I am outwardly—I am one among the crowd of poor—I am stricken, I am dying. But our souls know each other. They gazed in silence as those who have long been parted and meet again, but when they found voice they were assured, and all their speech is understanding. The life of Israel is in your veins. (633–4; ch. 46)

Deronda is not just any body to Mordecai; he is part of the same body: They have Israel in their veins. They quiver as one, and all their speech is understanding (they are already spoken for). They are leaves that quiver from a common stem (they are nonautonomous vegetation, not autonomous animals) and they touch each other with "invisible fibres," an image that borrows from the electric and magnetic language of

---

Eliot in several big-picture details, such as, "Throughout her work, familial and communal and cultural embeddedness is for Eliot both a fact of human existence and a value that must be cultivated in the face of modernity's damaging dispersions" (51). My argument about Daniel differs from Anderson's, though, in that a mystical plural identity need not preclude effective agency or individual personality. Autonomy is not a precondition of agency. See Amanda Anderson, "George Eliot and the Jewish Question," *Yale Journal of Criticism* 10.1 (1997): 39–61.

nineteenth-century mesmerism and spiritualism. Daniel becomes a materialization of the ghostly history of Israel. He cannot do otherwise in the novel (he is constantly described with an antinomian lack of free will) because he is historical materialism. He is a character who is in this novel only partially individualized.[17] He is not like, for instance, Grandcourt, an autonomous proprietor: He acts for and with Mordecai and his nation within. Israel is not a nation in a state, it is a diasporic nation located in Daniel's body. Daniel has far more ability to act as an agent than someone with no other one within—namely, the alienated Gwendolen whose story line unravels with the death of her husband and end of her marriage.

Daniel is also an incarnation of what has already occurred. He, in fact, does not say a thing in response to Mordecai's comment: "Deronda sat perfectly still, but felt his face tingling. It was impossible either to deny or assent" (634; ch. 46).[18] Eliot presents subjectivities that are not in history but are identical to history—a concept connected to the Kabbala, to Buddhism, and to Victorian spiritualism/mysticism.[19]

The kiss that ends *Daniel Deronda* is a rite of passage, allowing Mordecai's soul, through transmigration, to join Deronda's soul in Deronda's body. This kiss physically united souls that are already linked spiritually. It is not, then, just a symbolic act, it actually serves to transfer the title of Mordecai's agency and the life of Israel into Daniel's body within the mystical rhetoric and logic of this novel.

Daniel, as an executive self, represents all of Israel. His possessed individualism is an odd model for the nineteenth century self insofar as in England in the 1870s one must own property and be male to vote. Property rights lead to voting rights, and possessions, in this way, lead to the power of civic participation. However, the nineteenth century is also filled with extensive and absurd variations from this rule. It is the century where in the United States one black man equals three-fifths of a white man. It is the century when parliamentary debate in England states that it is as ridiculous to say that *woman* is contained in the word *man*, as to say that *cow* is included in the word *man*.[20] In other words, a century of representative democracy is marked by continual absurdities of both a mathematical and categorical nature. The mysticism of religion that is already supposed to transcend logic and rules is a theoretical equal to regulated political incommensurability. So if thinking of mysticism politically seems absurd, of course it must be, because the representative democracy of the nineteenth century is already logically absurd. To imagine Daniel's body as

---

[17] There are also characters outside of the Jewish plot line within in this novel who are only partially individualized, for instance, the entwined subjectivity of Rex and Anna Gascoigne.

[18] At this point in the novel, Daniel is still in *denial*, the anagram of his first name, about his ethnic identity.

[19] For further insight into the connections between Eastern and Western religious cultures within Victorian England, see the special topics issue on Victorian religion in *Victorian Literature and Culture* (2003), Cambridge online journal.

[20] See Susan Kingsley Kent, *Sex and Suffrage in Britain, 1860–1914* (Princeton, NJ: Princeton University Press, 1987), 187.

the property of Israel and of Mordecai means neither that Daniel is objectified nor that he is not an agent in this novel. Instead, through Eliot's mystically inflected characterization of Daniel, Eliot reworks the definition of an individual with agency. Partially she does this through the Jewish plot line of the novel, but she also does this by placing Judaism within the concept of pantheism.

Judaism as Pantheism: Civilization Outside of the Nation-state Paradigm

In preparation for writing *Daniel Deronda*, Eliot's notes indicate that she is taking different religio-philosophical trajectories (or potentially competing histories) and mapping them onto one another. Her novel seeks for what could be called social unification or the one-ness of creation through the tenets of pantheism. Specifically she was influenced by Charles Bray's version of pantheism. In addressing the *Kabbala* in her notebooks, George Eliot translates Heinrich Hirsch Graetz's comments on the *Kabbala*:

> The doctrines of the Cabbala are neither ancient Jewish, nor new-philosophical. The ideal potencies, the spiritual intermediators between the Divine fullness of light & the dim world—the pre-existence of the soul—the transmigration of souls—the magical operation of human actions on the higher world—all belong to the Alexandrian neo-platonic philosophy.[21]

In this note, Eliot's translation of Graetz makes a universalizing gesture: Ideal potencies, preexisting souls, transmigration, the effect of the humans on "the higher world," belong to neo-Platonism, rather than to an ancient Jewish or new-philosophical tradition. Eliot collapses several mystical traditions, including spiritualism and pantheism, into one another in *Daniel Deronda*.[22]

In fact, the "possessed" in possessed individualism is somewhat specific to Charles Bray's pantheism. Bray, the well-known Victorian free thinker and philosopher, had been a friend of Eliot's since 1841, when she and her father moved near Coventry;

---

[21]   Eliot quoted in Irwin, *Notebooks*, 175. Eliot's translation is of Heinrich Hirsch Graetz, *Geschichte der Juden von Maimun's Tod (1205) bis zur Verbannung de Juden aus Spanien und Portugal*, Part 1, 2nd edn 1873.

[22]   To portray Eliot as a spiritualist would be a misrepresentation, but she was interested in all sorts of mysticism, including spiritualism. As early as 1852, she writes that "indications of claire-voyance witnessed by a competent observer are of thrilling interest and give me a restless desire to get at more extensive and satisfactory evidence" (Haight 5: 45. 22 April 1852). Her 1878 novella, *The Lifted Veil*, originally written in 1859, explores clairvoyance. She was also well aware of the ongoing experiments with séances. Eliot, her companion, George Henry Lewes, and Charles Darwin, on a January evening in 1874, attended a séance together at Erasmus Darwin's house—she found it a sham and left in disgust. See Frederick R. Karl, *George Eliot: The Voice of a Century* (New York: Norton, 1995), 531.

there, she spent much time with the Bray family. Bray sent his book *Illusion and Delusion* (1873), a work that set about disproving spiritualism, to Eliot and George Henry Lewes in fall 1873, in return for Lewes's *Problems of Life and Mind* (1873), which was published as a three-part series: *The Foundation of a Creed* (1874), *The Physical Basis of Mind* (1877), and *The Study of Psychology* (1879–1880), which Eliot finished after Lewes's death. The starting point of Lewes's *Problems* is the goal of moving metaphysics from the realm of religion to science.[23] Bray similarly wants the "light of science" to be the standard by which the spiritual is assessed, arguing that "it will be found that all the ... attributes or qualities ascribed to matter are attributes of mind and not of matter, and that the world itself is but an illusion and delusion—a great ghost or mental spectre."[24] He argues that metaphysicians formerly sought "to divide the qualities or properties of matter into primary and secondary" (primary properties belong to the object and secondary properties to the observer) but that this distinction is false and that "all [properties] are equally dependent upon the action of the brain."[25]

Bray further argues that the way to increase aggregate well-being is not in the increase of wealth but through the genetic increase of the size of the brain.[26] He is a proponent of mind over matter and advocates an eugenic approach to social change. Bray's concept of civilization's relying not on the increase of wealth but on the increase of brain is echoed in *Daniel Deronda*. The question of subjectivity, of what creates an identity, is central in *Daniel Deronda*. Certainly, Uncle Hugo's quip about Napoleon's *mot*, "*Je suis un ancêtre*" does not satisfy Daniel or Eliot (201; ch. 15). The novel goes to great lengths to uncover Daniel's biological roots, rather than charting a process of Daniel's independent economic progress (or "where he is going to," even if this is Palestine). With this quest comes his cultural heritage. Daniel's increase in brain, to borrow Bray's model, occurs when his Jewish heritage, through the mind of Mordecai, transmigrates and moves into his body. Knowledge of cultural heritage becomes the preferred capital over property.

In Bray's radical, evolutionary view of subjectivity and the world it creates, he notes that:

> the will which originally required a distinct *conscious* volition has passed, in the ages into the unconscious or automatic constitution the fixed laws and order of nature. Here Materialism and Absolute Idealism meet ... As the world to us is the world only of our ideas, so the universe may exist only in the mind of God.[27]

---

[23]   Irwin, *Notebooks*, 17.

[24]   See Charles Bray, *Illusion and Delusion; Or, Modern Pantheism versus Spiritualism* (London: Thomas Scott, 1873).

[25]   *Ibid.*, 5–6.

[26]   *Ibid.*, 36.

[27]   *Ibid.*, 38–9, 42.

The framework of materialism and absolute idealism meeting in bodies that are part of the mind of God constitutes Bray's addition to the field of metaphysics and also presents a theme that *Daniel Deronda* explores.[28] In fact, Bray's metaphysics also helps delineate Eliot's preferred type of individual in this novel, which can be described as a multiple personality order. Bray's metaphysical paradigm can be applied to the concept of transmigration and the type of individual Daniel may be:

> We are part of all the forces around, and in direct and immediate connection with them, and but partially individualized. As star can act on star, at immeasurable distances, so can one mind upon another within more limited bounds, when such minds are *en-rapport*.[29]

Daniel and Mordecai are *en-rapport*, and Daniel is only "partially individualized." Daniel remains, though, an effective agent, but not an autonomous agent. Some of Daniel's freedom disappears with the knowledge of his bond to Mordecai and Israel. As Daniel explains to Gwendolen, "The idea that he is possessed with" makes "his task" his "duty" (875; ch. 69). Bray uses a quotation from Spinoza to make a consonant point about the illusory nature of free will: "'Human liberty, of which all boast,' says Spinoza, 'consists solely in this, that man is conscious of his will, and unconscious of the causes by which it is determined.'"[30] Daniel's actualization as a person comes when he becomes not only acquainted but also identified with the causes that determine his will.[31] He is forever in touch with the Mordecai within. Conversely, Gwendolen continues to think herself free throughout much of the novel without considering that she is not determining her own will but being instead conscripted by Grandcourt's will, both personal and testamentary.

Eliot and Bray both foreground the physicality of identity and identification through their discussions of shared bodies and souls. Bray explains a lack of autonomy in terms of people's being located in the unconscious extremities of God's body. He writes:

> As our body has a centre of volition and intelligence so may the universe have. Our earth moves round the sun, and all power comes to us from thence; but the sun moves round some other centre, and that probably round another, until we approach the great centre of

---

28 Bray's work contributes to the prehistory of psychoanalysis. Concepts such as Jung's collective unconscious appear both unoriginal and pantheistic in relation to Bray's work and other mid-nineteenth-century metaphysical treatises that directly led to the foundation of psychology as a discipline.

29 Bray, *Illusion and Delusion*, 31–2.

30 *Ibid.*, 35.

31 The reader could pit Anderson's argument that Daniel is an independent, rational thinker against Bray's quotation of Spinoza. Autonomous, rational identity would only equal false consciousness for Bray—and perhaps the same holds true for Eliot's characterization of independent thought in this novel.

all, where possibly God's power may be more directly exercised, and he may consciously govern all; here in the extremities, much of it seems to have passed into the automatic.[32]

In Bray's lengthy analogy and description of consciousness, Victorians are mere matter "in the extremities" of God's body. This view presents extrahuman organizational networks subsuming the individual. Eliot presents the same concept with Daniel: His will turns automatic when Mordecai and Israel inhabit him. Stronger volitions overtake him, and his body becomes an extreme outpost of an idea.

Bray helps read *Deronda* in the following terms: (1) If there is really no matter, then the logical conclusion is that the category of property (material possessions) becomes illusory and unimportant; and (2) if property is unimportant (because it is illusory), then a model of subjectivity predicated on possessive individualism becomes invalid. (Gwendolen, then, can never be happy marrying for property and power not only because the title is not transferred to her in the will but also because the *power* of property does not exist in a real sense.) This is to argue like a Victorian man of letters, though. This is to argue like Bray. All the same, Eliot does argue like Bray. At times she makes these two assumptions in presenting Daniel and Gwendolen. Eliot favors, in this novel, a world where imagination has more power than property. Eliot perhaps says it best through a typical Gwendolen comment: "'Imagination is often truer than fact,' said Gwendolen, decisively, though she could no more have explained these glib words than if they had been Coptic or Etruscan" (76; ch. 5). Coptic and Etruscan were just two of the ancient languages that represented partially known cultures in which Victorians were obsessively interested—making the additional joke that in representing cultures, imagination plays a bigger role than fact for Eliot.

One way to describe *Daniel Deronda* is to say that if a character is the aggregate of a person's perceptions, then this novel explores what happens when aggregate, competing perceptions/worldviews keep colliding even when they are a part of the same nervous system. Bray writes:

> The world, however, as we conceive it, is created by the peculiar constitution of the nervous system … There is not one world, then, but thousands of worlds, as each creature creates its own, and all made out of the same stuff, which is not matter, but mind. What we call MATTER is an illusion and delusion.[33]

Interacting characters, then, in common spaces in the novel, potentially can be viewed through Eliot's reading in metaphysics as not cohabiting the same real world but as cohabiting competing ideal worlds. Through this lens, Daniel may be understood as an allegory for possessed individualism.

Eliot also plays with the possibility of sharing ideal worlds. Bray's and Eliot's common link is a belief in collective identity. In fact, Bray ends his pantheistic essay

---

[32]   Bray, *Illusion and Delusion*, 42.
[33]   *Ibid.*, 7.

with the concept that a person is just a phenomenally changing part of the noumenal mind of God:

> We *are immortal*, for we are part of God himself, do we wish always to remain in the childhood of our present individual existence? ... As each of the countless cells in the human body has a separate life, and yet constituting the life of the whole, making one body, so the aggregate of individual creatures makes one great nervous system, every beat or change in which produces intense enjoyment, so great, indeed, that the necessary pain which we call evil disappears and is lost.[34]

Eliot presents "one great nervous system" in this novel that replaces a system with which she is nervous (namely, an English national center)—she is writing realism about a universe that is a very big body and has a mind of its own. Characters overlap, and the individual is not at the center of her psychological studies: Aggregate characters are. Daniel is not singular; instead he has a collective identity, a multiple personality order or civic polity constituted of Mordecai, medieval scholars (Kabbalists), his father, his grandfather, and Israel.

The complexity and heterodoxy of Eliot's religious research and views refigure the novel's politics. Her depiction of Judaism in this novel is unique because she imagines it subsumed by a bigger category of Eastern pantheistic world religions, as opposed to solely imagining it within its own traditional terms. At base, *Daniel Deronda* is a novel, a fictional account, and even major religious traditions depicted within novels can be uniquely fictionalized. Eliot models Judaism on Eastern as well as Western mystical traditions, from pantheism to neo-Platonism. Eliot scarcely seems to uphold England as a political ideal for anyone, including the English. Her ideas also do not uphold the Western political model of possessive individualism or uphold distinctly Western religious traditions over Eastern ones.

Proto-Zionism or Postnationalism?

Palestine is ostensibly where Daniel will go after the closing chapter of the novel, which serves as a metaphor for the way in which his body, like Palestine, is a place that can be colonized. In this way, possessed individualism is modeled after colonization. Yet this is a colonialism with a difference. The Jewish plot in *Daniel Deronda* is not actually about desiring a nation as much as it is about a desire for community, interconnections between individuals, and a definition for agency that surprisingly does not include autonomy. A lack of autonomy may also signal the removal of a desire for dominion, which is the state ownership of a territory.

Literary critics frequently discuss the proto-Zionism in this novel as a desire for nation and for exclusion of otherness. However, the impulse behind the Jewish

---

[34] *Ibid.*, 42–3.

plot in *Daniel Deronda* may also be read as an attempt to move beyond the concept of nation and its narrow concerns in favor of embracing individual and community identities that are more collective, less competitive, and not based on desiring a nation located in a state. What if the proto-Zionism in this novel is actually neither about a nation-making desire of European Jews to colonize Palestine nor about an impulse to exclude Jews from Western Europe?[35]

Wondering if proto-Zionism can equal an inclusive versus exclusionary plan is fairly counterintuitive in examining the scholarship concerning the Jewish question, genre, and gender in *Daniel Deronda*, a novel commonly accepted as dealing with Daniel's discovery of Jewish heritage and his desire to colonize Palestine with European Jews. For instance, Edward W. Said writes of *Daniel Deronda* that:

> Brightness, freedom, and redemption—key matters for Eliot—are to be restricted to Europeans and the Jews, who are themselves European prototypes so far as colonizing the East is concerned ... Humanity and sympathy it seems are not endowments of anything but an Occidental mentality; to look for them in the despotic East, much less find them, is to waste one's time ... Eliot is no different from other European apostles of sympathy, humanity, and understanding for whom noble sentiments were either left behind in Europe or made programmatically inapplicable outside Europe.[36]

Said further sees Eliot as in favor of a project of replicating England elsewhere and upholding the values of European ideas, noting that "Eliot was indifferent to races who could not be assimilated to European ideas."[37] Similarly, Susan Meyer writes, "Despite the feminist and anti-imperialist nuances that can be found at various points in the novel, and despite its moments of genuine interest in the Jews, when this novel comes to its closure it reinforces gender and race hierarchies and firmly draws national boundaries."[38] Meyer finds the proto-Zionism in the novel to be primarily

---

[35] Bruce Robbins describes the cosmopolitan subject as one who lives within and moves between multiple nations, affiliations, and civil identities. This definition could well describe the character of Daniel not so much because of his physical travel, though he frequently travels beyond the English nation-state, but because of his moving between multiple nations and civil identities within his own body. See Robbins's introduction to *Cosmopolitics: Thinking and Feeling Beyond the Nation*, ed. Pheng Cheah and Bruce Robbins (Minneapolis: University of Minnesota Press, 1998), especially pp. 3–10.

[36] Edward W. Said, "Zionism from the Standpoint of Its Victims," in *Dangerous Liaisons: Gender, Nation, and Postcolonial Perspectives*, eds Anne McClintock, Aamir Mufti, and Ella Shohat (Minneapolis: University of Minnesota Press, 1997), 22. This version of Said's essay is revised substantially in comparison to the original printing of this essay in *Social Text* 1:1 (Winter 1979), 7–58. His analysis of Eliot and *Daniel Deronda*, though, remains the same and I quote from the version of the essay in *Dangerous Liaisons*.

[37] *Ibid.*

[38] Susan Meyer, "'Safely to Their Own Borders': Proto-Zionism, Feminism, and Nationalism in *Daniel Deronda*," *English Literary History* 60:3 (1993), 752.

an impulse to exclude Jews from England and reinforce traditionally subordinate
roles for women.

Michael Ragussis, however, argues persuasively of *Daniel Deronda* that it is
Eliot's "attempt ... to expose English anti-Semitism and to celebrate Judaic culture,"
going on to note that:

> Eliot was favorably impressed by Harriet Beecher Stowe's *Uncle Tom's Cabin* as she was
> preparing for her own depiction of national life and national disgrace. In *Daniel Deronda*
> Eliot transforms Stowe's depiction of the American disgrace of slavery into the English
> disgrace of anti-Semitism. Eliot wrote to Stowe in 1876, "not only towards the Jews, but
> towards all oriental peoples with whom we English come in contact, a spirit of arrogance
> and contemptuous dictatorialness is observable which has become a national disgrace to
> us."[39]

The working of the influence of Stowe on Eliot, as demonstrated by Ragussis,
certainly provides a powerful counterargument to Said and Meyer. It suggests
Eliot's opposition to colonialism as a national practice. Eliot writing to Stowe that
she observes a disgraceful dictatorialness that the English have "towards all oriental
peoples" is significant in assessing the politics of *Daniel Deronda*. The reader of
Daniel Deronda is not encouraged, I believe, to identify exclusively with a particular
viewpoint in the novel, even though Daniel identifies with Mordecai's vision. Eliot's
politics are not solely ventriloquised by her characterization of Mordecai, Daniel,
or Gwendolen.

Eliot's treatment of colonization (Daniel's body is colonized, but a trip to Palestine
is elided) is different from other actual Victorian plans for Palestinian colonization,
a topic widely discussed in the 1870s.[40] Her treatment of colonization suggests
that her proto-Zionism might be a version of the postnational: a vision for polity
potentially free from a zeal for exclusionary politics.[41] It is important here to recall
that, for Eliot, Judaism is closely aligned with other communal mystical systems,
even beyond Bray's pantheism, as the following reference in Eliot's correspondence
will show.

Eliot was aware that archeologists and cartographers, working on site in
Palestine, were sending information back to England. Eliot followed these accounts
of exploration and biblical archeology in Palestine in the 1870s and of planned
colonizations. She knew of the career, for instance, of former MP Laurence Oliphant.
In 1867, in New York, Oliphant had joined a curious spiritualist group, a virtual sex

---

[39]   Michael Ragussis, *Figures of Conversion: "The Jewish Question" and English National
       Identity* (Durham, NC: Duke University Press, 1995), 265, 267. Ragussis's quotation from
       Eliot, in turn, comes from Gordon S. Haight, ed., *The George Eliot Letters*, 9 vols (New
       Haven: Yale University Press 1978), 6:301.

[40]   Proto-Zionism is a much more multivalent discourse for Eliot in terms of her reading and
       writing than it is in the description that Meyer gives to proto-Zionism.

[41]   For more about the concept of the cosmopolitan postnational, see Robbins.

cult, led by an ex-Swedenborgian minister, Thomas Lake Harris. Called the New Life, the cult moved to Santa Rosa, California, in 1875. (Recall the sister in the New Life with fairies in her body?) This group explored the concept of spiritual correspondences (having an invisible lover cohabiting one's body—a concept invoking transmigration) and sought a promised land. Oliphant was working on an economic and spiritual project of colonizing Palestine with European Jews—the same topic Eliot explores in *Daniel Deronda*.[42] Both Oliphant's and Harris's plans share a common Christian overlay of the utopian and imperialist project of building a new Eden.

Eliot's editor, John Blackwood, in a letter dated 8 August 1879 to her wrote, "Oliphant writes to me from our embassy at Constantinople. He has been all over Syria and Palestine and sends me some of the first fruits in a M.S. article to be followed by others and also by a book. You and he and Disraeli are all I fancy working to one end."[43] What could this "one end" toward which they are all working be in Blackwood's fancy? Zionism? Colonizing Palestine? An imagined utopia? Cosmopolitanism? Projects are, of course, imaginings with tangible impacts. Blackwood's remarkable claim of a common goal between MP Oliphant, prime minister and novelist Benjamin Disraeli, and Eliot deserves further attention, especially in light of the odd beliefs of the spiritualist cult the New Life, of which Oliphant was a member.

Thomas Lake Harris, the founder of the New Life, claimed that he could create a new mode of enlightened breathing, "open respiration," in his adherents and that he was God's only emissary here on Earth. Membership in this spiritualist group was one of Oliphant's prompts in a plan to colonize Palestine. Returning to the epigraph of this book, colonization is presented as filling up the open space of the body. This visionary type of colonization is described as the member of the Sisterhood in the New Life continues her journal entry:

June 9, 1881: ... Lately I have imagined a little fay; he is about as large as the point of a pin who comes out on the tip of the first finger of my left hand, and talks to me; he is exquisitely dressed; yesterday he told me about some new babies ... July 12, 1881: I can feel space in every part of my body which is not filled. I do wish I could give you some

---

[42]   As Eliot writes to Blackwood on 25 February 1879, "There is a great movement now among the Jews towards colonising Palestine, and bringing out the resources of the soil. Probably Mr. Oliphant is interested in the work, and will find his experience in the West not without applicability in the East" (Haight 7:109). As Haight notes, "Early in 1879 [Oliphant] took up a scheme for colonizing Palestine with Jews, and went to the East to examine the country and try to obtain a concession from the Turkish government." See Gordon S. Haight, ed., *The George Eliot Letters*, 9 vols (New Haven: Yale University Press 1978), 7:109. See also Laurence Oliphant, *Land of Gilead, with Excursions in the Lebanon* (New York: Appleton, 1881).

[43]   Blackwood quoted in Haight, *The George Eliot Letters*, 7:192.

idea of this feeling of space. I could not until I felt this space imagine how one could feel another within them, but now I know I have space and room for my counterpart ... August 15, 1881: [S]ince the breath came it has grown very much and my dresses have all had to be enlarged; it is the same with my sister, loose dresses are now too tight for comfort.[44]

Similar to the minim mammal visionary quotation from Eliot, with the tiny elephant adjacent to a finger in a glove, this also presents an intriguing account of tiny visionary suburbanite colonists living within the body. Harris has told this woman that two-in-ones, fays, can settle in bodies, build houses in bodies, plant fruit trees in bodies—expand space in bodies. This is an urban style of transmigration of souls, a nonbiological model of reproduction, and a model of colonization. A "two-in-one" (wherever it may have been previously) finds entrance to the body, builds a house and "then little baby fays would be born"—presumably from the single two-in-one rather than from a couple of two-in-ones—spontaneous generation. Or, as one reader put it, "This is a self-pollinating hermaphroditic vision."[45]

The sister's model of planned community provides a concept of utopian colonization. It is only after others started to live within the sister that she developed a group and state identity in her spacious body. So, too, with Daniel, who also could be described as a two-in-one. Once Mordecai breathes his soul into him, Daniel has an identity and a purpose: Traveling to the East. The Sister in the New Life becomes a fay city-state or polis just as Daniel Deronda becomes an Israel satellite with Mordecai's soul and the life of Israel nested in his body.

What does it mean to have a place inhabit a person? For Daniel it is as Mordecai tells him: "The life of Israel is in your veins" (634; ch. 46). Daniel's Jewish identity is about a place (the nation of Israel) embodying his person. This makes the idea of Israel, as it pertains to Daniel, a nation of diaspora: A nation that is a regenerating notion in Daniel's mind.[46] Having a place inhabit a person also means that a possessed person's agency is distinct from a singular autonomous agency and that any plans he or she may have—including colonizing—are mediated by having had one's own body colonized. Having a place inhabit a person means that for such a one he or she is always mediating and being mediated by a variety of allegiances. For instance, because Daniel knows his will is not his own, it means also that his identity is self-reflexive. His actions may be both more intentional and more responsible, resulting in his agency having less of a damaging effect on others.

Unlike the way we may understand object relations from Hegel or Lacan (there is a single individuated self; there is an other), the knowledge of their others, for both

---

44 Quoted in Herbert Wallace Schneider and George Lawton, *A Prophet and a Pilgrim* (New York: Columbia University Press, 1942), 525, 527–8, 530.

45 Ross Forman, phone conversation with author, 26 February 2003.

46 Diaspora as "regeneration through statelessness" (vii) is discussed in Daniel and Jonathan Boyarin, *Powers of Diaspora: Two Essays on the Relevance of Jewish Culture* (Minneapolis: University of Minnesota Press, 2002).

the Sister and for Daniel, does not lead to a greater sense of their separateness and self-actualization—at least, not in the way we understand self-actualization. Rather, the possessed understand themselves primarily through a semi-invisible group identity. The utopian Sister's account and Daniel's trajectory toward the East are not completely dissimilar to the plans that Western millenialist visionaries starting in the 1860s had for Palestine. For instance, the first modern Western European cartographer of Palestine, Claude Conder, about whom Blackwood wrote to Eliot, notes the existence of Western spiritualist colonies in Palestine set up by American Mormons in the 1860s and by the Temple Society (millenialist German Lutherans) in the 1870s. In a description of a Haifa Temple Society settlement, Conder writes:

> The little village of red-cheeked, flaxen-haired peasants, with cheery salutations, and honest smiling faces, is a pleasant place to visit; the women in their short skirts and brown straw hats, and the men in felt wideawakes and grey cloth, contrast most favorably with the dirty, squalid, lying Fellahin … A fresh sea breeze blows all day among the acacia trees which flank the dusty street … The whole colony is seen soberly marching down to the meeting-house, where they are weekly comforted, with the assurance that the end will soon come, and the Temple Colony be acknowledged, by God and man, to be the example of the whole world, and the true heir of the Holy Land and of Jerusalem.[47]

These clean, pleasant German utopians are not markedly unlike the Sister's exquisitely dressed fingertip fairy (except they are much bigger). They inhabit an idealized Holy Land (in Palestine) in a similarly incoherent spatiotemporal relation to their surroundings. I include Conder's depiction of Western utopian colonists in Haifa because the utopians who stay in the West and keep the topos within their bodies seem to be much less intrusive than those who move to Palestine and view the indigenous population as not entitled to their own homeland. Conder finds the German Temple Society preferable to and about to supersede the presumably indigenous "dirty, squalid, lying Fellahin" in Haifa.[48] Eliot's characters, unlike these colonists, never get farther than the Mediterranean. Eliot favors her *Deronda* characters when they are possessed and not when they are being possessive. Imagining a place at a distance or placing a nation or community within an individual (as is the novelistic project with Daniel) has lower environmental impact than packing up all of the "felt wideawakes" and moving to Palestine. Imagination is a more genuinely permeable colonization.

An inquiry into Eliot's political vision is implied by making these types of comparisons. If Eliot gives us an imaginary colonization, it is relevant to know what other, more typical imperialists, funded by the English government, who do not separate visionary from political plans, offer with their visions of colonization. Conder

---

[47]   Claude Reignier Conder, *Tent Work in Palestine. A Record of Discovery and Adventure*, 2 vols (London: Richard Bentley and Son, 1878), 2:306, 314.

[48]   *Fellahin* is an Arabic word denoting "farmers" and connoting "ignorant." Translation courtesy Mazen Naous.

feels that the purpose of the first map of Palestine, for which he was the principal surveyor, was to give the West remote access to Palestine.[49] Conder writes, "Palestine is thus brought home to England, and the student may travel, in his study, over its weary roads and rugged hills without an ache, and may ford its dangerous streams, and pass through its malarious plains without discomfort."[50] Palestine, then, more so than in its role in *Daniel Deronda*, is designed for the English consumer who is a virtual traveler—it is presented as an imaginary destination: "Palestine is thus brought home to England."[51] This also provides a model of imperial absorption that foreshadows the British mandate over Palestine that fell on the heels of World War I.[52] However, in this novel, Mordecai brings Israel into Daniel. Conder ends his work by reiterating the ideal dependence of Palestine on Western Europe. He writes:

---

[49]   Neil Asher Silberman in *Digging for God and Country: Exploration, and the Secret Struggle for the Holy Land, 1799–1917* (New York: Knopf, 1982), notes the popularity of works such as Conder's in London of the 1870s. The first such excitement occurred over the Moabite stone in January 1870. Silberman writes, "On January 16, 1870, under the by-line of Charles Clermont-Ganneau, and under the title '*La Stele de Mesa, roi de Moab, 896 avant J.C.*,' the Moabite stone was introduced to the western world. The London *Times* printed an article on the very next day containing the fantastic news … The dramatic proof of the historical accuracy of the Bible soon became a popular subject … in drawing rooms, dinner parties, and garden receptions throughout England. 'Like a lucky actress or singer,' wrote one contemporary commentator, 'it took us by storm'" (109). Thus the popular Victorian obsession with the idea of Palestine began.

[50]   Conder, *Tent Work*, I:xvi–xvii.

[51]   *Ibid.*, 1:xvi.

[52]   Denis Judd writes, "In November 1917, Balfour, serving as Foreign Secretary in Lloyd George's wartime coalition government, issued a declaration in which Britain pledged its support to 'the establishment in Palestine of a national home for the Jewish people.' The foundation of a Jewish homeland in Palestine, although fraught with various risks and dangers, offered many potential advantages to Britain and the Allies. Jewish opinion in the United States and Russia was expected to be favourably impressed. More important still, the settlement in Palestine of substantial numbers of Jewish immigrants, drawn mostly from Europe, would guarantee Britain a continuing strategic and commercial state in the area" (251). This account of the British mandate in Palestine provides a vision of Zionism that is the familiar and nationalistic version of the term. See Denis Judd, *Empire: The British Imperial Experience, 1765 to the Present* (New York: Basic Books, 1997), 251. Furthermore, Rachel Hallote, historiographer of biblical archeology, through her research on mid-nineteenth century biblical archeology places the start date of funding for biblical archeology at 1840 with Lord Palmerston's formation of the "official protectorate of the Jewish community in Jerusalem" which provided initial funding for biblical archeology and established Britain with an economic stake in the Middle East. See Hallote's book, *Bible, Map and Spade: The American Palestine Exploration Society, Frederick Jones Bliss and the Forgotten Story of Early American Biblical Archaeology* (Piscataway, NJ: Gorgias Press, 2006). Phone interview with author, July 2005.

The happiest future which could befall Palestine seems to me to be its occupation by some strong European power, which might recognise the value of the natural resources pointed out above; but until some such change occurs, the good land must remain a desolation. "And thorns shall come up in her palaces, nettles and brambles in the fortresses thereof, and it shall be an habitation of dragons, and a court for owls" [Isa. xxxiv. 13].[53]

Conder presents Palestine as a space for economic ventures, a desert waiting to be economically and spiritually colonized by "some strong European power." Conder is imagining a strong Western power that can replace the weak and decadent Ottoman empire, rehearsing a familiar geopolitical stereotype. Although Eliot's novel ends with Daniel and Mirah headed to the East, the same imperialist tone that is present in Conder is not present in Eliot: In fact, the word *Palestine* only occurs in *Daniel Deronda* twice. It first occurs at the beginning of Chapter 41 when Daniel considers his budding relationship with Mordecai in comparison to imagining a young man "centuries ago in Rome, Greece, Asia Minor, Palestine" or "Cairo" (41). The second reference is in Chapter 42, when Gideon, a Jew at "the Philosphers" club says to Mordecai:

I know you are not for the restoration of Judea by miracle, and so on; but you are as well aware as I am that the subject has been mixed up with a heap of nonsense both by Jews and Christians. And as to the connection of our race with Palestine, it has been perverted by superstition till it's as demoralizing as the old poor-law. (593, Ch. 42)

In each of these references, Zionist leanings are quite different than they are in Conder.

Daniel Deronda in part chronicles Daniel's discovery of his Jewish ethnicity and his decision to take over Mordecai's planned pilgrimage to the East. But by the novel's end, he never gets there, perhaps because Eliot values Palestine as an idea that can come and embody her characters rather than as a realist's geographic place. Of course, Daniel does intend to get to the East as he tells Gwendolen:

The idea that I am possessed with is that of restoring a political existence to my people, making them a nation again, giving them a national centre, such as the English have, though they too are scattered over the face of the globe. That is a task which presents itself to me as a duty: I am resolved to begin it, however feebly. I am resolved to devote my life to it. (875; ch. 69)

Daniel is possessed with an idea—a comparative political idea at that. He wants his people, who are scattered over the globe like the English are, to have a national center and a political existence. Daniel's views are proto-Zionist in this regard, but Eliot does not seem to argue for a replicated English political system for Palestine. For one thing, she was well aware of how England had mistreated English Jews for hundreds

---

[53] Conder, *Tent Work*, 2:332.

of years.[54] For another, she was aware of women's disenfranchised status in England and how such a system disabled a character like Gwendolen. She saw the inequities of English economics and politics; her Victorian England was not a prototype for a new Jerusalem. It is somewhat easy to forget that Daniel, even after he takes on Mordecai's vision, remains an English citizen. Yet, he feels suddenly disenfranchised once he knows he is Jewish, in spite of his privilege, gender, English education, and English citizenship. His statement that he desires for Jews to have a national center like the English do, is predicated on the assumption that English Jews, like himself, his wife, Mirah, and the Cohen family are precluded from fully participating in the English national center because they are Jewish.[55] In this sense, a desire for a Jewish national center may have more to do with feeling alienated from English political participation than it does with the potentially exclusionary impulses of Zionism.[56] Eliot's view on colonization in this novel is visionary, and the promised land remains, at the end of this novel, a vision.

The promised land's remaining vision retains a very distinct politic from that of Zionism. "In an important essay informed by the history of the Jews and Israel in the twentieth century, Daniel Boyarin and Jonathan Boyarin have argued for a conception of Jewish identity that is based not on achieved nationhood but rather on unending diaspora," writes Amanda Anderson.[57] She continues, "Deeply suspicious of European models of nationhood and cultural identity, the Boyarins seek to define Judaism against what they construe as a somewhat monolithic Western Europe."[58] Anderson's presentation of the Boyarins' definition of Judaism as relying on unending diaspora, as opposed to relying on Zionism, is a dominant definition of Judaism in *Daniel Deronda* as well. Anderson does a succinct job of explaining when and how ethnocentricity can be an ethically appropriate discourse, as opposed to an ethically problematic discourse:

> For Boyarin and Boyarin, a "particular discourse of ethnocentricity is ethically appropriate only when the cultural identity is an embattled (or, at any rate, nonhegemonic) identity." Favoring a notion of cultural belonging based on generational connection rather than

---

54 Eliot quoted in Irwin, *Notebooks*, 85–7. Here Eliot notes R. Hirschfeld, *Das innere Leben des modernum Judenthums*, about the history of Jews in England and of London synagogues.

55 Of side interest here is Eliot's implication that "pure English blood" cannot be produced by "leech or lancet" (582; ch. 42) potentially separating the term *English* from the category of ethnicity.

56 For instance, Irwin writes, "In *Daniel Deronda*, George Eliot occludes doctrinal issues, presenting without comment a broad range of Jewish observance" (78). Furthermore, I note in "the Philosophers" Club, Chapter 42, 572–99, a wide range of Jewish political views (from assimilation to going to the East to form a Jewish national center) are presented.

57 Amanda Anderson, "George Eliot and the Jewish Question," *Yale Journal of Criticism* 10.1 (1997), 57.

58 *Ibid.*

autochthony, the Boyarins see Zionism as a betrayal of the Jewish culture rather than its culmination.[59]

Following this line of thought, I argue that Judaism in *Daniel Deronda* looks distinct from the Zionism that seeks to colonize the space of Palestine, because bodies rather than lands are being colonized. In this Eliot novel, bodies are lands, and lands are ideas.

Eliot's novel brings to light the contrast between a possessed individual and a possessive individual. Real empowerment, in Eliot's presentation of these characters, is not centered in an individual's possession of property but in being conceptually possessed, for example, Daniel's kissable self who becomes an "executive self" (530; ch. 38). Individualism need not be landed (or grounded); it is a collectively shared cultural/historical/political body that ends up being located in the person of Daniel—who has a Theban Mordecai within (527; ch. 38).

Eliot's Realism in *Daniel Deronda*

Daniel and Gwendolen both self-contain/represent incommensurate political systems. Both Daniel and Gwendolen represent themselves, to borrow Marx's definition of civil society, by what they do and who they are.[60] Although they are in different extremities of the same body, to borrow Bray's pantheistic vision, they have no necessary relation to one another because the identity that connects them is too large to be recognizable. *Deronda* is a realist novel that describes a very big system. They might not know they are in God's body, to take Bray somewhat seriously with his pantheistic universality. To consider Marx seriously is to imagine the way in which *Daniel Deronda* enacts the decentralization of the sociopolitical through embodiment. Kristin Ross says, in reference to Marx writing about Hegel, that:

> If the separation between state and civil society does not exist, then politics becomes just another branch of social production. Political emancipation means emancipation from politics as a specialized activity. Marx concludes his critique of Hegel with the suppression

---

59   *Ibid.* In turn, see Daniel Boyarin and Jonathan Boyarin, "Diaspora: Generation and the Ground of Jewish Identity," *Critical Inquiry* 19 (1993): 718.

60   Karl Marx in his 1843 critique of Hegel writes, "Alternatively, civil society is the *real* political society. If so, it would be senseless to insist on a requirement which stems from the conception of the political state as something existing apart from civil society [for here] the *legislature* entirely ceases to be important as a *representative* body. The legislature is representative only in the sense that *every* function is representative. For example, a shoemaker is representative in so far as he satisfies a social need ... In this sense he is representative not by virtue of another thing which he represents but by virtue of what he *is* and *does*" (Marx in Kristin Ross, *The Emergence of Social Space* [Minneapolis: University of Minnesota Press, 1988], 24).

of politics and the extinction of the state ... When Marx takes the Commune seriously, he
must confront the possibility of a multiplicity of roads replacing the unique Highway of
History; he must give new significance to the decentralization of the socio-political.[61]

In this rubric, the political is released from a necessary tie to centralized governance
and simply represents itself as a social production. In this model, history becomes
multiple and not singular; it becomes decentralized; it moves away from the central
nervous system of any given body (or nation) and out into the extremities. History
becomes possessed with multiple personalities, and the political becomes a social
production. The nation fades from view and something else, more complex and harder
to define, takes its place—a certain type of new group formation and commentary. If
sociopolitical power is decentralized and politics suppressed, then civic centers are
moved into bodies that self-represent: possessed individualism, as is the case with
Daniel.

Eliot's novel presents the conflict between possessed and possessive individualism
remaining outside of a totalizing political schema. This narrative is marked by
partialness, interstices, silences, and contingencies. Her characterization fascinates
because it suggests that a big, tangled skein may be at the center of the individual and
at the center of historical narrative.

The Realism of Collective Identity

Eliot presents Gwendolen alone and without collective identity. Eliot sacrifices her
at the altar of possessive individualism. Unlike Daniel, she does not prosper: She
is not possessed by thoughts. Gwendolen is not sociable and does not like people,
but is an independent thinker until her thoughts disintegrate. She and Daniel do
spend a fair amount of time talking to each other in this novel. Yet, unlike other
frequent talkers who share or come to share an identity (Mordecai and Daniel, Rex
and Anna), Gwendolen and Daniel never become aggregated. Why is this? How
do we describe their interaction? They speak some of the most tortured dialogue in
the annals of the Victorian novel because they represent incommensurate concepts
of a political self. They do not speak the same language—Daniel and Gwendolen
remain in separate spaces; they inhabit competing ideal worlds. They represent
colliding ideologies.

One way to describe their failure to connect is to say that both of their colonial
desires have been altered. Daniel is colonized by Israel, and Gwendolen does not
"win empire." If their desires are colonial, perhaps it is helpful to think what sort of
space they occupy.

Social geography was a topic of intellectual thought in the 1870s. In *The
Emergence of Social Space*, Kristin Ross, discussing the development of the social

---

61   Ross, *Emergence*, 24–5.

science of geography in 1870s France, notes a difference between definitions of geography as landscape and geography as social space. In the early 1870s, Vidal de la Blanche presented the definition that "geography is the science of landscape."[62] Ross describes the Vidalian model as ahistorical and one that removes alterity and particularity from geography. She juxtaposes this definition with the slightly later anarchist geography of Elisee Reclus, who defines geography in 1872 as "nothing but history in space," which should consider everything: "Science should be a living thing or else it is nothing but a scholastic misery. Like a plant that draws its nourishment from afar through all its roots as well as through the pores of its leaves, geography should begin by everything at once: cosmography, natural history, history, topography."[63] This second definition of geography is social, particular, and broadly seeking.

Daniel Deronda takes on social geography, specifically colonization, as a focal concern. However, it seems to be a reverse colonization. As we see in the case of Daniel, Israel colonizes him; he does not visit it, or describe it, or colonize it, or map it. Israel, instead, visits Daniel, describes him, colonizes him, maps him. Daniel's body becomes the geographical space of a particularized (if not singular) Israel. He is possessed. He fits nicely within the paradigm of Reclus's geography; he is "nothing but history in space." "Space" becomes specified here as "the body."

Gwendolen's body is different. She does not become embodied like Daniel; she does not receive social space either. Her body becomes an unspeakable alterity. How to theorize her body—in what terms to map it—becomes a conundrum. Gwendolen is exiled from the social space of the novel. She is removed from a social topography. In terms of the political economy of mysticism, she is not a possessed individual. She is the exile who, unlike Mordecai, does not gain admission/access to Daniel's being at the end of the novel. Instead, she has tried to work within the political economy of possessive individualism. She has sought to be the synecdoche of Grandcourt's position (as a possessive individual) through her (brief unhappy) marriage to him. The relations she pursues with others, such as Grandcourt and Daniel, seem to stand in for her identity—identification replaces identity (as it had with the young Daniel before identification changes to identity when Mordecai's soul moves into his body). Gwendolen is marked not by the network of love but the alternative emptiness of hate: "I shall never love anybody. I can't love people. I hate them" (115). She does not connect. Gwendolen belongs in a Vidalian geography of landscape, ahistorical but with all the alterity and particularity you could hope for. She stands as a geography of outer space:

> The little astronomy taught her at school used sometimes to set her imagination at work in a way that made her tremble: but always when some one joined her she recovered her indifference to the vastness in which she seemed an exile; she found again her usual world in which her will was of some avail, and the religious nomenclature belonging to

---

62   *Ibid.*, 86.
63   Reclus in Ross, *Emergence*, 91.

this world was no more identified for her with those uneasy impressions of awe than her uncle's surplices seen out of the use at the rectory. With human ears and eyes about her, she had always hitherto recovered her confidence, and felt the possibility of winning empire. (95)

This is Gwendolen, nearly lost in space and struggling at the edge of pantheism. Consider Bray: "The human body is a perfect cosmos, an epitome of the action of the forces of the whole world."[64] Gwendolen is spinning around in outer space. Time and again, she is described as an exile.

Inclusions and Exclusions: Aggregate Characterization

But what about Gwendolen's grief? Claiming that Daniel has a happy-ever-after because he has become the embodiment of an ideology does not ameliorate Gwendolen's despair and isolation.[65] All the same, it does point out an important element in relief, namely, that Gwendolen *is* a character in the isolationist tradition of possessive individualism, and she embodies this ideology perfectly. In fact, the novel would have been vastly different if it had been named after Gwendolen Harleth. Interestingly, we have a fascinating, vital, possessive individual (*sans* voice), Gwendolen, stuck in a genre that does not privilege her economic organization. The supreme achievement of this novel is that it succeeds at being a compelling portrayal of alternative organizations for political identity. However, the system Gwendolen represents fails. No *bildungsroman* for her—no diachronic narrative of her winnings or even of her irregular, growth-enhancing fortunes—but only an unpleasantly fitting genre, like a shoe two sizes too small. In this novel, Eliot does not seem concerned with having one vital personality in one body—better to put two in one—or have Gwendolen *in absentia*. After all, by the end of the novel, Gwendolen's increasing incoherence is telling. The main problem she may have is she is not a political theorist. At the end of the novel, when Gwendolen claims that it will be better for her having known Daniel, she may be partly right, if she means understanding him structurally (882, ch. 70). If she thinks in terms of insinuation, knowing how his body is structured could become a model for absorbing others—realizing that particular compound combinations of characters in a single body is a model for the creation of a type of political representation. The possessed individual does not necessarily choose his or her preferred political schema at the outset, as one would under a Lockean system, where the necessary preconditions for Locke are economic, either in fact or

---

64 Bray, *Illusion and Delusion*, 39–40.
65 Things might go differently in the hands of another novelist. For instance, in Dickens, Gwendolen might be Mrs. Lammle of *Our Mutual Friend*, or in Trollope, she might become Lizzie Eustace of *The Eustace Diamonds*.

by analogy.[66] In possessed individualism, the system can choose the individual, and this constitutes a departure from earlier theories of political economy. The necessary preconditions of forming a body politic beyond a possessive logic are mystical and therefore elusive in *Deronda*.

This conflict between ideologies is not simply a plot device for keeping a desired tension between Daniel and Gwendolen. Other characters in the novel also can be described as models of possessed individualism. Daniel's feature of one body not equaling one person occurs with other characters, also would-be colonists who do not or cannot stand alone. This seems to be Eliot's preferred organizational structure for characterization. It is not, then, only the mystically active who become possessed. These characters have an inverse structure to that of Daniel himself. Daniel has plural souls in one body. Some characters, in contrast, share one soul between them—they are automatic and can't quite think on their own (suggesting that being political is never solitary and rarely typified by independent thinking). For example, Gwendolen's young cousins, Rex and Anna Gascoigne form a sort of circuit that defines subjectivity and historical narrative in terms of shared utopian space.[67] Eliot writes, "I like to mark the time, and connect the course of individual lives with the historic stream, for all classes of thinkers" in reply to Anna's thought that running off to the colonies, with her brother would absolve her of crinolines and the enlarged public spaces which they require (121–2; ch. 8).

Rex and Anna think in shared time and space as a single, speculating unit. As an elucidation of the model of identity as synchronic complicity, we can consider a scene between Anna and Rex after Gwendolen has rejected Rex's love and he desires to leave England for the colonies:

> "I'll tell you what I am thinking of, Nannie. I will go to Canada, or somewhere of that sort."
> (Rex had not studied the character of our colonial possessions.)
>   "Oh, Rex, not for always!"

---

[66] See John Locke, *Two Treatises of Government* (London: Everyman, 1998). Locke writes, "Since all princes and rulers of independent governments all through the world, are in a state of nature, 'tis plain the world never was, nor ever will be, without numbers of men in that state. I have named all governors of independent communities, whether they are, or are not, in league with others: for 'tis not every compact that puts an end to the state of nature between men, but only this one of agreeing together mutually to enter into one community, and make one body politic; other promises and compacts, men may make with one another, and yet still be in the state of nature" (121–2). Locke's "state of nature" is a phrase that describes social atomism. Even if subsequent decisions are not independent once one is part of the body politic, becoming part of that body is, for Locke, a distinctly volitional act. Gwendolen wants to be part of the same body with Daniel but that is not a decision that Daniel can make. She does not realize that Daniel's entering into the same body politic with Mordecai was partially a nonvolitional act because of the transmigration of souls.

[67] Eliot frequently organizes siblings *en masse* as a unit of soul—such as the Meyrick girls or the Tullivers in *Mill on the Floss*.

"Yes; to get my bread there. I should like to build a hut, and work hard at clearing, and have everything wild about me, and a great wide quiet."

"And not take me with you?" said Anna, the big tears coming fast.

"How could I?"

"I should like it better than anything; and settlers go with their families. I would sooner go there than stay here in England. I could make the fires, and mend the clothes, and cook the food; and I could learn how to make the bread before we went. It would be nicer than anything—like playing at life over again, as we used to do when we made our tent with the drugget, and had our little plates and dishes."

"Father and mother would not let you go."

"Yes, I think they would, when I explained everything. It would save money; and papa would have more to bring up the boys with." … Rex would have seemed a vision of the father's youth, if it had been possible to imagine Mr. Gascoigne without distinct plans and without command, smitten with a heart sorrow, and having no more notion of concealment than a sick animal; and Anna was a tiny copy of Rex, with hair drawn back and knotted, her face following his in its changes of expression, as if they had one soul between them.

"Yes; to get my bread there."

"I could learn to make the bread before we went." (117–19; ch. 8).

Anna's response to Rex's plan is a sophisticated if unwitting joke: Rex means to make a living in the colonies by saying "to get my bread there"; Anna seems to argue that "to make a living" is "to make-up a living": Rex does not need to get his bread in Canada, if Anna already knows how to make bread in England. Making a life is placed in the domain of make-believe: "It would be nicer than anything, playing at life over again," as Anna argues. She cannot keep the fantasy of playing at life over again under the rug/drugget. Also of note is that her fantasy is not separate from but coincident with Rex's fantasy, as if "they share one soul between them": Their preferred history is one of shared subjectivity and "repeats" rather than one of moving through a linear progression. They want to go off to the colonies, "the empty places," which are free of the limitations of civilized English life.

This thematic refrain of make-believe is an allegory that is repeated throughout the novel between other sets of people who either have, like Rex-and-Anna and Ezra-and-Daniel, "one soul between them," or who are contractually bound to auditing each other's narratives, as are Daniel and Gwendolen. This pattern defines history as shared identity or contractual conversation: In other words, history is not a narrative of time but is a narrative about shared space—or intersubjectivity. Inversely, identity is defined in terms of having a shared history of being a part of a larger body (to believe one's private life is carried along by some extrahuman script, such as operates with manifest destiny, for example). History's being embodied in persons stuck together, limpetlike, is explored through the case of Ezra Mordecai and Daniel. History becomes a map of this shared space; a limpet attaching to a political body: "If the swiftest thinking has about the pace of a greyhound, the slowest must be supposed to move, like the limpet, by an apparent sticking, which after a good while is discerned to be a slight progression" (771; ch. 58). Part of Daniel's story is that his individualism comes to him as a process of thinking that is a progression to the idea of Zionism; he is like the limpet slowly sucking on Mordecai and Israel. Daniel is involved in thinking that is collective: He doesn't just possess thoughts; thinking possesses him. Eliot gives us a definition of history that is radically localized and privately subjective, yet rarely typified by independent thought. History, thus, is a transferred narrative between bodies and not a narrative written in stone.

I end this consideration of the problems of historical progression and shared subjectivity in *Daniel Deronda* with an Eliot anecdote from late 1869 and early 1870:

> The Ban-Hamideh could not understand the irresistible attraction that the [Moabite] stone held for the Europeans. Nothing of value could be seen on its surface, though perhaps it concealed something more valuable inside. The Bedouin hoisted the stone onto a blazing fire. When it became red-hot, they dumped it into a trough of water. Again and again this procedure was repeated. Cracks began to develop; the stone was beginning to reveal the secret of its contents. But when it finally split apart into dozens of fragments with a hiss of steam and a final splash into the water trough, the Ban-Hamideh found nothing. The stone, now nothing more than a water soaked pile of black fragments, clearly contained no gold or treasure. The larger pieces were quickly distributed among the clan members for hiding in various places around their encampment. All that was left open to the light of day after the Bedouin had left was an innocent scattering of black gravel among the ruins at Dhiban.[68]

This is a depiction of the fate that the Moabite stone, probably the most significant find in Victorian biblical archeology, underwent in the year 1869. A Palestinian nomadic tribe, the Ban-Hamideh, became suspicious of the very interested would-be buyers from Germany, France, and England. The stone's surface of Moab writing (which corroborated the "truth"/accuracy of biblical narrative in Kings II in a non-Hebraic account) from the ninth century BCE was worthless as a document to the tribe and, in a *Maltese Falcon* scenario, the tribe broke the stone and looked inside for treasure, wondering if secret valuables inside were what made Westerners so eager to buy it. Unfortunately, there was no hidden treasure. The stone's surface treasure of nonbiblical evidence for the historical accuracy of the Bible became shattered, a physically fragmented form. The irretrievability of the past, in an ironic tour-de-force, is evinced in a broken stone.

Eliot notes her introduction to the stone in her journal of May 1870, following a trip to Oxford:

> After lunch we went to the Bodleian, and then to the Sheldonian Theatre, where there was a meeting apropos of Palestine Exploration. Captain Warren, conductor of the Exploration at Jerusalem read a paper, and then Mr. Deutsche gave an account of the interpretation, as hitherto arrived at, of the Moabite Stone. I saw "squeezes" of this stone for the first time, with photographs taken from the squeezes.[69]

---

68   Silberman, *Digging*, 107.
69   Haight, *Letters*, 5:100, 25–28 May 1870.

The stone is like the fragmentation of the narrative in *Daniel Deronda*, which in turn parallels the fragmentation of political economy, identity, and selfhood. The story of this stone seems to parallel the historical conclusions of Eliot's final novel: Histories are plural; history marks spaces and rests in subjects, but it cannot tell time. In fact, in her notebook, her entry for the Mesha-Stone has a "marginal pencil line beside the account of the shattering of the stone": "When the English, Prussians & French were trying to get possession of it the Arabs became suspicious & angry, made the stone hot, poured cold water on it & thus shattered it."[70] In one sense, the stone may be a metaphor for Eliot's novel; perhaps it is only a shattering of a shattering, but not the destruction of a dream. Gwendolen, Grandcourt, Daniel, Mordecai, Rex, Anna, Lydia, and Mirah are aggregates exploded and repieced together, and something like a story is squeezed out of them. Unlike the Moabite stone, they are not simply surface; they represent complex often incommensurate political economies and social geographies. This reading profoundly changes a realist text into something not entirely conventionally recognizable to the reader as realism.

Daniel Deronda is one long narration about who shares which stories with whom. Characters in *Daniel Deronda* see themselves as narrative chunks: fragments of stone. Consider this interaction between Daniel and Mordecai:

> "Everything I can in conscience do to make your life effective I will do."
>
> "I know it," said Mordecai, in the tone of quiet certainty which dispenses with further assurance. "I heard it. You see it all—you are by my side on the mount of vision, and behold the paths of fulfillment which others deny."
>
> He was silent a moment or two, and then went on meditatively—"You will take up my life where it was broken." (600)

These two characters, on their "mount of vision," have to become aggregated to speak: They know their "broken" edges and search for a fit. This model marks their search for possessed individualism when they fuse into an executive self.

Artist Hans Meyrick explains alternatively what happens to characters like Gwendolen. He explains to Daniel his portrait series of the story of Berenice (who was "beautiful, popular, and ambitious" and forced to leave her husband) for whom he has used Mirah as his model. He says:

> "No, no; a few mature touches to show the lapse of time. Dark-eyed beauty wears well, hers particularly. But now, here is the fifth: Berenice seated lonely on the ruins of Jerusalem. That is pure imagination. That is what ought to have been—perhaps was. Now, see how I tell a pathetic negative. Nobody knows what became of her:—that is finely indicated by the series coming to a close. There is no sixth picture." Here Hans pretended to speak with a gasping sense of sublimity, and drew back his head with a frown, as if looking for a like impression on Deronda. "I break off in the Homeric style. The story is chipped off, so to speak, and passes with a ragged edge into nothing—*le neant*; can anything be more sublime, especially in French? The vulgar would desire to see her corpse and burial—perhaps her

---

70   Irwin, *Notebooks*, 416.

will read and her linen distributed. But now come and look at this on the easel. I have made some way there." (514; ch. 37)

This is a novel where a story is told by the transfer of a soul into a body. Some fragments (like Gwendolen) are chipped off and stay that way. Daniel ends with an extra soul in his body, and Gwendolen ends without any body. This novel is really most striking, though, beyond the unique fates of Gwendolen and Daniel and beyond the jagged texture of the narrative. This novel tells us something about the direction of the late Victorian novel, in general, in terms of plot and character, and about changing views of political economy.

Identity in this novel is primarily political. The political is enabled by a mystical embodiment that some can experience (like Daniel) and some cannot (such as Gwendolen). Introducing "the mystical" into "the political" revolutionizes the model of political economy and disables an established discourse of entitlement in the novel. Compare, for instance, the difference between *Middlemarch* (1871–1872) and *Daniel Deronda* (1876). The entire central plotline of *Middlemarch*, almost from the first page to the last, revolves around the effects of Mr Casaubon's will on his young widow, Dorothea. In terms of wills, far more disastrous things happen to Gwendolen—another young, beautiful, and intriguing widow. Yet it is unthinkable to imagine Eliot's structuring the plot of *Daniel Deronda* around the testamentary fate of Gwendolen. Comparing the political economy in these two novels shows a world turned upside down. The central structural feature of the one, the effects of a disagreeable husband's will on a young widow, is really only a minor part of the structure in *Daniel Deronda*, relegated mainly to Books 1 and 7. Instead, the central structuring theme of this novel is the intersection of the mystical and the political. Namely, the romance, visions, and happy ending of this book are all about a new political alliance: the mystical, invisible, historical community within Daniel's body.

Political economy has been transfigured by the mystical, and politics has become the new romance and religion (and not just for Trollope's Plantagenet Palliser).[71] Political efficacy happens through a mystical passage, and to be a individual in Eliot's last novel requires becoming a plural political entity. *Daniel Deronda* points to a change of course in both the domestic novel and political identity.

Conclusion

The only way Eliot's characters in *Daniel Deronda* can be successful is when they serve as outposts for the ideas of invisible communities, narratives, and pasts. Eliot wrote a new type of realism, not just the careful description of the psychological functions of a closed community, as she does in *Middlemarch*. Rather, she wrote

---

[71] Compare the experiences of Plantagenet Palliser in Anthony Trollope's six Palliser novels (1864–1880), which portray high Victorian English parliamentary political society.

realism about an extrapersonal, pantheistic system. Each character is a tiny working in the mind of a large, invisible central system. Because her characters overlap and meld or disappear, the individual, either in tragic straits or triumphant circumstances, is not at the center of the psychological studies—aggregate characters are. These aggregate characters people a postnationalist civilization that is not grounded in nation-states but in bodies.

The whole text in its fragmentation is like a new history/telling of modern political economy. This novel gives the reader the chance to look anew at concepts like possessive individualism and the private individual. Eliot ultimately favors possession over possessiveness in a plot so radical that the reader can view an invisible sphere subsuming the divide between the public and the private sphere. Through the Jewish plot, Eliot tells the stories of competing political logics. The mystical, for Eliot, comes out on top. Characters are not integral and whole: They are partially imprinted, partially effaced, and ultimately fragmented to be remade. For Eliot, in *Daniel Deronda*, the individual does not provide the key to interiority; the combination of all the characters and their grand, invisible, extrasensory, combined agency does.

The next chapter, "Worlds Apart," continues to focus on Victorian views of the possessed individual and shared spaces, with an emphasis on women's subjectivity through a consideration of the extra spheres of invisible culture.

SECTION TWO

EXTRA SPHERES

Chapter 2

Worlds Apart: Invisible Culture and Extra Spheres

Frequently, mystical practitioners explored a new mystical concept of natural order that subsumed the visible world to the order of a more powerful extra sphere, making the real world and civic order undesirable by comparison. Their accounts describing seeing the invisible and mystical extra spheres frequently imagine women, as well as the future of society, to be outside of history and linear time. For instance, Florence Marryat writes against the powers of organized religion and against the reassurance of recorded history, arguing that:

> there must be a big screw loose somewhere in the various religions presented to us, which profess to give us everything but this—vague hopes, threatening fears, promises of reward, and dread of punishment, but not *an atom of proof* that, having passed out of this body, we shall exist either to enjoy the one, or endure the other ... And though history may be sufficient for us, when we are asked to believe that William the Conqueror landed in England in the year 1066 (because, if the truth were told, we do not care one jot nor tittle if he ever landed here at all), it is *not* enough to rest all our hopes of a future life upon, for ourselves and those we love.[1]

Marryat's comment raises several questions: How should the anachronistic impulse that she and other mystical writers favor be interpreted? Is it revolutionary? Solipsistic? Utopian? Serving as protest? This chapter will address some of these possibilities, while at the same time recognizing that these options are not mutually exclusive. The extra spheres provided by mystical accounts of spirit possession are rarely stable and fixed but are instead quite dynamic. Although the generic features across a wide array of accounts are surprisingly similar, the worlds they proffer and their authors' political views are disparate and distinct. The utopian removals that define accounts of spiritual vision and extra spheres against that of realistic portrayals of the public sphere both show how political life may be uniquely imagined as part of one's physical body and indicate how Victorian subjects desired to see political life changed. The first section of this chapter will describe the visual theories through which spiritualists imagined they could literally see the invisible. Invisible sights in turn led to new worldviews in the extra spheres of mystics that will be treated in the second section of this chapter.

---

[1]   Florence Marryat, *The Spirit World* (Leipzig: Bernhard Tauchnitz, 1894), 7, 9.

Invisible Culture

A basic yet crucial question arises when considering interactions between people and spirits: How was it supposed to have occurred? Spiritualists literally had an alternative worldview through their distinctive and extensively described theories of spiritual or inner vision. To fully understand the power and persuasion of their beliefs, it is important to see the fluid boundary they described between what could be seen by all with their outer eyes and what, while seeming invisible to most, might be visible to some through inner vision.

Received theories of vision were tested throughout the nineteenth century by scientists and by spiritualists. The Enlightenment concept of vision, where a singular observer would respond in a predictable way to a given stimulus, was being questioned in the experiments of scientists and in the experiences of practicing spiritualists. Scientists were working in the fields of optics and physics to provide new hypotheses about the workings of vision.[2] Spiritualists, in contrast, were turning to their personal experiences with inner vision, second sight, to explain how they could see the invisible. Both of these nineteenth-century groups were finding vision to be subjective. Johannes Muller, an early nineteenth-century theorist of physiological optics, worked on the theory of specialization of sensory nerves, arguing that a given stimulus would generate distinct sensations when applied to different types of sensory nerves; for example, the given stimulus, electricity, would produce one sensation when applied to the skin and another when applied to the optic nerve. Muller was describing an arbitrary relationship between stimulus and sensation, a theory that upset the stability of the Enlightenment singular observer and suggested that an eye that perceived differences as equivalencies had an innate capacity to misperceive.[3]

---

[2]   See Jonathan Crary, *Techniques of the Observer, On Vision and Modernity in the Nineteenth Century* (Cambridge: MIT Press, 1990) for his fascinating discussion of early nineteenth-century optics, from which I draw all material on Johannes Muller, Augustin Jean Fresnel, and Pierre Flourens.

[3]   Crary discusses the work of Johannes Muller at length writing, "His fame came to rest on his theorization of ... specialization: The doctrine of specific nerve energies (*spezifische Sinnesenergien*) introduced in the *Physiologie* ... It asserted quite simply—and this is what marks its epistemological scandal—that a uniform cause (for example, electricity) generates utterly different sensations from one kind of nerve to another. Electricity applied to the optic nerve produces the experience of light, applied to the skin the sensation of touch. Conversely, Muller showed that a variety of different causes would produce the *same* sensation in a given sensory nerve. In other words, he is describing a fundamentally arbitrary relation between stimulus and sensation. It is an account of a body with an innate capacity, one might even say a transcendental faculty, to *misperceive*—of an eye that renders differences equivalent" (90). In turn, he references Johannes Muller, *Zur vergleichenden Physiologie des Gesichtsinnes des Menschen und Thiere* (Leipzig, 1826) and *Uber die phantastischen Gesichterscheinungen* (Coblenz, 1826).

The precursor to Muller's theory was a switch to believing that light could not be described as singular any more than the body's sensations could. Augustin Jean Fresnel theorized that light did not move as longitudinal rays but as transverse waves. Thus, light could no longer be said to move directly from one source to one observer, and more important, it no longer had an independent physical description—it moved the same way as a number of other things, such as other electromagnetic waves.[4] Another nineteenth-century scientist, Pierre Flourens, theorized that different brain/ perceptual functions were localized; under his theory the body and its vision became subjective.[5]

The theories of nineteenth-century optical scientists, such as Muller, Fresnel, and Flourens, suggest that vision is a construction and that it might be difficult to have a single viewer attend to a certain sight, especially when other things might be pulling his or her attention away. A spiritualist who *sees* spirit materializations is a good (albeit atypical) example of this distraction. Stimuli automatically and simultaneously pull a subject's attention in too many directions. If one cannot claim a person's attention, controlling him or her becomes difficult. One of the largest objectives of Victorian primary optical research, according to Crary, was to discover as much as possible about visual attention, what the viewer could focus on and for how long. With this information, science sought ways to "control" the attention span of the new Industrial Age worker to increase productivity.[6] The Victorian spiritualist's use of vision was quite different. Spiritualism further theorized vision as subjective, distinguishing between outer (material) and inner (spiritual) eyes.

Spiritualists believed the dead and disembodied could "materialize" at a séance or that their words and deeds could be channeled through the mouth and body of the medium who could see them. This whole construct called into question the very meaning of vision and changed the spiritualist's concepts of visible culture while creating an invisible culture for the practitioner. The concept of inner vision, as defined by the practices of Victorian spiritualists, became highly destabilizing. The claim that the invisible spiritual realm can be seen upsets stable concepts of

---

[4] Crary, *Techniques*, 86–8. Crary, in turn, cites Edward Frankel, "Corpuscular Optics and the Wave Theory of Light: The Science and Politics of a Revolution in Physics," *Social Studies of Science* 6 (1976): 141–84; G.N. Cantor, *Optics after Newton* (Manchester: Manchester University Press, 1983), esp. 150–59; and R.H. Silliman, "Fresnel and the Emergence of Physics as a Discipline," *Historical Studies in the Physical Sciences* 4 (1974): 137–62.

[5] Flourens named the cerebellum the motor center and the cerebrum the perception center (Crary, *Techniques*, 82). Crary references Pierre Flourens, *Recherches experimentales sur les proprietes et les fonctions du systeme nerveux dans les animaux vertebres* (Paris: Crevot, 1824).

[6] See Crary, *Techniques*, 85. Crary's book argues that optical science in the 1820s and 1830s provided the theory that the senses were localized and, because what was seeable relied on the viewer's specific optical organization, that in turn upset the concept of a unified Enlightenment observer who could attend to common visual stimuli.

what is external, such as the existence of a known history or the concept of national or other earthly government in many Victorian accounts. The 1850s to 1870s were a time of great flux in political representation—in terms of suffrage campaigns as well as in class consciousness, industrialization, and, in the United States, abolition. The spiritualist medium's perceived ability to see spirit communicants who come to Earth with verbal directions for life—and to consider these communicants to be as real as the living—changed concepts of received order and of a fixed subjectivity.

Various nineteenth-century views on the nature of spiritual vision focus in part on the influence spiritual vision had on theology and on why and how it would be possible—or impossible—to see the invisible. The 1871 writing of mesmerist Professor G.G. Zerffi, *Spiritualism and Animal Magnetism*, argued a spirit could not be seen. Camilla Crosland in her 1857 work, *Light in the Valley*, claimed that a spirit could be seen by a spiritualist and Sophia DeMorgan in her 1863 book, *From Matter to Spirit*, went even further by claiming that the question of seeing a spirit was one that had been effectively theorized by reputable philosophers long before the nineteenth-century began. It is this intellectual debate that frames the contradictory viewpoints the Croslands—both Anglicans and spiritualists—held about seeing spirits. After examining Newton Crosland's views on inner vision, I address the phenomenon of spirit photography in the 1870s to show one intersection of mysticism and technology. Finally, this section will address Camilla Crosland's provocative beliefs concerning spiritual vision and theology.

Spiritualist Views on Seeing the Invisible

In 1871, Prof. George Gustavus Zerffi, a popular mesmerist who was investigating spiritualism, gave his explanation of why it would be technically impossible for a person to see a spirit. He argues that although spirits may exist and even may be able to make themselves felt by the effects they produce on matter, no one can see these spirits. He writes:

> What is the supernatural? ... If the rays of the sun, at a distance of 95,000,000 of miles, by influencing our globe can produce rocks, plants, animals, and vary these products according to the angle at which they touch our earth, the question may suggest itself to the thinking mind, why should some magnetic force not stream out from our own bodies and produce strange effects on others ...? To attribute, however, such phenomena to *spirits*, is in itself a mere phraseological caprice. Spirits as such may exist, but if they exist, they can only make themselves felt by changes produced on matter, that is by effects.[7]

---

[7]   George Gustavus Zerffi, *Spiritualism and Animal Magnetism: A Treatise on Dreams, Second Sight, Somnambulism, Magnetic Sleep, Spiritual Manifestations, Hallucinations, and Spectral Visions* (London: Hardwicke, 1871), 117. Zerffi lived from 1821 to 1892.

Zerffi sets down the argument that a spirit does not possess a material body as the sun does, and therefore it is not possible to see or touch a spirit. From the point of view of critics (such as Zerffi), Victorian spiritualists make an irrational attribution of cause and overvalue a delusional world because of it.[8] Zerffi depicts spiritualists as afflicted:

> Our Spiritualists ... are distinguished by a pallid countenance, an oppressed respiration, dilated pupils, nervous twitchings, and all those symptoms ... which are common to those afflicted with second sight, whether prophetic or retrospective ... This phenomenon [is] a reaction against the growing materialistic and utilitarian tendencies of our times, which threaten to destroy all the good livings of metaphysicians held in the region of shadows. Imagination is to be altogether destroyed ... These minds labour under the misapprehension that only fancy has poetical charms.[9]

Zerffi attributes the faulty vision of spiritualists to a reaction against a growing materialistic and utilitarian tendency of the time that he feels was threatening metaphysics and imagination. Simultaneously, he himself believed that magnetic rays streamed out of the human body. In the twenty-first century, believing in spirits or emanating magnetic rays may seem equally unusual and not evidently spiritualist/materialist opposites (see Figure 2.1).

In contrast to Zerffi's view, many Victorian spiritualists, such as Camilla Crosland, value and participate in the extra spheres they discern with their inner eyes. Camilla Crosland in 1857 describes spiritualist vision:

> My own impression, both from observation and report, is, that as the spiritual eye is opened the material eye is closed, and that just in proportion to the power and privileges of the medium is the perfect or the partial opening of the one and the closing of the other ... The phenomena ... of clairvoyance, and even of ordinary dreaming, suggests how completely the spirit eye can see, totally unaided by outer light.[10]

Camilla claims that the inner and outer eye (the spiritual eye and the material eye) can work simultaneously and that the material eye, which sees "mundane details," is in the service of the spiritual eye. Whereas Zerffi is claiming that spiritualists are wrong to believe that spirits are the cause of the phenomena they see and wrong to assume

---

[8] This practice of valuing the truth of delusion over the reality of the "outer world" is what some Victorians defined as constituting insanity. Even the staunch Anglican Newton Crosland, Camilla Crosland's husband, who was also a spiritualist and whom I will soon discuss, notes, "The *Encyclopaedia Britannica* says, that 'the true theory of apparitions is the same as that of insanity'." See Newton Crosland, *Apparitions; a New Theory* (London: Effingham Wilson, 1856), 30.

[9] Zerffi, *Spiritualism and Animal Magnetism*, 106, 102.

[10] Mrs Newton Crosland [Camilla Toulmin], *Light in the Valley. My Experiences of Spiritualism* (London: Routledge, 1857), 83–92.

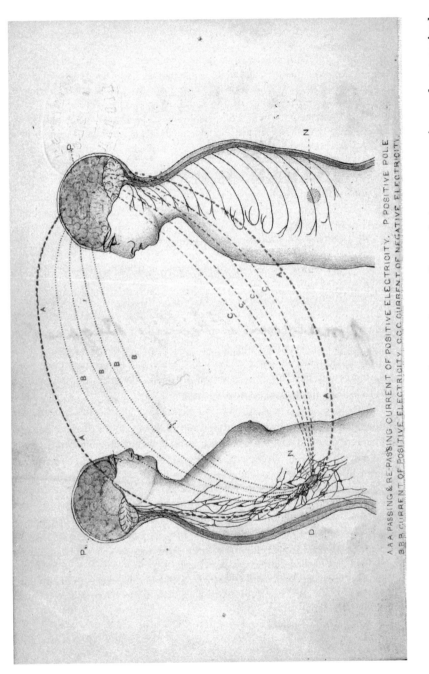

AAA PASSING & RE-PASSING CURRENT OF POSITIVE ELECTRICITY.   P POSITIVE POLE
B.B.B. CURRENT OF POSITIVE ELECTRICITY.   C.C.C. CURRENT OF NEGATIVE ELECTRICITY.

Figure 2.1   Zerffi's mesmeric chart of the transference of magnetic rays between mesmerizer and mesmerized

that the phenomena are real, Camilla claims that spirits are the cause and are more real than the things seen by the material, physical, "outer" eye. She defends her position by saying, "The truth is, that talking of Spiritualism to those whose spiritual faculty is thickly encrusted with materialism, is something like talking of flashing jewels to one who has never seen; but none should despair of a human mind, sooner or later, shaking off its encarnalizing scales."[11] Her beliefs about inner vision are thus protected from the onslaught of detractors by her claim that such critics are physically unable to comprehend spiritualism—because of vision blocked by materialist encrustations. Though Camilla Crosland and Zerffi certainly disagree about spiritualism and whether it provides fact or fantasy, their positions about magnetism and the subjectivity of vision are not inconsistent. Camilla writes that:

> the spirits have declared that magnetism and electricity, though not spirit, are the media by which spirit acts on matter ... It would appear that there is a soul ... which permeates through the body in life, and it is on or by this atmosphere that disembodied spirits are permitted to communicate with mortals.[12]

In this quotation, Crosland imagines the soul as an atmosphere that permits disembodied spirits to communicate through the media of magnetism and electricity, just as Zerffi assumes that the medium of magnetism is what permits one material body to stream out rays that affect another body.

What makes mediums and the adherents of spiritualism such as Camilla Crosland so challenging to mesmerists such as Zerffi is that they enact a localization of the senses outside of a materialist frame. They may see what others see with their outer eye and simultaneously see something entirely different with their inner eye. A medium cannot be subjected to external regulation because she does not see what another sees, and even when she does, she will not focus her attention on common visual imperatives. She thinks, via sensory localization, locally.

Sophia De Morgan, the first historian of spiritualism and herself a Victorian spiritualist, likens the radical sensory locality of spiritualists to that of philosophers. In 1863 She categorized spiritualists as neo-Platonic intermediate idealists:

> The soul, with all the memories and impressions of which it has become the storehouse, takes its place, and the more internal spirit developed and advanced animates the 'spiritual body.' But according to the belief of thoughtful men, mental philosophers are of three classes: the *Idealists*, who believe, with Berkeley and others, that ideas are communicated without any real substratum; the *Realists*, who hold that we perceive outer things as they really are; and a third, who may be called *Intermediate Idealists*—of this class are the great majority of philosophers, who believe that matter is *a something* external to ourselves which produces its appropriate impression or idea on the sense and mind, but which requires its appropriate receptivity in the mind to give it form and character. The *ideas* of Plato show

---

11   *Ibid.*, 39.
12   *Ibid.*, 31, 33.

that he belongs to this third class, and the observations of phrenologists, which prove a variety of susceptibilities to impressions, are strongly in favour of this doctrine. We are, even in this earthly life, the architects of our own surroundings; external nature supplies the *cause* whose effect is produced through the senses and brain, according to a *type* or *idea* in the mind.[13]

De Morgan presents the theory that the external world is perceived in accordance with an idea in an individual's mind. Mediumship then becomes the outgrowth of something inherent in the individual—a special sensory organization. Mediumship provides a competing visual and somatic technology for how to process reality.

The somatic technology of mediumship allowed each practitioner to interpret what he or she was seeing and relate it to personal beliefs about inner sight and its meaning. This in turn created a junction between spiritualism and Christianity in mid-nineteenth-century England that speaks of God and Jesus being best accessed outside of organized religion. This juncture is particularly apparent in the writings of Camilla Crosland and her husband Newton Crosland.

Newton Crosland's Theory of Apparitions

The Croslands were a prominent mid-Victorian theologically inclined couple living in London. Newton Crosland was a pious adherent of the Church of England, and his wife, Camilla, whose views this section has already partly examined, was a literary woman, noted for her children's books, biographies, and her personal acquaintance with such famous activists as Harriet Beecher Stowe and Margaret Fuller.[14] The Croslands held complicated (and antagonistic) theologically inflected interpretations of spirit manifestations.

Newton Crosland's *Apparitions; A New Theory* (1856) blends the budding technology of photography with the epistemologically—and theologically—

---

[13] D.C. [Sophia De Morgan], *From Matter to Spirit. The Result of Ten Years; Experience in Spirit Manifestations. Intended as a Guide to Enquirers* (London: Longman, Roberts, and Green, 1863), 209.

[14] Camilla Toulmin, who was born in London in 1812, married Newton Crosland in 1848. She had been making her living as a writer for several years following the death of her father. See her autobiography, *Landmarks of a Literary Life: 1829–1892* (New York: Charles Scribner, 1893). Her works mainly relate to conditions of the poor and to spiritualism. They include biography: *Memorable Women: The Story of Their Lives* (New York: G.P. Putnam and Sons, 1860) and children's books such as *Stories of London Re-told for Youthful Readers* (London: W.H. Allen, 1880) and *The Island of the Rainbow. A Fairy Tale. And Other Fancies* (London: Routledge, 1866). She also translated and published Victor Hugo's *Hermani: A Tragedy* (London: G. Bell and Sons, 1887). For a listing of her published works, see S. Austin Allibone, *A Critical Dictionary of English Literature and British and American Authors ... to the Latter Half of the Nineteenth Century* (London: J.B. Lippincott, 1908), 418.

established ethic of learning by example.[15] Starting in the 1870s, spiritualists were producing photographs that contained the image of a living sitter surrounded by images of the spectral. However, even by the 1850s, some spiritualists were starting to discuss the spiritual through the new technology of photography. Newton elucidates his photographic spirit theory as follows:

> The scoffing logician ... exclaims—"I have no objection to believe in the apparition of the soul of your grandmother, but don't tell me that you really and literally saw the ghost of her night-cap and apron!" ... To meet the difficulty, I venture to offer as a solution the following hypothesis: that every significant action of our lives—in the garments we wear, and in the attitudes and gestures of our humanity—is vitally photographed or depicted in the spirit-world; and that the angels, under God's direction, have the power of exhibiting, as a living picture, any specific circumstances or features to those who have the gift of spiritual sight, and who are intended to be influenced by the manifestations ... What an idea of infinity and divine government does it give us, to suppose that after death we shall move through a grand picture-gallery of our own deeds self-delineated! What a subject of contemplation and awe to those who are debating in their own minds the character of their actions! What a check to those who have not yet quite decided to perpetrate something unworthy of future exhibition! And what a consolation to believe that true repentance for any vicious deeds may secure the removal of the portraits of such deeds from this gallery of celestial art![16]

Crosland's bold theory is simultaneously technologically progressive and religiously conservative. He is ready to incorporate new mystical experiences and emerging photographic technology into an existing framework of Christian education. Spirits appear as if at a slideshow of the moral past life. The beatified, repentant, soberly attired spirit indicates high points of the soul's earthly tenure. "What a consolation to believe that ... repentance for any vicious deeds may secure the removal ... of such deeds from this gallery." In this scheme, spirit visitation is as innocuous as the family portrait gallery and potentially leads to redemption. Photographic ephemerality—already uncanny—is reinstated into a heavenly context where the ghostly is reassuringly domesticated. All the grandmothers (in all their nightcaps) peacefully people eternity—offering picture-book guidance to their earthly progeny.

Crosland offers us a beguiling question: What kind of an idea of infinity and divine government does it give us to suppose that after death we shall move through a grand picture gallery of our own deeds self-delineated? It gives us a divine government that

---

[15] Newton Crosland's other published works include *The Eltham Tragedy Revued by C.* (London, 1871); *Apparitions: An Essay Explanatory of Old Facts and a New Theory; to Which Are Added "Sketches and Adventures"* (London, 1873), an extension of his 1856 work; *Pith: Essays and Sketches, Grave and Gay: With Some Verses and Illustrations* (London, 1881); *The New Principia; or, The Astronomy of the Future* (London, 1883). As cited in Allibone, *Critical Dictionary*, 418.

[16] Newton Crosland, *Apparitions; A New Theory* (London: Effingham Wilson, 11, Royal Exchange, 1856), 28–30.

in fact does not substantially differ from the idea of Victorian earthly government: hegemonically inscribed grannies eternally wearing their aprons. The celestial imitates and celebrates the terrestrial. No revolutionary changes or acts are required; heaven is a well-edited strolling gallery run by the divine government with angel docents. Christian *telos* is nothing but the divine reinscription of a preexisting respectable England.

Spirit Photography

Even as odd as the technology to which Newton Crosland alludes—spirit photography—may seem, it became a popular London practice in less than two decades after his writing in 1856.[17] England's first spirit photographer, Fred A. Hudson, of 177 Holloway Road, London, experienced a booming business in summer of 1872. Fritz, in his book *Where Are the Dead? Or Spiritualism Explained*, notes:

> Mr. Hudson has taken a great number of spirit photographs, and his rooms for many months in the summer of 1872 were crowded with Spiritualists from all parts of the country, anxious to be photographed … The form of a spirit came out distinctly upon the plate immediately on the likeness being "developed."[18]

The verb *developed* is duly noted to emphasize, no doubt, the Victorian trope of development as well as the chemical process of bringing forth the image. One striking feature of the description of Hudson's business is the likelihood that the sitter will recognize the spirit that is developed beside him or her on the photographic plate. In this case, the spirit materialization will not just be available to one with the gift of spiritual sight but to everyone. Often one's dead children, as for Swedenborgian medium Mr Howitt, or ancestors whose likeness is only known to the sitter and not to Mr Hudson, will appear in the spirit photograph. The lesson of the spirit photograph seems to be that it will document the persistence of ancestral ties and familial identity beyond the vale. Spirit photography describes the photograph as under the influence of the sitter who is looking back at the camera—it seems as though the camera is temporarily the mesmerized or the mediumized, and the spiritualist sitter is the mesmerizer or spirit control producing extra images on the plate by force of thought. As in mediumship, the physical organization and force of thought of the sitter was believed to materialize the thought-about spirit or object.

---

[17]   See Martyn Jolly, *Faces of the Living Dead* (London: British Library, 2006) and Pierre Apraxine, et al., *The Perfect Medium* (New Haven and London: Yale University Press, 2005) for recent work on Frederick Hudson as well as on the spirit photography of William Mumler of New York and of Parisian Edouard Buguet. Buguet and Mumler, unlike Hudson, underwent trials for fraud.

[18]   Fritz, *Where Are the Dead? Or, Spiritualism Explained* (London: Simpkin, Marshall, 1873), 81–2.

Through the 1880s and well into the twentieth century, with such famous proponents as Sir Arthur Conan Doyle, spirit photography remained quite popular. In 1882, Georgiana Houghton published *Chronicles of the Photographs of Spiritual Beings and Phenomena Invisible to the Material Eye.*[19] This work, not unlike Camilla Crosland's accounts of spiritualism, reads like a memoir or autobiography chronicling Houghton's social circle and mystical episodes of particular interest. As Camilla's accounts will also show, Houghton's episodes recount frequent interactions with ancestors, dead children, deceased historical personages, and new acquaintances who serve as spirit controls. Houghton's work intersperses the narrative with six pages (nine photographs each) of images that loosely provide the album that goes along with the memoir (see Figure 2.2). Eight photos depict the living with a dead parent, grandparent, or ancestor. Another seven show a living sitter with a dead sibling or child. Historical spirit figures who are photographed include St John the Evangelist, Joan of Arc, and the Day Star (Lucifer, a.k.a. Satan). Famous Victorians photographed with spirits include scientist Alfred Russel Wallace, Mr Hudson (probably Fred Hudson the spirit photographer), famous Swedenborgian minister Mr Howitt, and famous mediums, including Mrs Guppy (see Chapter 3). There are also several photographs that leave the relationship or history of the subject poorly annotated, noting only partial details, such as "Alexander Calder, Esq., and spirits" or the "unclad spirit," or "Alas! For her whose white robe of innocence became a rag," or "Charlie [a spirit] embracing me." In fact, the annotations are of the informal style one might expect if one were ushered through someone's family picture album. The surprising feature here is that the ghostly and the uncanny, just as often without a known history as with one, are made familial, intimate, trusted, and have implied ties to the earthly sitter.

Certain inherent life factors, such as death, historical time, and the demographic situation of the living (or the dead), no longer matter. If the Evangelist appears to one, why read the Bible? If Joan of Arc is back, what difference does heresy or execution make? In this belief system, can history still teach lessons; do the dead have a fixed echo and valence of meaning? Do the dead remain in the past tense? What types of transgression, shame, illegality, or honor have a universal identity? Why did one spirit's "white robe of innocence" become "a rag" (a reference to prostitution)? In short, how does interacting and being seen with spirits in a séance or a photograph define or redefine one's social, spiritual, and moral topography? When the "past" of the "historical past" returns, it enables spiritualists to reconceptualize world order through imagining history only through spiritual synchronicity.

---

[19]   Georgiana Houghton, *Chronicles of the Photographs of Spiritual Beings and Phenomena Invisible to the Material Eye: Interblended with Personal Narratives* (London: E.W. Allen 1882). Many of the spirit photographs that appear in Houghton's book were taken in Hudson's studio, as several of the sitters Fritz discusses in *Where Are the Dead?*, such as William Howitt, are included in Houghton's plates of spirit photographs.

Figure 2.2   One of the six plates from Houghton's book showing from left
to right and from top to bottom: **The Day-Star; Mrs Ramsay
and Môtee; Geraldine Cope; Mrs Clarke (of California) and
spirit; Maurice Joseph, Esq., and spirits; Captain Fawcett, RN,
and son; Mrs Guppy, Tommy, and Katie; Spirit, with American
photographs; Mr Howitt and his daughter, with spirit of his son**
Courtesy of the Bryn Mawr College Library.

Spiritual vision provides the surprising atemporal return of ghosts and images from the past. This methodology in its neo-Platonism is ahistorical. Take, for instance, Houghton's spirit photograph of Joan of Arc (Figure 2.3). Joan, in terms of historical reception and as a culturally produced icon, can truly be all things to all people. For Houghton she is just one of many images that is part of the family picture album: She is transmogrified from medieval France to Victorian England in this spirit photograph, one of many of her simulations for which no original exists. In terms of Joan of Arc's reception culturally over the past six hundred years or so, she is a veritable Cindy Sherman from days of yore. In terms of Houghton's spirit photograph of Joan of Arc, Joan may appear to be quite specifically like a modern-day self-photographer: She is in the studio, producing a staged self-portrait from beyond this world. Of course, it must be noted that this type of "reading" of a spirit photograph focuses on its cultural reception in the 1870s and early 1880s when the discourse of "evidence" and "truth" did not yet apply predominantly to a photographic image that most twenty-first-century viewers quickly would identify as a double exposure.[20]

Writings on spirit photography such as Fritz's and Houghton's discuss spirit photographs in the 1870s and early 1880s primarily as mementos or souvenirs of mediumship as well as memorialization of the dead who come back for a spirit photograph, not unlike the postmortem photography popular at the time. Studio photography up through the 1880s follows the compositional conventions of painted portrait miniatures, which had been popular as a portrait format, by amateurs and professionals through the 1840s (see Figure 2.4). During the 1840s, the popularization

---

[20]   For a discussion of the technique of producing spirit photographs, see Robert Hirsch, *Seizing the Light, A History of Photography* (Boston: McGraw Hill, 2000), 32–3, 128–9, and William C. Darrah, *Cartes de Visite in Nineteenth-Century Photography* (Gettysburg, PA: W.C. Darrah, 1981), 41–2. Hirsch, for instance, includes an albumen silver stereograph of the Ghost of Milton, measuring 3.5 by 7 inches, by an unknown photographer, published by New "Spirit" Photographs, now in the George Eastman House collection. Hirsch comments, "Ghosts were created when a veiled figure entered the scene for a portion of the exposure, producing a transparent phantom. To maintain believability, less scrupulous operators concealed their methods from the public and used ploys such as a plate with a previously recorded ghost image, a transparency of a ghost image placed in front of the lens, a miniature ghost transparency placed behind the lens, or a ghost image reflected into the lens during exposure" (129). Additionally, on the technique of spirit photography, Darrah, citing *Photographic News* 1:11 (1858), writes, "Brewster had discovered that if a person stood in a position before the camera for a second or less while the exposure continued for a time thereafter, a 'ghost' appeared in the negative. The person simply walked off the setting, resulting in under-exposure of his figure. Many humorous and sentimental stereographs utilizing this idea were produced between 1854–1858" (42). He further notes that some photographers, such as O. Erekson of Bridgeport, CT, and G.L. Lape of New York "produced similar portraits, some serious sentimental mementos, not to deceive but to please the family, and some intended to be humorous, such as the ghost pointing an accusing finger at a person" (42). Many thanks to Pansylea Willburn for bibliographic suggestions on early photography.

Figure 2.3   **Spirit photograph of Joan of Arc**
Courtesy of the Bryn Mawr College Library.

From a miniature painted in 1848 by Mrs Pitt

Camilla Crosland

Simpson Low, Marston & Co. Ld.   Swan Electric Engraving Co.

Figure 2.4   **From a miniature painted in 1848 by Mrs Pitt of Camilla Crosland**

of photography began to supplant painting in portraiture. Beginning in the late 1860s, debates about the reality versus fraud of spirit photography began to come to the fore with the trial of William Mumler.[21] But neither Fritz nor Houghton are concerned with this controversy in their writings. Although debates, especially in France and America, did consider the authenticity of spirit photography, many writers, readers, and viewers of spirit photographs in 1870s London would not have found spirit photography any stranger or more contrived than studio photography in general—both are highly staged in terms of the idioms of portraiture.[22]

The practice of spirit photography, with visitors from the past returning to the present, rests on the Kantian assumption that time does not matter or come to bear on the existence of a thing. Zerffi explains Kant's view on time and reality, "Kant's theory is confirmed by many facts that are adduced. For if time is not essential to the reality of a *thing*, past and future have no signification with reference to it. According to this any event may be seen whether it has already happened or not."[23] This conception of timelessness provides a powerful critique of the importance of the historical past, one that Marryat, who did not care a jot about William the Conqueror, also utilized. In spiritualist reasoning, temporality and the reality that comes with it have no bearing on what does or does not exist or on what has or has not occurred—creating space for the radical reconceptualization of history and social order. Taking this as a possible assumption creates for the spiritualist a wildly different view of the relationship between time and place, the living and the dead, as it does for Camilla Crosland.

---

21   These debates continue well into the twentieth century. See, for instance, Arthur Conan Doyle, *The Case for Spirit Photography* (New York: George H. Doran, 1923).

22   See Katherine Coombs, *The Miniature in England* (London: Victoria and Albert, 1998) and Claudia Brush Kidwell with Nancy Rexford, "Foreword," in *Dressed for the Photographer, Ordinary Americans and Fashion, 1840–1900* (Kent, OH: Kent State University Press, 1995). Coombs observes, "Miniature painting was supplanted in emotional and cultural life by photography. In a painting by John Everett Millais from 1871, *Yes or No* (Yale Center for British Art), the heroine does not hold a miniature of her lover but a *carte de visite*, a small photograph on a card" (117). Not only did photography supplant portraiture, but photography also continued in the idiom of portraiture. As Kidwell and Rexford write, "Even for portrait photographs, both photographers and sitters considered it perfectly appropriate to arrange reality for the photographic occasion ... In the 1870s and 1880s photographers often provided painted backdrops to simulate an attractive setting, whether indoors or out ... The use of such props and backdrops shows that photographers were consciously working in a portraiture tradition borrowed from painting" (xii).

23   Zerffi, *Spiritualism and Animal Magnetism*, 67.

Camilla Crosland's Millenarian Theology

Camilla Crosland's beliefs call into question Newton Crosland's explanation of the meaning of spirit manifestations. Without temporality, history becomes a nonissue for interpreting a manifestation. The removal of history makes the contemplation of what society is or might be a vital question for some spiritualist theologians. Unlike her husband, who saw spiritualism as upholding the historical past and traditions of honorable (dead) elders, Camilla viewed her experiences with spiritualism as the revelation of a new order. In the mid-1850s she became quite involved with spiritualism because it provided a mode for the reconsideration of temporality through the redefinition of physical laws. In fact, she gives the following surprising depiction of natural law:

> The laws of the spiritual world do—under certain conditions, and finding, there is reason to suppose, their *tertium quid* in magnetism or electricity—very often control and supersede the common laws of matter. And thus it comes to pass that I, with hundreds of others, am able to testify that heavy articles are frequently suspended in the air by invisible means; that a musical instrument has been played by invisible fingers; that by those peculiar concussions which spiritualist agree to call raps, messages proceeding from disembodied intelligences are frequently delivered; and, in short, to certify to more interesting phenomena than it would be easy to catalogue or classify.[24]

The claim that unlikely events outlined in *Light in the Valley*—such as spirit rapping, levitating objects, invisible musicians—can be witnessed and testified to trumps the Victorian trope of empirical evidence. The concept of natural law's superseding civic order is nonchalantly presented. There seems to be a gendered program fulfilled by this spectacular power of natural law. Camilla speaks elsewhere of woman as being closer to the spiritual than man (see Figure 2.5). She writes that the "laws of the spiritual world ... supersede the common laws of matter,"[25] a theme that Lois Waisbrooker addresses several decades later in specific reference to Darwin. Nature (and the history of civilization with it) becomes a radically changeable record that is subject to arbitrary and entertaining uncanny performances. The laws by which instruments are invisibly played and heavy furniture is lifted by thought alone reorganize and vitalize domestic space. Camilla Crosland's view of the inexplicable but superior spiritual powers of women challenges the concept of a knowable historical world.

She writes of a unique fate for women, "On a particular occasion Vastness [her spirit communicant] gave us the following message: '... Woman also represents the church. The church is militant, and woman is militant; when the church is triumphant, woman will be triumphant.'"[26] This vision makes women spiritually closer to the divine and

---

24 Crosland, *Light in the Valley*, 81–2.
25 *Ibid.*, 81.
26 *Ibid.*, 94.

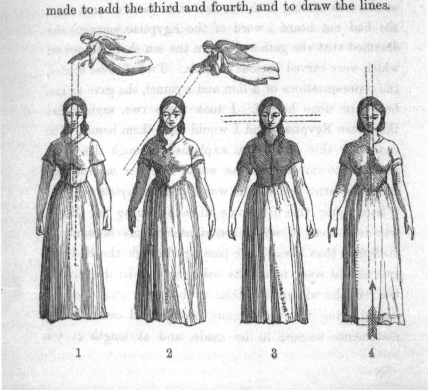

I traced out two figures, and my little girl (aged 10) was made to add the third and fourth, and to draw the lines.

1   2   3   4

Figure 2.5 **Illustration of Crosland's classification of four types of women mediums. Drawings by Camilla Crosland and her ten-year-old daughter**
Facsimile courtesy of Watkinson Library, Trinity College, Hartford, CT.

destined for dominion through their affiliation with the church.[27] The stylistic of inevitability echoes a Marxist historical determinism as well as the inevitable ascension of the natural and the godly. In Camilla's view individual women actually adhere to a revolutionary "woman is militant" institutional future. These women, unlike those of Mr Crosland, do not people heaven in nightcaps and aprons.

---

27 Likening Christ to women, through emphasis on Christ's maternal behavior, is not unique to Camilla Crosland in Victorian writing. Consider Christina Rossetti's prose and poetry. For more information on Rossetti's religious views, see Frederick S. Roden, "The Kiss of the Soul: The Mystical Theology of Christina Rossetti's Devotional Prose," in *Women's Theology in Nineteenth-Century Britain*, ed. Julie Melnyk (New York: Garland, 1998).

A further sign of a challenged terrestrial order is apparent in the structure of the séance itself as Camilla describes it:

> I must observe that the dictation was taken down from the lips of the seeress in my presence, the gentleman—a clergyman of the Church of England—who was the amanuensis, being the only person besides ourselves present ... The spirit who showed this vision is known to us by the name Vastness.[28]

The reader may wonder who in fact the amanuensis from the Church of England is. This man is busy, in any event, with transcribing messages from the sensual seeress's lips. Camilla's higher spiritual laws have subsumed the representative of the Church of England.

What seems to be most striking about the spiritual realm with which Camilla presents is not so much the content of the visions she describes but the implied structure of the higher spiritual realm she depicts. In the practice of the vision, the clergyman is only an amanuensis; the invisible controls the visible; women are natively closest to the celestial and will rule; and even the vision itself is viewed through the vehicle of a crystal likened to a hen's egg. She explains this in detail:

> A novice in Spiritualism will very naturally inquire the manner in which the foregoing vision was presented to the seeress. I answer, through an oval crystal about the size and shape of a hen's egg ... I may describe that when a vision is about to be presented the crystal appears to expand, and then that it disappears; nay, that surrounding objects seem likewise to give way, and only the spiritual world to be visible.[29]

It is interesting to note the concept that all vision, such as political vision, is a version of dreaming, half image, half volition. The rather homely hen's egg crystal becomes transcendent—serving as the gateway to inner vision and higher law.[30] In fact, no shortage of dignitaries appear to the seeress in this fashion. Surprisingly, included on this distinguished list is Christ himself. The simultaneous orthodoxy and heterodoxy of this Christ serve as the basis of a compelling, original, revolutionary theology (see Figure 2.6).

Let us meet this Christ:

THE BEARDED CHRIST: "I am that I am ... I was rejected, I was betrayed, I was misrepresented, I was slandered,—even more, I was crucified. I was buried, I was resuscitated, I was made evident unto woman, being the nearest approach to the spiritual;

---

[28] Crosland, *Light in the Valley*, 83.

[29] *Ibid.*, 91–2.

[30] The crystal egg that enables spiritual vision is also likely based on the philosopher's egg of metaphysicians, according to anthropologist Sasha Welland (personal interview with author February 2004). See, in turn, the entry for "Philosopher's Egg," in Lyndy Abraham, *A Dictionary of Alchemical Imagery* (New York: Cambridge University Press, 1998).

THE BEARDED CHRIST

Figure 2.6   Seeress's spirit drawing of the bearded Christ
Facsimile courtesy of Watkinson Library, Trinity College,
Hartford, CT.

… To another in the body, in the last or the closing of the outer upon the inner world, I gave in charge the keeping of My mother. She lived seven epochs, or years, according to your calculation of time; after that she was translated, but her spirit descended in various ways to help in the Christianizing or polarizing of the earth and its inhabitants to God … I, by the telegraphic communication between the Father, His Spirit, and Myself, preserved My own oneness … I was linked with God … with everything that exists in creation, because they are from and part of God, the Outer and the Inner … I will marry the outer to the inner, and the innermost; I will etherealize, I will spiritualize, I will mentalize My chosen, My predestined, My pre-called. They are many, they are numerous; they are more than many—they are great."[31]

The first somewhat surprising statement this Christ makes is that he was "made evident unto woman, being the nearest approach to the spiritual." The Bearded Christ, who speaks to Camilla through Vastness, credits woman with the capacity for correct interpretation. In fact, this narrative states that Christ's crucifixion occurred because he was misrepresented. As if to foreground the issue of representation, Christ goes on to note, when speaking of the Virgin Mary's assumption into heaven, that "she was translated, but her spirit descended in various ways to help in the Christianizing or polarizing of the earth and its inhabitants to God." Again, representation is at the fore; Mary is reinscribed into a new language system: translated, as if staying just the same in meaning while changing form into a sign only occasionally recognizable to her old sphere, the world.

In Camilla's document the Passion becomes a series of perpetually reperformed speech acts that are available to interpretation, not a set of previously narrated historical events. Also noteworthy about the translated Mary is that her intercessions and appearances on Earth involve her in an act of polarizing (or Christianizing) "of the earth and its inhabitants to God." Like a magnet or a cathode ray, the spiritual function of this Mary is described through the metaphors of electromagnetism as a mechanistic inevitability. Natural law is again being figured as socially disruptive.

Camilla Crosland's religious history has a certain undeniable Calvinist tone. She has found an all-powerful Christ who remarks that He "will etherialize … spiritualize … mentalize [His] chosen, [His] predestined, [His] pre-called." Just as spiritual laws can control natural ones, Christ can supersede free will. In fact, for Camilla, human history becomes solely a part of the mind of God in a massive project of pantheistic unification.[32] Christ was linked to "everything that exists in creation, because they are from and part of God."[33] Camilla's millenarian view corresponds to her interpretation of events occurring within her own home. In her theology she and other women are

---

[31] Crosland, *Light in the Valley*, 136–8.

[32] For a very detailed depiction of this philosophical trajectory, see Charles Bray, *Illusion and Delusion; Or, Modern Pantheism versus Spiritualism* (London: Thomas Scott, 1873). Bray was friend and correspondent of George Henry Lewes and George Eliot.

[33] Crosland, *Light in the Valley*, 134.

not subjected to the will of God because they are already part of the will of God—predestination, because of this interdigitation of subjectivities, resembles autonomy of Christ's large "social" body. In fact, the illustration titled the Crucified Woman in her book visually links Christ and woman as part of the same crucifixion and places them both in the stained glass of a church window (see Figure 2.7).

The real Victorian world is subsumed under the ideal umbrella of the mind of the Godhead in Camilla's scheme. Whereas Newton's spirit world is a photographic record of the past, of the celestial turned terrestrial, Camilla's is firmly in the present tense with predestination having become a sharing in the will of God.

For the Croslands, as well as for countless other Victorians exploring the mystical, there was a common belief in the possibility of seeing the invisible. Their accounts often place differing and conflicting views about the *meaning* of mystical experiences, of their perceptions of what they saw with the outer eye and what they saw with the inner eye. These Victorian spiritualists were investigating new spaces between the natural and the supernatural; in the process, they were redefining their individual lives in the temporal world. They were focusing on concepts of what was and what their inner visions told them could be. These mystical experiences and beliefs were disruptive to a public and private sphere construction in Victorian life and brought into question received theories of science, religion, and government. For Victorian mystics, everything was subject to change. In this sense, they were typical of much that was happening in the mid-nineteenth century when concepts of the rational, the ordinary, the natural, and the historical were fluid and frequently debated.

When the ideal became more tenable to practicing mystics than the real, it changed their theology, and it affected not only their subjectivities but also their views about history, reflection, and action. Their beliefs about vision created for them extra spheres beyond the public and private spheres in which nineteenth-century life is so often classified.

Extra Spheres

The language of imagining a connection between the invisible and the visible or the spiritual and the natural is a unifying paradigm across a range of accounts that describe spirit manifestations and other visions. A wide range of experiences and distinct worldviews are enabled by this common structural assumption. Lois Waisbrooker, a sympathetic medium, completely redefined natural selection. Harriet Martineau, a political economist, was cured of a long-term illness. Florence Marryat experienced new communities and new definitions for friendship. The disparate examples that will next be examined share the common structural assumption that the ideal precedes and governs the real. When the ideal precedes the actual, as De Morgan explained it, all sorts of unusual experiences can become easily normalized because of a new understanding of the hidden and then revealed power that the spirit realm holds in shaping the real. De Morgan's concept seems to be shared by many mystics who

THE CRUCIFIED WOMAN

Figure 2.7 **Seeress's spirit drawing of the crucified woman**
Facsimile courtesy of Watkinson Library, Trinity College,
Hartford, CT.

believe that their unique spiritual vision allows them to be philosophers and activists who move between invisible extra spheres and the real world.

Spiritual Darwinism

One such mystic, Waisbrooker, used her interactions in and conceptualizations of extra spheres to revise the definition of natural law. Waisbrooker as sympathetic medium and social radical had an ontological resistance to political and religious order because she felt her power and identity came from another source. She viewed herself as embodied by the sexually evolved and as becoming so herself. For her, sex is the way to heaven and is also the vehicle through which spirits rule the world, making women a natural, sexually active, sexually evolved part of divine order. This notion of women being closer to the divine is a common Victorian notion that is open to the most circumscribed readings, such as viewing a woman as "The Angel in the House." However, the trick and the slip of what Waisbrooker so intriguingly accomplishes in her publications is that understanding the connection between the divine and the natural can lead to an enlightened woman who completely redefines nature and along with it natural order. Suddenly, nature cannot be understood outside of the spiritual, and it is an experimental playground that promotes not the survival of the fittest but survival of the most spiritually sexual.

Born Adeline Eliza Nichols, Waisbrooker had working-class parents who were poorly educated. She writes, "I did not come of a literary stock of ancestry. My parents worked hard for daily bread, had but little education, and less time to use it."[34] Waisbrooker herself already had children at the age of 26 when she took up her education. Although Waisbrooker suffered a lifetime of weak health, she needed to work for a living. She taught black schoolchildren while she was still young, and she was also a domestic servant. Waisbrooker did not start writing until the 1860s. She considered her primary vocation to be that of a working radical.[35] By the 1880s, "Waisbrooker was an active leader in Boston's free love and spiritualist communities."[36] From 1901 to 1904, she lived in the anarchist colony of Home, Washington. Waisbrooker died at her son's home in 1909 when she was 84 years old—she was destitute.[37] I begin by focusing on her biography because she is not only a little-known radical but also a widely published nineteenth-century spiritualist.[38]

---

[34] Lois Waisbrooker, *Suffrage for Women: The Reasons Why* (St Louis: Clayton and Babington, 1868), 25.

[35] Lois Waisbrooker, *The Fountain of Life, or, The Threefold Power of Sex* (Topeka, KS: Independent Publishing, 1893), 136.

[36] Pam McAllister quoted in Lois Waisbrooker, *Sex Revolution*, intro. by Pam McAllister (Philadelphia: New Society Publishers, 1985), 38.

[37] McAllister in *Sex Revolution*, 46.

[38] See Logie Barrow, *Independent Spirits: Spiritualism and English Plebeians, 1850–1910* (London: Routledge and Kegan Paul, 1986), and Anne Braude, *Radical Spirits: Spiritualism and Women's Rights in Nineteenth-Century America* (Boston: Beacon Press, 1989), for

In many ways, Waisbrooker, though a radical, theorized her views from dominant Victorian ideologies. Her works provide an example of the way in which dominant trends in nineteenth-century thought are continuous with radical social thought.

Her prose provides a radical revision of Darwin's evolutionary theory. Waisbrooker develops a theory of what I call sex evolution in her works *The Fountain of Life, or the Threefold Power of Sex* (1893) and *My Century Plant* (1896). Building off the works of Swedenborg, Darwin, and Galton, Waisbrooker believed that the only way to salvation and spiritual enlightenment is through refined sex acts in which spiritual (rather than material) fluid is exchanged, a partner sex act she calls Dianism. Unlike Darwin and Galton, she was not interested in physical evolution or breeding but instead was interested in spiritual evolution and spiritual enlightenment. Taking her cue from Swedenborg, she defined the spiritual as the most real and placed the physical and the actual under its control, redefining natural law and marshaling the force of a uniquely described Mother Nature. She threads her vision of spiritual enlightenment through the needle of sex. Her writings do not promote social law but her own unconventional definition of natural law. By redefining nature and what is natural to the world and for women, she finds authorization for decades of radical activism and her anarchist viewpoints. She wrote in the models of allegory, philosophical treatise, and biblical exegesis to explain the conjunction she viewed between material and spiritual science.[39]

Waisbrooker's strategic use of "Mother Nature" in her writing and her related redefinition of natural law indicate the rhetorical room for unconventional Darwinian argumentation in the late-nineteenth-century popular press. Her writings also show a clear departure from the Cartesian tradition by negating the possibility of mind-body dualism by claiming the mind's advancement relies on the body having sex. A closer study of her work, then, helps rethink the utility of the frequent scholarly retrojection of mind-body dualism onto the nineteenth-century subject. Instead, her prose foregrounds the role that physicality plays in a quest for salvation and enlightenment.

Waisbrooker referred to herself as a sympathetic medium because she claimed that when she channeled the spirit of a deceased person could completely embody her. Spiritualism was based on a neo-Platonic belief that the spiritual is real and that the physical can be in conversation with it and potentially under its influence. Waisbrooker

---

further discussion of working-class activism and spiritualism in England and in the United States. For more information on free love radicalism and anarchism that occasionally mentions Waisbrooker see Hal D. Sears, *The Sex Radicals: Free Love in High Victorian America* (Lawrence: Regents Press of Kansas, 1977), James Malin, *A Concern about Humanity: Notes on Reform, 1872–1912, at the National and Kansas Levels of Thought* (Lawrence: Regents Press of Kansas, 1964), Margaret S. Marsh, *Anarchist Women, 1870–1920* (Philadelphia: Temple University Press, 1981) and Charles Pierce LeWarne, *Utopias of Puget Sound, 1885–1915* (Seattle: University of Washington Press, 1975).

[39]   Waisbrooker, *Fountain of Life*, 125.

felt particularly authorized in her anarchist views and opposition to organized religion because of her physical aptitude for mediumship. She found spiritual and social authority elsewhere.

Her writings were far from esoteric. She saw a direct link between her theology and her action. Her spiritualist beliefs resulted in her taking a direct social role as an activist and advocate for women's sexual and reproductive rights. Her explicit written views on sex led to her arrest on at least three occasions for violating anti-obscenity laws. In the 1890s she was arrested at least twice under the Comstock Anti-Obscenity Act of 1873.[40] Waisbrooker was a good friend of radical press publisher of *Lucifer*, Moses Harman. From the 1890s on, she was a contributor and sometimes editor of *Lucifer the Light-Bearer*, a free-love journal that in 1907 had turned into the *American Journal of Eugenics*. Her guest editorship of *Lucifer* led to her own arrest, following her printing of "The Hundred Dollar Article." McAllister explains that in 1892:

> Waisbrooker, aged sixty six, was asked to serve as guest editor of the free love journal *Lucifer* while its editor, Moses Harman, himself aged sixty two, was in and out of jail on obscenity charges. Waisbrooker accepted the job and almost immediately, in her effort to dramatize the ridiculous inconsistencies of the Comstock act, reprinted an excerpt about horse penises from a Department of Agriculture report. In her editorial she pointed out that the government report contained descriptions, which, if applied to human organs, would have been immediately censored. She was right: the issue was barred from the mails.[41]

In Waisbrooker's 1896 book, *My Century Plant*, she provides the account of her second arrest, again while editing *Lucifer*, this time for reprinting "That Hundred Dollar Article" as well as "The Markland Letter." "The Markland Letter," the one for which Moses Harman had been arrested for publishing because it contained the word *penis*, was the story of a marriage that resulted in legalized rape and murder. The inflammatory passage, which follows the anecdote of how the husband rapes his wife, is as follows:

> What is rape? Is it not coition by force, not having a legal right?
>
> Can there be legal rape? Did this man rape his wife? Would it have been rape had he not been married to her?
>
> Does the law protect the person of woman in marriage? Does it protect her out of marriage? …
>
> If a man stabs his wife to death with a knife does not the law hold him for murder?
>
> If he stabs her to death with his penis, what does the law do? …

---

[40] Anthony Comstock was responsible for the US Federal Anti-Obscenity act of 3 March 1873, also known as the Postal Censorship act of 1873, which made it illegal to send obscene material through the US mail. See Edward DeGrazia, *Censorship Landmarks* (New York: R.R. Bowker, 1969), 153.

[41] McAllister in *Sex Revolution*, 40.

Can a Czar have more absolute power over a subject than a man has over the genitals of his wife?[42]

Waisbrooker remarks that for publishing this, "Moses Harmon spent his 65th birthday in prison and is still there December 27, 1895!"[43] Waisbrooker was additionally arrested for supporting Dianism in a publication.[44] She was repeatedly subject to arrest and harassment for her activism that sought to stop rape in the marriage bed.[45] Waisbrooker's activism was based on her mystical, fringe theology. Her beliefs about the other world fueled her activism in the "real" world. An intriguing self-styled Swedenborgian worldview inspired her radicalism.

Emanuel Swedenborg gave Waisbrooker the genesis of her ideas about the paramount importance of the ideal rather than the real.[46] Swedenborg envisions a world, the Earth, that is a metaphor for heaven.[47] To him, the unseen is real, literal; the earthly is figurative, derivative subsistence. Waisbrooker made this assumption the point of departure for her own work and belief in the ascendancy of natural law. Her unique contribution to this theory is her attempt to connect the spiritual and earthly realms by reasoning the boundary between the dead and the living. In a most unusual trajectory, she saw this connection and the fulfillment of natural law as being actualized solely through the act of sex, an act she defines as ideally going beyond an act of the flesh.

At a base level, finding the church and the government to be evil, Waisbrooker defined her beliefs as anti-Christian. Yet she saw an implied connection between

---

[42] Lois Waisbrooker, *My Century Plant* (Topeka, KS: Independent Publishing, 1896), 223.

[43] *Ibid.*, 224.

[44] *Ibid.*, 243.

[45] *Lucifer* is the only journal in the late-nineteenth-century American radical press that I have seen referenced in secondary literature as dealing extensively with the issue of marital rape. Also important to know is that *Lucifer*'s violations of the Comstock Act, though intentional, were probably not mailed directly to Comstock. Comstock seems instead to have actively hunted down obscenity, such as the instance of jailing Victoria Woodhull for publishing the details of minister Henry Ward Beecher's adultery in *Woodhull and Claflin's Weekly*. See John D'Emilio and Estelle B. Freedman, *Intimate Matters: A History of Sexuality in America* (New York: Harper and Row, 1988), 156–67.

[46] Swedenborg was an eighteenth-century Swedish mystic, who apparently for the last half of his life subsisted solely on a diet of bread, milk, and coffee. Starting in the 1750s, he began to have daily visions of heaven and the other parts of the spiritual realm. He recorded his unique encounters in his most famous work, *Heaven and Its Wonders and Hell; from Things Heard and Seen* (1758), trans. from original Latin by John C. Ager (Westchester: Swedenborg Foundation, 1995), and also in *The Spiritual Diary of Emanuel Swedenborg*, trans. George Bush, ed. Samuel Beswick (Boston: Henry H. and J.W. Carter, 1877). By the 1790s, there was quite a Swedenborgian rage in radical England, and the Church of the New Jerusalem was formed. It had such famous adherents as William Blake and Thomas Paine. This church is still active in England and the United States today.

[47] See Swedenborg, *Heaven and Its Wonders and Hell*, 68.

the spiritual and the sexual (which is integral to her own beliefs) in most Christian doctrines. She writes:

> In analyzing this question of sex I catch glimpses of its meaning in every Christian doctrine almost. No, I am not a Christian. I repudiate the claims of the church as utterly subversive to the welfare of the race, but I do not repudiate the truths of nature's laws of which the Christian system is the distorted shadow.[48]

Though she is anti-Christian, her identity as a radical does not map neatly or fully onto the ideologies of given nineteenth-century communities of American radicals—such as free-love radicals and anarchists. She is socialist as well as anarchist, and her eugenic theories are not Galtonian. She cares about the *spiritual* evolution of the race through sex—not about *physical* procreation, which would create a more evolved race. She glosses the term *race* as "human race" across many of her works.

Waisbrooker explains her concept of the intricate relationship between sex and the spiritual through positing that there are three connected sexual centers in the human body: the brain/intellect, the heart/soul/spirit, and the genitalia/physical/animal.[49] Furthermore, Waisbrooker claims that because these centers of brain, soul, and genitalia are linked, the only way to the spiritual is through the sex act. She writes, "There can be no living, growing spiritual life without a clean, active sex life."[50] She feels that sexual variety (concurrent multiple partners) is counterproductive because it leads to mixed-up magnetism. Sodomy is also evil in her philosophy—it seems by a Waisbrookerian logic of physics—adding a positive to a positive charge. Women are desiring subjects for her because they are more spiritually refined. A medium, who may be a woman or a man, is defined in her magnetic trope as being negatively charged and receptive. She also defines all women as being negatively charged and receptive. The sexes, for Waisbrooker, have an inherent electrical charge. Sexual magnetism, though, also contains content. One can receive deceitful magnetism from a lying lover, for instance. Believing, as she did, that spiritual growth can only be attained through sexual intercourse, it became very important to her that sex only occur under ideal, spiritually felicitous conditions.

Additionally, the reader is told that sex is not limited to this body in this life but transcends death. She explains that individuals do not need bodies and continue to have sexual desires after death.[51] She also feels that perfect sex acts lend to spiritual evolution in life after death, writing, "A perfect union between two persons, man and woman, of these three sex centers can alone develop the threefold power of sex and evolve therefrom the triune power which can overcome all evils and secure the inheritance which the intuitive soul of the race is struggling to gain."[52] Sex can

---

48 Waisbrooker, *Fountain of Life*, 57.
49 See *Fountain of Life* (1893) for greater detail.
50 Waisbrooker, *Fountain of Life*, 59.
51 Waisbrooker, *My Century Plant*, 129.
52 Waisbrooker, *Fountain of Life*, 37.

overcome death by a mechanism of evolution. According to Waisbrooker, there is one soul to the race, and it can only become transcendent through sex acts that enable spiritual evolution. In reference to spiritual evolution, Waisbrooker provides the following anecdote:

> A gentleman who has a most lovely family, in commenting on Swedenborg's statement, says: "Without the action of the positive on the negative everything in nature would be barren, and, as the spiritual is the real, the physical, as it were, only the result of the action of the psychical, it must necessarily follow that the union of the male and female on the spiritual plane will also result in spiritual fruition."[53]

Sexual union, in the specific way Waisbrooker defines it, is not one way to enlightenment, it is the *only* way. She also does not adhere to a stereotypically Christian view that children, through their purity or even their humanity, might have a chance at salvation. She writes, "Strange that long ago mankind has not seen this that a life of celibacy cannot conduce to spirituality ... It will be of little use trying to make our children more spiritual. We will have to wait."[54] Children cannot be spiritual because they are not yet sexually active. Spiritual evolution can only be achieved through the transfer of immaterial magnetism for the Dianistic adult. Of this ethereal magnetism she notes:

> We can not see this sex magnetism but we can feel it, feel it even in the presence of the loved one—more in the clasp of the hands, in the pressure of the lips, and when bodies blend the acme is reached. Some element must pass from one to the other or this could not be.[55]

Waisbrooker inhabits an epistemologically challenging world where the dead are in the realm of the living and the only way to the spiritual is through refined sex acts. These sex acts can occur between two living people or between the living and the spirit of a dead person by the initiative of the dead. This alternative natural sexual order serves as the basis for her imaginative beliefs.

Her concept of spiritual evolution and of the sex act's leading to spiritual enlightenment have undeniable Victorian eugenic undertones, typical of late-nineteenth-century sex radicals. The term *eugenics* was coined in 1883 by Charles Darwin's cousin Francis Galton, who was also famous for his early contributions to the developing field of statistics.[56] Galton was obsessed with quantification, particularly the ways that it could be applied to genetic inheritance. Furthermore, he felt that social law should go about encouraging births among those with great reputation

---

[53]   *Ibid.*, 60.

[54]   Waisbrooker, *My Century Plant*, 129.

[55]   *Ibid.*, 54.

[56]   Justin Wintle, ed., *Makers of Nineteenth Century Culture, 1800–1914* (London and Boston: Routledge & Kegan Paul, 1982), 235.

and discouraging it among the poor and ordinary. He thought in this manner that the species could be improved overall, much as in cattle breeding.[57]

Unlike Galton's fascination with statistically quantifying races and classes of people as a whole, Waisbrooker is always primarily interested in the individual's experience. More specifically, she supports spiritual rather than physical eugenics. For Waisbrooker, humanity will be improved through individual spiritual enlightenment; she argues for the experience of distinct refined sex acts with no progeny. For Waisbrooker, spiritual evolution works through Dianism, not through selectively begetting better babies. Seemingly unconcerned about physical evolution, she was obsessed with spiritual evolution.

There is also a very obvious link between Galton's work and radical thought in late Victorian England and the United States on human breeding as a means of an improved species. For instance, historian Daniel Kelves remarks of a very famous free-love radical: "In the United States, Victoria Woodhull repeatedly invoked before lecture audiences 'the scientific propagation of the human race' as reason for sexual education and the emancipation of women."[58] Waisbrooker agreed with Woodhull on matters of social policy, supporting both contraception and suffrage for women.[59] It was not for the reason of better breeding, however, but for spiritual enlightenment. John D'Emilio and Estelle B. Freedman explain the link between the free-love movement and eugenics quite succinctly:

> Despite its opposition to marriage, the free-love doctrine was rooted in a perfectionist notion of the family in which the "true love" of a man and woman would produce not only morally stronger characters but also biologically superior children. Free lovers, social purity advocates, suffragists, and some utopians combined this romantic vision with late-nineteenth century Darwinian theories of natural selection to create what historian Hal Sears has termed "anarchist eugenics," the forerunner of the Progressive-era eugenics movement ... Despite the persecution of free-love anarchists, their values were not entirely incompatible with those of most Americans. Indeed, by 1907, when *Lucifer* became the *American Journal of Eugenics*, free love had ceased to occupy the radical fringe. Its once threatening message of sex education, birth control, and the romantic union of love and sexuality was about to become the dominant middle-class sexual ideology. Along the way, however, the central anarchist theme of individual freedom would be discarded.[60]

Waisbrooker was one such anarchist whose radical social views would become discarded, but with the additional difference of caring more for spirits than bodies. While Galton explored eugenic Darwinism and Herbert Spencer developed what

---

57   Daniel J. Kelves, *In the Name of Eugenics* (New York: Knopf, 1985), 12–14.

58   *Ibid.*, 21.

59   For an excellent look at the career of Victoria Woodhull, see Mary Gabriel, *Notorious Victoria* (Chapel Hill, NC: Algonquin Books, 1998).

60   D'Emilio and Freedman, *Intimate Matters*, 165–6.

comes to be known as social Darwinism, Waisbrooker supported a concept of what I would call spiritual Darwinism.[61]

Perhaps Waisbrooker's radical writings are most surprising in the way that some of them are so typically Victorian. One likeness hinges on her agreement with Darwin. Just as Darwin uses an exemplary style in his writing, so does Waisbrooker: hypothesis, observation, and conclusion. Both place evidence in the domain of anecdote. The key concept for both, though differently defined, is natural selection. Darwin's premise that "the relation of organism to organism is the most important of all relations" is also Waisbrooker's assumption.[62] However, for Waisbrooker, an organism can be living or dead; it does not matter in her view because death does not limit the ability of the organisms to interrelate with the living. This marks a slight but completely essential difference between Darwin and Waisbrooker. Natural selection, for Waisbrooker, now contains spiritual organisms, not just living ones. In other words, her natural selection operates for the living and for the dead. This, then, leads to a very different imagining of what selection might be like as an operation (select for the extinction of all bodies? forget breeding?) and also what survival might mean (survival as life after death, death communing with life, death before life, death instead of life). Waisbrooker, unlike Darwin, believes in a perfectible humanity sponsored by a literal Mother Nature who protects her human children, instead of promoting competition and survival of the fittest. She writes:

> A mother, when her child tries something new, will assist it till the *how* is learned and then it is left to decide for itself if said new thing is best or not. Mother Nature does the same thing. She stores up in the bodies and brains of her human children a reserve force to be used in exigencies, or for experiment.[63]

Here, unlike in Darwin, we get a Mother Nature who is helpful and tries to be a conservator of life, rearing humanity and always looking out for its best interests. Waisbrooker assumes that there is one creation of collective (rather than individual) history. Furthermore, she sees no need for this collective history to be based on competition: This specification of her belief seems to be the root of her prosocial vision and radical activism.

---

[61] See Herbert Spencer, *The Study of Sociology* (New York: Appleton, 1875). For an overview of Herbert Spencer's philosophy, see *Social England: A Record of the Progress of the People in Religion, Laws, Learning, Arts, Industry, Commerce, Science, Literature and Manners from the Earliest Times to the Present Day*, vol. 6, section 11, ed. H.D. Traill (London: Cassell, 1909), pp. 676–9. See Francis Galton's *Essays in Eugenics* (London: Eugenics Education Society, 1909) for an overview of his theories.

[62] Charles Darwin, *On the Origin of the Species by Means of Natural Selection* (London: Murray, 1859), as reprinted in *The Essential Darwin*, ed. Robert Jastrow with Kenneth Korey (Boston: Little, Brown, 1984), 95.

[63] Waisbrooker, *The Fountain of Life*, 120.

Waisbrooker's spirits, whom she describes meeting at séances in several of her writings, are part of Mother Nature's reserve force of bodies and brains with which she experiments. These spirits depend on the agency of chemistry for their ability to materialize. Her views align nature and immaterial spirits as having a common, larger-than-mortal agency. She writes, for instance, of séances:

> As I understand the philosophy of modern Spiritualism, the physical phenomena are the experimental efforts of a class of spirits who are studying the laws of matter with the intent of learning how to so control it as to stand in our midst as resurrected spirits when they so choose.[64]

For her, séances are practice runs for spirits to take on physical bodies of the medium or of the combined ectoplasmic aura of the sitters, to better understand the scientific laws of matter. Manifestations are caused by spirits and not by the sitters. Additionally, from Waisbrooker we learn that:

> The ascension robes of our spirit friends are being woven in the loom of time by the fingers of chemistry. Chemistry is shown to be the agent that enables a disembodied mortal to condense, through the union of the male and female aura, enough of matter to clothe itself temporarily. But what is the character of this aura? Like the purpose of the honest sitters at the time, spiritual, spiritualized sex aura.[65]

In other words, a manifestation works as spiritual evolution does—through sexual chemistry. It takes the combination of male and female spiritualized auras to present an enlightened and refined spirit in the séance room. It is an odd science, a systematized blending of the material and the immaterial, enabled by chemistry, refinement, and sex.

A manifestation is not, however, simply chemistry at work. Deeply influenced by Swedenborg, Waisbrooker upholds the concept of chemistry with forethought. She writes, "It can readily be understood that the idea of a thing must exist before it can be actualized."[66] This likens her thinking to a common Kantian assumption of spiritualists about the ideal preceding the real, a view shared by De Morgan and Camilla Crosland. Waisbrooker believes in a perfectible humanity that is destined by cosmic forethought to become so: It is a foolproof model for progress. It also meshes well with her anarchist beliefs that civil law and the church are "subversive to the welfare of the race."[67] She believes, alternatively, that only sex is the redeemer and that true freedom comes from obeying nature.

---

64   *Ibid.*, 69.
65   Lois Waisbrooker, *Bible Truth Bursting Its Shell That It May Express Its Larger Meaning*, n.p., n.d. [Chicago, Center Research for Libraries: CRL A–10613, Cat. C].
66   Waisbrooker, *Fountain of Life*, 68.
67   See Waisbrooker, *Fountain of Life*, 100–30, for more details.

Waisbrooker is an example of a nineteenth-century woman who sought her political self through her mystical obsession. She also serves as an example of what can happen when beliefs about a sexual practice (such as Dianism) lead directly to concrete political action. She is not just embodied by mysticism, though; she theorizes it by building off of the works of Swedenborg and Darwin. Using the idea that the ideal precedes and governs the real, she sets up an alternative paradigm for describing power. She also follows Swedenborg's example by imagining the spiritual individual, as indeed she is, as a special conduit for receiving and interpreting visions. Using many of the same rhetorical formulations as Darwin, such as making exemplary arguments, she uses familiar and persuasive techniques for forwarding her unique spiritual views about sexual evolution.

Harriet Martineau and Mesmeric Cure

Even though it is less radically political, Harriet Martineau's cure from a severe stomach complaint in an extra sphere provides similarly disruptive understandings of unfixed human hierarchical relationships.

Socialist and political economist Harriet Martineau (1802–1876) was also a prolific journalist. She published over 1,400 articles in the *Daily News* between 1852 and 1866, interpreting economic, social, and political practices and theories of the day.[68] Deaf from the age of 14 and financially on her own following the death of her father when she was 24, she wrote for a living. She became one of the best-known authors of her period.

Raised as a Unitarian, Martineau later became influenced by the Positivism of Auguste Comte, whose book she translated into English in 1853. Comte presented a vision of progress in which scientific attitudes would win over the domestic forces of what he considered to be delusive theology and metaphysics.[69] Martineau also published a book on agnosticism.[70]

Martineau's most important work was in what were considered the radical causes of the time: better working conditions for domestic farm and factory workers, the abolition of slavery in America, and "the woman question." Throughout her life she

---

[68] Her reputation as an intellectual was established when she published *Illustrations of Political Economy, of Poor Laws and Paupers, and of Taxation* (London: Charles Fox, 1832–1834). Many feel that this work "opened up new material for Victorian fiction, anticipating the novels of industrial conflict, of politics, and of social issues." See Paul Turner's *English Literature 1832–1890, Excluding the Novel* (Oxford: Clarendon Press, 1989).

[69] Auguste Comte, *The Positive Philosophy of Auguste Comte, freely translated and condensed by Harriet Martineau* (London: J. Chapman, 1853). For a further discussion of the works of Martineau and Comte, see *Makers of Nineteenth Century Culture 1800–1914*, ed. Justin Wintle (London: Routledge and Kegan Paul, 1982).

[70] Harriet Martineau, *Letters on the Laws of Man's Nature* (London: J. Chapman, 1851).

wrote about and actively participated in causes that would improve the situation of women. Her concerns crossed class lines; she favored fairness for working women, such as seamstresses, governesses, and domestic servants. She signed the first petition in 1866 to go before Parliament seeking the vote for women, a bill sponsored by John Stuart Mill. She traveled both to America and to the Near East. Like other intellectuals of her time, she was open to new ideas, often presented as advances in science or medicine, such as phrenology and mesmerism.[71]

Martineau was quite ill in the early 1840s and felt she was cured by mesmerism—a practice that relies on one person's having sway over the mind and body of another.[72] The story of her cure is rather mystical and shows the dynamism and play involved with taking a trance state seriously. Martineau, who was originally under the care of mesmeric physician Mr Spencer T. Hall, gives us the following account of her cure:

> First, the outlines of all objects were blurred; then a bust, standing on a pedestal in a strong light, melted quite away ... I feared to move my eyes, lest the singular appearance should vanish, and I cried out, "O! deepen it! deepen it!" supposing this the precursor of the sleep. I could not be deepened, however; and when I glanced aside from the luminous point, I found that I need not fear the return of objects to their ordinary appearance. While the passes were continued, the busts reappeared ghost-like, in the dim atmosphere, like faint shadows, except that their outlines and the parts in the highest relief, burned with the same phosphoric light. The features of one, an Isis with bent head, seemed to be illumined by a fire on the floor, though this bust has its back to the windows. This appearance continued during the remaining twenty minutes before the gentlemen [Mr Hall and a male assistant] were obliged to leave me. The other effects produced were, first, heat, oppression, and sickness, and, for a few hours after, disordered stomach, followed, in the course of the evening, by a feeling of lightness and relief, in which I thought I could hardly be mistaken.[73]

The mesmeric passes do not make the room disappear for Martineau; they only change the appearance and function of the room's elements. For instance, Isis, the Egyptian goddess, begins to glow, illumined by a fire on the floor. In *The Golden Bough*, Frazer notes that "Isis, goddess of corn, was revered for increasing fruitfulness of the earth

---

[71] For more information on the life of Harriet Martineau, see Theodora Bosanquet, *Harriet Martineau* (London: F. Etchells and H. Macdonald, 1927); R.K. Webb, *Harriet Martineau: A Radical Victorian* (New York: Columbia University Press, 1960); and Valerie Kossew Pichanick, *Harriet Martineau and Her Work, 1802–1876* (Ann Arbor: University of Michigan Press, 1980).

[72] First called "animal magnetism," it was used as a medical treatment to reduce pain. This system, popularized by Austrian physician E.A. Mesmer (1734–1815), used a hypnotic state that was induced by the influence of an operator over the will and nervous system of the patient. See also Alison Winter, *Mesmerized: The Powers of Mind in Victorian Britain* (Chicago: University of Chicago Press, 1998) for a historical account of mesmerism.

[73] Spencer T. Hall, *Mesmeric Experiences* (London: H. Bailliere, 1845), 71.

in many ways."[74] A goddess of fruitfulness and harvest food becomes illumined for Martineau who, by the descriptions, sounds as if she were suffering from a severe and chronic stomach complaint. The mesmeric state creates a receptive place for the literal rather than symbolic interaction of myth and medicine.

What may be stranger to ponder, though, is that Martineau's maid takes over her medical care. No reasons are given; the new "doctor" is only parenthetically noted. Martineau reports:

> Within one minute (after the maid began) the twilight and phosphoric lights appeared; and in two or three more, a delicious sensation of ease spread through me—a cool comfort, before which all pain and distress gave way, oozing out, as it were, at the soles of my feet. During that hour, and almost the whole evening, I could no more help exclaiming with pleasure, than a person in torture crying out with pain. I became hungry, and ate with relish, for the first time these five years.[75]

Then, "her maid had carried on the cure pretty far, when a benevolent lady came to her aid, out of pure zeal and kindness, and proceeded with it." She says she cannot "feel sufficiently thankful for such a resurrection." Finally, in a letter to Mr Hall, she reveals that she had "the day before walked nearly five miles" and that she "continued quite well, feeling *nothing* whatever of her late complaints."[76]

Martineau not only recounts a remarkable recovery, she also lists a remarkable host of makers and witnesses to her cure, from doctor to maid to benevolent lady. Her switch in primary health care provider from doctor to maid and then to lady marks an affront to the growing professionalization of medicine in the nineteenth century. Professional medical expertise, in this example, becomes less important for Martineau; she instead favors the amelioration of pain through mesmerism provided by her maid at home. Direct spirit communication does more for her than professionalized medicine. Her case is also a record of ecstasy: "I could no more help exclaiming with pleasure, than a person in torture crying out with pain." It would seem to be a success story for the efficacy of trance and the unquestionable power of one person's head and hands, whether those of a professional doctor or a servant, to overpower and control the patient. It is interesting that Martineau calls this experience a séance. It is also an instance, by extension, that raises provocative questions about other types of mystical experiences, such as those at the spiritualist séance table.

If we read "medium" for Martineau and "spirit" for the doctor, maid, or lady, we quickly realize how promiscuous the claims of the séance experience are. In a similar way, the respectable spiritualist housewife turned medium or control for the table is inviting anyone from the beyond, good or bad, high or low, to have the total use of her

---

[74] J.G. Frazer, *The Golden Bough: A Study in Comparative Religion* (London: Macmillan, 1890), 314.

[75] Hall, *Mesmeric Experiences*, 73–4.

[76] *Ibid.*, 74.

body. Martineau, the entranced subject, just like any medium, is the completely open recipient of outside influence. This scenario also seems analogous to viewing women as privately owned objects, acted on, except here the women have no fixed owner—and being possessed without legal ownership is a crucially disruptive difference to social order. Martineau, as Miss Showers's case (discussed shortly) will also indicate, presents a female subjectivity that is not terribly singular. Only by the community of women mesmerists and statues, which oversee fires in her home, does Martineau's mesmeric cure come to pass. It is only through a state of ecstasy where pleasure becomes as inevitable as her pain has been that she ritualistically passes into health. It is as if her post-Mr Hall "doctors" remain nameless to emphasize their significance as maid and lady; as women enacting on her body a certain type of supreme relief from pain and resulting pleasure.

What seems to be a symbolic or actual sexual act (one minute after the maid began doing what?) here becomes associated with healing Martineau's body. In her "fancy," the long illness is ended. In this case, it is through her membership in a radically mystical, mythical, mostly female community that Martineau regains health and connection to the larger human family. As in the séance situation that Camilla Crosland presents, Martineau also experiences a present tense with a supernatural quality: Efficacy of mystical intervention seems boundlessly influential. In Martineau's account, we gain a strong sense of the subjectively invisible superseding the visible. In better health, Martineau returned to her work. A year later she was well enough to start an arduous tour of Egypt, Palestine, Syria, and Lebanon.[77] An even more extreme example of imagining bodies as permeable is provided by Florence Marryat's séance experiences.

Florence Marryat, the Professional Medium, and Promiscuous Community

Daughter of famous Victorian adventure novelist Captain Frederick Marryat, Florence Marryat was also a writer.[78] Married twice, her first husband was Col. Ross Church

---

[77]   In 1846, Martineau built a home in Ambleside in the Lake District where Charlotte Brontë and George Eliot visited her and from where she wrote to Elizabeth Barrett Browning expressing her happiness with her new home. Her work as a writer and reformer continued for the rest of her life. See Harriet Martineau's *Selected Letters*, ed. Valerie Sanders (New York: Oxford University Press, 1990).

[78]   For a discussion of Captain Marryat's works, including his story for boys, *The Settlers in Canada* (1844), see Elleke Boehmer, *Colonial and Postcolonial Literature: Migrant Metaphors* (Oxford and New York: Oxford University Press, 1995). Boehmer writes that Captain Marryat's fiction often thematized the "fragility of the civilized state" and that "contact with the Other created vulnerability" in his stories (34). Florence Marryat's writings on spiritualism, conversely, celebrate the vulnerability séance interactions with the dead, who are a type of "Other," pose to the English social order (see Marryat quotation from the first page of this chapter).

of the Madras Staff Corps; they lived and traveled extensively in India, and some of her experiences there are reflected in her stories.[79] Her second husband was also a military man, Col. Francis Lean, of the Royal Marine Light Infantry. Marryat's definite flair for the dramatic can be seen in the 44 popular romance stories she wrote from 1868 to 1886, many of which were published in serial form in periodicals and gave her a large and enthusiastic reading audience.[80] Of a social nature, she edited *London Society* from 1872 to 1876. Well known as a dramatic reader and singer, she wrote and acted in her own drama, *Her World*, produced in London in 1881.

Besides being a prolific romance writer and actress, she was also a spiritualist and close friend of certain mediums, including the well-known public (professional) medium Miss Showers. Marryat seems to prefer the immediacy of semi-visible community in extra spheres to the promises of history and Christian tradition. In her work of 1891, *There Is No Death*, she recounts her personal experiences with several trance mediums. Miss Showers, one such medium, is the passive receptacle for the spiritual other while also the producer of the spectral. The medium wavers, being at once both subject and object. Present at the table while vacantly waiting for an unseen spirit to employ her body, the medium embodies a complex system of exchange. The "invoking, flaming lips of the medium" produce spectra illustrating an imaginary host of spirits, who evoke amazingly complex and diverse relations with and within the medium's body. Although Marryat is not a medium herself, but only near mediums, the context of the séance provides a dynamic space for role-playing and social interaction.

In one account involving Miss Showers, Marryat is instructed by materialized spirit emissaries to explore the body of the entranced medium:

> Then someone else grasped my other hand, and Peter's voice said, "We've got you safe. We want you to feel the medium." The two figures led me between them to the sofa on which Miss Showers was lying. They passed my hands all over her head and body ... When my hands were placed upon it [her heart], it was leaping up and down violently, and felt like some rabbit or some other live animal bounding in her bosom ... There was no doubt at all of the abnormal condition into which the medium had been thrown, in order to produce these strong manifestations, which were borrowed, for the time being, from her life, and could never (so they informed me) put the *whole* of what they borrowed back again.[81]

This description is noteworthy not only for its depiction of Marryat's noninteractive bodily contact with materialized ectoplasms and the medium but also because it offers a scenario in which Miss Showers, while still Miss Showers, is also inhabited

---

79 See Florence Marryat, *Gup: Sketches of Anglo Indian Life and Character* (London: R. Bentley, 1868).

80 See Allibone, *Critical Dictionary*, 983, for a detailed list.

81 Florence Marryat, *There Is No Death* (London: Kegan Paul, Trench, Trubner, 1891), 152.

by another creature (like a rabbit) that is stealing away or "borrowing" from her vitality and not leaving her body as the spirit found it. Her identity is not single or fixed at this moment. The use of the verb *borrowing* is common in describing what the medium gives in many accounts. This verb also places the séance in the realm of economic exchange. Certainly, it seems with Miss Showers that what is borrowed from the body is lost in speculation. I mean *speculation* both in the sense of philosophical insight and in the sense of some sort of strange futures market. Perhaps this represents an alternative idea of how political representation and selfhood could be described—self-possession of something intangible and morphing—an unfixed selfhood.

Marryat is not, after all, stopping the life-stealing practice of mediumship—she is aiding and abetting it. Like the force within Miss Showers's body, something active and "abnormal," or perhaps atypical, also is going on outside her body that is busy being observed and touched in a scene of active frottage. Marryat also remains outside Miss Showers's body, to prove that there is no more room *inside* the medium's body: Miss Showers is not alone. Her body is an active bus(y)ness.

The medium's body has become the site of spiritual exchange and a place that Marryat believes spirits to inhabit. If, as Marryat believes, Miss Showers's body becomes a locus of spiritual interaction, and if, as she also assumes, this takes away part of Miss Showers's life, then what does Miss Showers get in return? What is her new identity? Considering this spiritual question yields an interesting possible reply. In effect, through Miss Showers's mystical practices as a medium, she is removed from a context of private, domestic space on a Victorian sofa in a boudoir and replaced into an active, semi-visible ectoplasmic community, placed among rather busy and energetic spirits. The séance room, though semi-private, transforms through séance practices of calling up and embodying spirits, into a public, imaginary, democratic space, where any number of spirits, with any number of opinions and desires, descend on the entranced body for a congress of sorts. The singular body is the location for civic polity and representation instead of representing one individual who becomes a part of civic polity (a possibility that although mundane, mediumship in no way precludes). The mystical medium, in return for her body and her role in domestic space, gets an imaginary spiritual life elsewhere. The implication is that a woman, by renouncing or complicating her ties to this world, gets an active role in a concurrent, extra, spiritual world.

Three years after publishing *There Is No Death*, Marryat published a sort of apologia for this work, titled *The Spirit World* (1894), in which she herself theorized the theology of mediumship. She directly (unlike Camilla Crosland's pro-Christian writings some 40 years earlier) pitted spiritualism against the promise of Christianity and of British history. Her perceived enemy of power is the Church rather than the government, and this substitution is interesting. Although, for instance, Waisbrooker saw the government as directly responsible for unreasonable limitations on civil rights, in *The Spirit World* Marryat argues that the Catholic Church knows of and denies the power of spiritualism. She claims that the Church does this because the common practice of spiritualism would reduce the power of Catholicism and because spirits supersede the Church's spiritual authority.[82] She writes, "They [spirits] come to teach us, not to be treated like servants to run messages, or gratify idle curiosity. They are the higher powers, we the lower. They the preachers, we the congregation."[83] Marryat thus defines her own mystical practices and writings as a direct challenge to the authority of the Catholic Church. However, the spirits also do not in any way mirror impersonal institutional authority. They instead offer hands-on opportunities for radically reimagined social interaction.

On one occasion, for example, Miss Showers, busy at work as a medium, asks Marryat "to put [Marryat's] hands up her [Miss Showers's] skirts and convince [her]self that she was half-dematerialized."[84] Marryat does as she is told "and felt that [Miss Showers] had no legs, although she had been walking around the room a few minutes before. [Marryat] could feel nothing but the trunk of a body, which was lifted completely off the ground."[85] These are just two of numerous examples of Showers and Marryat's physical union during the act of mediumship. It is as if Marryat were appointed bodyguard to keep the spirits from entirely carrying off her friend. The rapport between the women extended beyond the séance room. Marryat writes:

And I may mention here that Miss Showers and I were so much *en rapport* that her manifestations were always much stronger in my presence. We could not sit next each other at an ordinary tea, or supper table ... A hand that did not belong to either of us, would make itself apparent under the table-cloth between us—a hand with power to grasp ours.[86]

The spirits in this narrative seem to play the role of constant third-party "Lucky Pierre" between or over these two women. The spirits, in these accounts, are constantly demanding, facilitating, or creating physical contact between the two. Perhaps they seek, in this narrative, to keep Miss Showers in the material world, to convince Marryat that the immaterial can embody and replace the material, or to illustrate that the immaterial may be materially known.

The acts of these two friends indicate same-sex desire and romantic friendship. Their eroticism, though, is not just a coupling of two: Showers and Marryat are only two of many participants. There are also the ostensibly disembodied yet materialized spirits within Miss Showers's body. As noted, one of Marryat's functions is to prove that there *are* others inhabiting Miss Showers's body at the same time. Showers and Marryat's union serves as an addendum to the union of spirits and the medium during the séance. Their physical contact not only represents a same-sex erotic act but also suggests an (auto-)erotic mystical community all (self-)contained by Miss

---

82 *Ibid.*, 12–13.
83 *Ibid.*, 14.
84 *Ibid.*, 152.
85 *Ibid.*, 152.
86 *Ibid.*, 148.

Showers's flesh.[87] The multiple subjectivities that form an identity within a single body within Miss Showers's body posit an ontological resistance to political order. To figure resistance as a nonvolitional aspect of being is predicated on an alternative definition of selfhood in a time when women were not considered fully entitled political individuals under the law. It seems that a Victorian woman's very selfhood needed to become plural to achieve civic parity. More than one feminized being could equal one man, whereas one woman could not. The drawing room séance involves these Victorian women in complicated, mystical subjectivities. In fact, these subjectivities are not only defined by interaction but also sometimes become the encompassing preserve of imagination: a transcendent place of action.

Conclusion

Mystical theories of seeing, such as those provided by Zerffi, the Croslands, De Morgan, and spirit photographers, present an invisible culture in the nineteenth century. This culture that some could see enabled the descriptions of extra spheres by the Croslands, Waisbrooker, Martineau, and Marryat. Their mystical spirit possession redefines the category of subjectivity as possessed. Not only did these mystics make a single identity impossible and replace it with a plural one, they also turned a person from an "is" to a "does." No longer could these Victorian women of the mystical fringe be held accountable to a fixed definition of identity. A person became a *process* of exploring different identities within the one body, as well as becoming a place, a space where multiple spirits commune. The woman's body became uncanny: unfamiliar at the place where it once seemed at home.

The women in all of the accounts treated herein can leave their bodies, join other bodies, or have others within their bodies. This sort of mixture marks a radical imagining of women's potential for mass political identity. It is also destabilizing because it takes a belief system out of the domain of representations and institutions and places it instead in the domain of dynamic and dramatic personal experience and revelation.

Yet in the accounts at hand, it is more a political modeling that is radical, rather than its outcome. These texts, and many others of the period, take a serious interest in judging and challenging worldly authority, as it exists in nation-states. They posit instead the power of a universal, natural order through expanding a notion of empire

---

87   For discussion on the early twentieth-century attraction that spiritualism held for lesbians, see Terry Castle, *The Apparitional Lesbian: Female Homosexuality and Modern Culture* (New York: Columbia University Press, 1993), esp. 48–9, 176–7, and 247, n. 21, and Bette London, *Writing Double: Women's Literary Partnerships* (Ithaca, NY: Cornell University Press, 1999), esp. 130–31. London's *Writing Double* provides a fascinating expanded discussion of the writing partnership (including posthumously) of Somerville and Ross (Edith Somerville and Violet Martin).

and women's social latitude. This focus on collectivity and alternative politics seems to be not only fantastic but also distinctly modern, as shown, for instance, in the case of *Daniel Deronda*'s proto-Zionism. It does not seem discontinuous in its impulses, for instance, to the collective political action of suffrage campaigns or to the contemporary theoretical interest in the postnational and in ways of imagining citizenship in a postcolonial world.

The rest of this book will look more specifically at the ways possessed individualism and extra spheres reconfigure subjectivity and the idea of characterization outside of the concept of autonomous agency. "Tables with Contents" will explore the refiguring of the concept of community through the radical continuity between person and thing when *one person* does not equal one body.

SECTION THREE

SUBJECTIVITY
RECONFIGURED

Chapter 3

Tables with Contents

> The most revealing testimony can be found in "the furniture of daily life" ... all the things we look at hourly without seeing ... Dickens could even write a story in *Household Words* about a talking hat stand which consoled the narrator when he was crossed in love.[1]

There was a discrete but noteworthy publishing phenomenon in the 1850s of animate séance table accounts.[2] These writings show how popular mystical practices distinctly break down a certain boundary, just as other sorts of mystical practices in other types of accounts question other boundaries. Daniel Deronda's possession, for instance, creates a continuity between public and private through his becoming an "executive self," possessed by the spirit of all of Israel. The Croslands, Marryat, and Waisbrooker challenge the boundary between visible and invisible through their theories of vision, community, and millenarian history in which invisible forces can directly affect the personal and social politics of the visible world.

Accounts of walking and talking séances tables, though at first glance seemingly silly and absurd, are also boundary breakers. They blur the categorical distinction between subject and object. Taken as a whole, then, popular mystical practices function to unite spirits, persons, and things to create a highly pervasive and distinct metaphysical worldview: *metaphysical* both in the sense of supernatural and in the sense of theoretical. The number of beings with agency, seen or unseen, living or not living, far outpaces the number of human bodies in mystical and "realistic" Victorian narratives. This proliferation of agents actually takes on a categorically radical politics that serves as a critique of public polity in the absence of civic parity. These tables are at the center of the articulation of both a new understanding of women and of the commodity.

---

[1] Asa Briggs, *Victorian Things* (Chicago: University of Chicago Press, 1988), 28, 33.

[2] Most of these accounts were published between 1853 and 1857. The account I will discuss in this chapter was published in 1863 and does not appear in catalogs through a search of "table turning" or "table tipping," though these are the search terms through which these types of essays and short books usually appear. Most of the accounts published in 1853 and 1854 were English ministers debating whether table turning was satanical. Accounts beginning in 1855 also consider whether animate tables are the result of parlor magic. Searching through both OCLC/World Cat and the British Library's catalog, somewhere between fifteen and twenty mid-Victorian publications can be found that consider table turning.

The slippery continuity between person and thing in accounts of table turning means that nouns and verbs that do not usually go together can do so in the context of the séance. A table can throw a tantrum and stomp across the room. Séances, through every subjectivity from the medium or the ectoplasm right down to the furniture in the room, play out manifold scripts for how a self might behave. Partnership can become liberal indeed, linking the living, the dead, and the living room. For many Victorians on the religious fringe, the boundaries of personal identity, the importance of community, and the self-defining identification with the invisible all diverge from what we would call autonomous subjectivity. Furthermore, the feminized subjectivity of walking and talking séance tables indicates that a woman's subjectivity is transferable and that identity in this context is truly performative. Just as labor that goes into producing something is the secret that adds mystical luster to a commodity, according to Marx, women's expression is the hidden, displaced power that adds mystical animation to the séance table (see Figure 3.1). The alternative sociability of this extra sphere in turn places stress on the public sphere by calling into question who a social actor should or could be.

To some Victorian mystics, a woman's use value became a central focus. If a woman was not a voting citizen or not exclusively a domestic self, what type of citizen was she? More centrally, of what type of social order was she a citizen? A medium's surprising embodiment of others set her up as a model for society in a single body. But why, then, should tables also be modeled as agents and gendered at times as women? In fact, should the treatment of Victorian tables relate at all to the subjectivity of Victorian women? Considering an interpersonal relationship between women and furniture is counterintuitive. An extended case, however, for such a relationship was being made by mystics, who were writing not only about the connection between the real and the imaginary but also about the commensurability of people and things. Their inquiry into animate inanimacy became a logical response to centuries of civil inequality for women. There was an air of possibility: Women and wood both found themselves in the subjunctive. Inequality opens the door to women being not only negatively objectified but also interestingly objectified. Their use and exchange values, like those of objects, can be expressed. The séance is an alternative place where a woman could express her spiritual use value through exchanges with people and things. These possibilities violated common Victorian expectations about order, classification, and taxonomy. Identity, like value in Marx's "Commodity," is based on exchange. Strange commensurabilities measured by exchanges mark the texture of social interaction and define the fleeting, insubstantial, and unfixed nature of a woman's identity. The economics of the political market enforce the vagaries of the Victorian mystical woman—like a commodity, she can only be understood in arbitrary relation to others, both human and thing.

If being possessed rather than possessive made a political individual in mystical accounts, there were implications for other categories, such as property. If possessions (symbols of wealth because of their exchange value) were no longer the central definition of an individual's identity and value, then the role of property could be radically reconsidered and reworked. Consider a table: What does a table do? A

TABLE TIPPING.

Figure 3.1   **Medium, sitters, and animate séance table**
Frontispiece from Searcher after truth, *The Rappers* (New York: 1854). Facsimile courtesy of Watkinson Library, Trinity College, Hartford, CT.

table is a social space. Ideas go on the table; things go on under the table. Arms and hands rest on it. It is a surface for eating and working; feet are only rudely placed there. People meet around it to play games and make deals. Tables are sites of consumption, production, and exchange. When a Victorian spiritualist believed tables to be possessed, tables, gendered as female, became personified and could often do as they pleased—serving as an iconographic representation of the subjectivity of Victorian women themselves.

Tables

> We can charge a table with brain or nervous force, and our volition can act or produce motion through that medium without the aid of the motor-nerves and muscular contact. In electro-biology the same thing takes place, one brain becomes charged with nervous force from another, and the whole of this force is under the direction of one will. We are surrounded by an atmosphere, the result of cerebration, its character depending upon the nervous centres or mental faculties from which it emanates. We all have felt the effect, more or less, of coming into each other's atmospheres ... So brain force may be carried through the same ether inducing consciousness, and carrying ideas in all sorts of ways, at present unknown to us.[3]

Charles Bray, George Eliot's lifelong friend with a pantheistic worldview, here speaks casually about charging a table with nervous force: the power of positive thinking. He is one of many Victorians who were very matter-of-fact about animate inanimacy. Tables could move on their own—distantly influenced by the nervous force of cerebration: thinking. Tables have always been celebrities, philosophically speaking. Their animation and pregnant meaning have been explored by Plato, Thomas DeQuincy, Karl Marx, Sigmund Freud, and Virginia Woolf, just to name a few. In the mid-nineteenth century they become the mystical life of the party at séances, suggesting that a conflation of subject and object is not necessarily unusual but could be normative.

For example, spiritualist Florence Marryat recounts an experience where she and her friend, professional medium Miss Showers, are alone in the drawing room.[4] They are attacked by spirits in the dark; their clothes are torn off; they are beaten: Miss Showers sits on the middle of the table for safety, having been removed from Florence's circling arms by the unseen. Why is the table safe? Why is it a party to the interaction? How does it save the girl? Why does furniture console? Why is the table the consistent site of the action? What does it mean for a subject to be on the table?

---

3   Charles Bray, *Illusion and Delusion; Or, Modern Pantheism versus Spiritualism* (London: Thomas Scott, 1873), 32.
4   Florence Marryat, *There Is No Death* [1891] (Philadelphia: David McKay, 1920), 113–14.

This decisive interaction between the table and Marryat and Showers seems natural to the women. The reason is perhaps that like them, the table is imagined as holding subjectivity and a communal nature.

Some people in the nineteenth century were obsessed with imbuing the insensitive with sensation. Shelley's poem, "The Sensitive Plant" (1820), for instance, uses the metaphor of the sensitive plant, an actual leafy green plant that recoils when touched, to explore the ideal of sensibility (or rather susceptibility) in a subject.[5] For some Victorians, this idealization of responding to touch was not just metaphorical when describing plants or the inanimate.

For instance, Dr Guppy, a spiritualist and the hydropathist of George Henry Lewes, when explaining why his séance table had started to move and communicate, says that the table, made of wood, has come from a plant that like the sensitive plant can feel. For many personified objects, like wooden furniture, it was possible for a spiritualist to imagine the objects not only feeling but also acting. With the rise of Victorian drawing room rituals and entertainments, such as table rapping, the wood texture seems to have felt itself and expressed its feelings to human companions.[6]

The implications of the subjectivity of wood reach into everyday life: If a Victorian spiritualist's parlor furniture can talk, there is no excuse for having a silent house—the absence of noise, on the part of furniture anyway, becomes resistance (pouting), or contentment (an afternoon nap), or ignoring (day-dreaming), or some other sort of silent treatment.

Victorian spiritualists were thinking about furniture in a way that suggests the absurd full extension of Marx's concept of commodity fetishism. Marx writes in *Capital*:

> If, by our process of abstraction, we ignore its use-value, we ignore also the material constituents and forms which render it a use-value. It is no longer, to us, a table, or a house, or yarn, or any other useful thing. All the qualities whereby it affects our senses are annulled. It has ceased to be the product of the work of a joiner, a builder, a spinner; the outcome of some specific kind of productive labour. When the useful character of the labour products vanish, the useful character of the labour embodied in them vanishes as well.[7]

Marx argues that use value calibrates the value of a man-made object. He claims that in a process of abstraction, people lose a sensual relationship to things and to their makers. He further claims that in the process, the specificity and qualities of an object

---

[5] Percy Bysshe Shelley, *The Complete Poems of Percy Bysshe Shelley*, with notes by Mary Shelley (New York: Modern Library, 1994), 627–34. The first four lines are as follows: "A SENSITIVE Plant in a garden grew, / And the young winds fed it with silver dew, / And it opened its fan-like leaves to the light, / And closed them beneath the kisses of Night" (lines 1–4).

[6] "How does texture feel to itself?" Eve Kosofsky Sedgwick posed this question, which initially made me think about the subjectivity of the séance table.

[7] Karl Marx, *Capital, Vol. 1* (New York: E.P. Dutton, 1939), 6.

become unrecognizable. How does this relate to the spiritualist Victorians who believed in mystical, personified tables? A table that can walk and play musical instruments does have a sensual and specific tie to its owner, if not its producer.

Marx further argues that commodities cannot express their own value, except through their relation to other commodities, and furthermore these comparative commodities must form a qualitative identity and be commensurable. He explains:

> Since no commodity can function as equivalent for itself, can make of its own bodily shape an expression of its own value, every commodity must (to express its value) enter into relation with some other commodity as equivalent, converting the bodily shape of that other commodity into the form of its own value ... [Aristotle] sees, further, that the value relation represented by the phrase "5 beds = 1 house" implies a qualitative identity between house and bed; he recognises that, different though the two things are to our bodily senses, they must have a common essence, for otherwise we could not relate them one to another as commensurable magnitudes. He says: "There cannot be exchange without equality, nor equality without commensurability."[8]

Dissimilar matters, then, cannot communicate or express themselves in terms of one another. Marx's assumption that there can be no exchange without equality is both a widely accepted ideal view and inaccurate. Politically speaking, there are all sorts of exchange without equality. But in this quotation, equality, which prefigures the possibility for exchange in an economic sense, is presented as something that is universally observable (recognized?) and conventionally agreed on. That is to say, one would only need to know what goes on the other side of the equals sign from *x* to know what *x* could or could not be exchanged for. However, the political context of Victorian England provides a counterexample: Women and men were not equal, and equality did not prefigure exchange because women and men had all sorts of exchanges: economic, social, sexual, and legally contractual, which were not necessarily commensurate. Due to civic inequality, there was a question mark on the other side of the equals sign from Victorian women, who were not equal to men. In the idealized belief that every commodity must (to express its value) enter into relation with some other commodity as equivalent, a thing might be exchanged for a woman. In relief, identity can have no stable, independent meaning, but must by logical necessity be performatively constructed through understanding in which type of exchanges it participates.

Regardless of the embedded assumption of requisite homogeneity in Marx's "Commodity," it suddenly seems clear why people at a séance and drawing room tables should become fast friends. The séance implies an equivalency and commensurability between commodities and persons. Victorian séance tables do not seem to focus on their exchange value but do value exchanges. Some of the Victorian women at a séance want to communicate with the dead who are quick. The table in the drawing room, like the quick dead, has had a former life. It began when its seed was planted;

---

8   *Ibid.*, 27, 30.

it grew up and lived for seasons as part of a specific family and then was cut down in the prime of life, rent asunder, and turned into something else—transferred from the realm of the living to that of the dead. Its form has changed. Marx writes:

> For instance, the form of wood is altered when we make a table of it. Nonetheless, the table is still wood, an ordinary palpable thing. But as soon as it presents itself as a commodity, it transformed into a thing which is transcendental as well as palpable. It stands with its feet solidly planted on the floor: but at the same time, over against all other commodities, it stands on its head; and in that wooden head it forms crotchets far stranger than table-turning ever was.[9]

Palpable wood is rather beyond ordinary wood. Marx's words raise a question: Is the wood palpable because it can be touched, or is it so because it is palpating and feeling? A table is planted on the floor and, insofar as it is made from cut-down timber, it may now be standing on its head (as opposed to its roots). Marx argues that in its head, or its top, it forms strange *crotchets* (a word with double meaning: a whimsical notion or a Y-like juncture shaped like a crotch, also possibly linking the table to a person's crotch and to the concept of whimsy or insanity). I am not sure what Marx means by this, but neither are others. Derrida, for example, writes:

> It is a great moment at the beginning of *Capital* as everyone recalls: Marx is wondering in effect how to describe the sudden looming up of the mystical character of the commodity, the mystification of the thing itself—and of the money-form of which the commodity's simple form is the "germ." He wants to analyze the equivalent whose *enigma* and mystical character only strike the bourgeois economist in the finished form of money, gold or silver. It is the moment in which Marx means to demonstrate that the mystical character owes nothing to a use-value. Is it just chance that he illustrates the principle of his explanation by causing a table to turn? Or rather by recalling the apparition of a turning table.[10]

Marx argues for a transcendental table, and Derrida argues that this table represents the mystical character of commodity, divorced from its use value. To be touched in the head, to have a crotchet, or to be turned is to have gone crazy. Some séance tables are mad, bad, and dangerous to know—with a head full of (feminized?) crotchets. Marx's table, however, is still circumscribed by the commodity culture circles in which it moves.

The final point that Marx makes in his "Commodity" chapter concerns the exchange value of a commodity. He writes:

> If commodities could speak, they would say: "Our use value may interest human beings; but it is not an attribute of ours, as things. What is our attribute, as things, is our value.

---

9   *Ibid.*, 44.

10   Jacques Derrida, *Spectres of Marx, the State of the Debt, the Work of Mourning, and the New International*, trans. Peggy Kamuf (New York and London: Routledge, 1994), 149.

Our own interrelations as commodities prove it. We are related to one another only as exchange-values."[11]

The fact that Marx actually gives commodities dialogue to speak is symptomatic not only of the alarming strangeness of table-turning that he earlier dismisses but also of the problem that just as subjects might become objectified, commodities might become subjectified. Certainly a well-schooled Marxist table would say that its use value, as contrasted with its exchange value, might interest humans, but it seems most tables in Victorian séance circles were not Marxist.[12] So what does the economically "other" table have to say for itself? In fact, the séance table defies Marx and takes an active interest in performing its own use value. Not only does it stand as the place for civic interactions, it walks and talks and draws and plays and is referred to as feminine. What does this, in turn, imply about Victorian women? Is it that a woman equals her inheritance? Equals her husband's economic power? Equals her dependency? Or perhaps through spiritualism and other forms of conceptually mystical interdependence, she equals or stands in synecdochal relation to the collectivity of which she is a part and which she represents. A woman can be touched, and she has subjectivity like palpable wood. Some Victorian laws, however, involving women failed to recognize them as individuals who were part of a community. For example, rape remained legalized within marriage. In this instance, a woman was a possession of the husband, not an equal individual. For Victorian women, inequality prefigured all exchanges; use value was by necessity, then, the alternative focus of expression.

Some Victorian tables were more transcendental than others. Let us look at tables to explore their use value and identity. The oeuvre of table criticism to date is rather slim, including the work of Daniel Cottom, who makes the following points about spiritualism and tables:

Spiritualists turned nature, the supernatural, human beings, and the world all together into public scenes unregulated by social and sacramental conventions ... This movement made spiritual ideas speak through the stupidest objects and people while at the same time suggesting that this world, the world that goes without saying, might actually be unreliable and disoriented: a world, in Emerson's outraged conclusion, with "no police, no foot-rule, no sanity,—nothing but whim and whim creative." ... If tables, trumpets, ordinary Joes, children's slates, and all the rest of the furniture of our lives could become philosophical mouthpieces, other objects—the objects of science, philosophy, religion, art—might appear as nothing more than the furniture of professional people, who gathered around it to be moved by the sorts of spirits they happened to prefer.[13]

---

11   Marx, *Capital*, 58.
12   It seems that we might be able to consider séance tables as predicting neo-Marxist critique, such as Baudrillard's, that commodities can function as part of a sign system, independent of people. This, however, is outside the scope of the present study.
13   Daniel Cottom, "On the Dignity of Tables," *Critical Inquiry* 14 (Summer 1988): 769, 772, 777.

Cottom argues for the emblematic role of tables in a spiritualist construction of meaning that posed a threat to the constructed reason of other professionalizing institutions.[14] Rather than focusing on social institutions, I explore the grounds for understanding identity—who or what is endowed with subjectivity and what that subjectivity resembles. The reason for this emphasis is clear: The definition of subjectivity becomes a focal issue because equality did not exist. The issue for Victorian women became with whom, if it were not a man, she could be equal and/or create a social order in which she could potentially express her use value or functional essence. Cottom's point about the spiritualist world being unreliable and disoriented and Emerson's point about it being a place of creative whim seem on target. It is even more important to stress that the animation embodied in a table that talks and dances or in a medium that exudes ectoplasms (moments of movement or of movement by remote control) is that these acts go against established Victorian regimes of order, which fall in the domain of a masculinized public sphere. Anyone or anything can be in on the act, part of a promiscuous, unsettling, viable community. If walking tables violate order, then, by extension, so do the women who talk to them—they are accomplices. Also, in this disoriented spiritualist world, things and people formerly known by one name start going by other names—tables become girls; girls become ghosts. The interactions between tables and women are based on a surprising fluidity of exchange that by extension points to the absurdity of civic inequality between women and men. Everyone and everything in a Victorian mystical fringe setting can be on the move—actively mingling in the most surprising manner: mixing living and dead, animate and inanimate—and this movement, physical and metaphorical, directly acts as political critique. This mixing of unlike things is a new incarnation of a political movement.

These mixers take place in the sanctified Victorian home with lofty explanations. Elizabeth Barrett Browning writes that:

> the common objection of the degradation of knocking with the leg of the table, and the ridicule of the position for a spirit, &c., &c., I don't enter into at all. Twice I have been present at table-experiments, and each time I was deeply impressed—impressed, there's the word for it! The panting and shivering of that dead dumb wood, the human emotion conveyed through it—by what? had to me a greater significance than the St. Peter's of this Rome. O poet! do you not know that poetry is not confined to the clipped alleys, no, nor to the blue tops of "Parnassus hill?"[15]

The panting and shivering poetic table is here extolled. This view fits nicely into a Romantic poetic tradition celebrating the spiritual interplay of people and things.

---

14 For another excellent article concerning French séance tables in part, as well as spiritism, Marx, and Victor Hugo, see Jann Matlock, "Ghostly Politics," *Diacritics* 30:3 (2000): 53–71.

15 Elizabeth Barrett Browning quoted in Cottom, "On the Dignity of Tables," 778–9.

Browning does not even pause before saying that a table can express human emotion. Her claim extends the concept of commodity fetishism—subjects do not only worship objects; objects become subjects and they worship together.[16] Browning's words provide a clear sense of the romantic Victorian concept of the ascendancy of the thing: metaphorical and yet also actual, the object is the vehicle for discussion of spirit, desire, abstract concepts, and the world frequently employed by Romantic and Victorian poetry.

This, however, does not answer why Victorian tables specifically were chosen to be such moving orators. Part of the reason is not just that tables are sensitive wood and have heads, feet, and legs like people, but also that they are a particular locus of human interaction—places of contract and community. Robert Hare writes, "The table still draws about it the inmates of every human dwelling, at all seasons, and in every kind of weather ... At tables, moreover, conferences are held, contracts and deeds signed ... It was at a table the Declaration of Independence was signed."[17] The table is a site of civic polity, then, and a place for making social laws and contracts: It is simultaneously legal and public, intimate and private. It is also a place that is an emblem of domestic space and a place of ritual observance.

That spirits should embody tables is a concern that Victorian literary woman Camilla Crosland (discussed in Chapter 2), an ardent Church of England member, considered at length when she wrote:

Perhaps there has been a good deal of thoughtless ridicule heaped upon the word Table. How apt we all are to undervalue common things! Is there no reverence for that mysterious table which was made by God's own order, as part of the Tabernacle furniture?* (*Exodus, XXV). No tender interest in that modern thing which must somewhat resemble the board at which our Blessed Lord himself broke bread, and bade His followers do the same in remembrance of Him? The vein of thought which opens up on rightly contemplating this subject is rich in imagery and association,—so rich that I should have been little likely to hit on it myself, but owe its wealth to a conversation with one of our greatest living Poets, who, in answer to the ridicule hurled at the table pleaded its sacred character. In deed, the table is the household altar. At the table we read ... Round the table family and friends gather ... Why, the phrase "our circle" is an idiom of the language, and, instinctively, congenial natures gather together to form it ... Mark if discord or unhappiness arises, how the chair is drawn back, the circle broken! ... Knowing, however, the objections which are commonly raised to table-rapping ... one evening, when in communication with a very high Spirit, I

---

16 Asa Briggs notes the further development of this trend in the hands of Victorian authors such as Thomas Hardy: "Hardy himself was well aware of what he conceived of as the poetry of simple things. After a friend in the course of a conversation on comparative culture had suggested that Dorset peasants held to 'the barbaric idea that confuses persons and things,' Hardy wrote in his diary that 'this barbaric idea ... is, by the way, also common to the highest imaginative genius—that of the poet.' If people could be treated as things, things could sometimes behave like people" (Briggs, *Victorian Things*, 18).

17 Hare quoted in Cottom, "On the Dignity of Tables," 779.

inquired what answer I should make ... The answer spelt out was—"If we came with more solemnity, we should awe you too much."[18]

The table, then, to Crosland becomes the emblem of everything domestic, holy and yet approachable. At every turn, the table is feminized. It is "mysterious," closely associated with the family "circle," should be treated with "tender interest," and is likely to be "undervalued." Crosland affiliates the table with Christ's sacrifice. The Eucharist takes place at the table. The table becomes the place where Christ is ritualistically translated from subject to object to subjects, and some of this subjectivity seems to wear off on the table. Also, the table itself seems filled with a desire for equality. Its words, speaking through a spirit, are that it does not want to overawe with solemnity.

The Guppys' Table, Mary Jane

Dr Samuel Guppy, George Henry Lewes's hydropathist, presents and theorizes the unique example of his drawing room table, which he names Mary Jane, in an essay that goes about explaining her identity.[19] The Guppys were in many ways a typical, middle class, mid-Victorian family. They had several children, and Dr Guppy was a fashionable provider of water therapies. Mrs Guppy was a well-known London medium. I provide a lengthy discussion of Dr Guppy's essay on their séance table because he gives such a detailed account of her identity that it leads to theorizing the qualities of other animate séance furniture. Although the account is atypical in terms of providing a characterization of the table, it is typical in terms of its description of what a séance table can do. For example, Mary Jane tilts, spells out messages, creates drawings, and plays music; these activities are characteristic of many other séance tables. Guppy's further analysis of the character of his table shows both how and why a woman (in this case, primarily Mrs Guppy) would communicate with a commodity (in this case, a table).

---

[18] Mrs Newton Crosland [Camilla Toulmin], *Light in the Valley. My Experiences of Spiritualism* (London: Routledge, 1857), 19.

[19] Both Dr Guppy and George Henry Lewes were Victorian men of science. Dr Guppy practiced a form of medical treatment, hydropathy, which started in Germany in 1825, involving internal and external application of cold water as treatment for disease. Lewes, the longtime companion of George Eliot, was a patient of Dr Guppy. Lewes investigated marine biology, psychology, philosophy, and physiology. Unlike Dr Guppy's enthusiastic embracing of the séance table, Lewes, when asked to participate in 1874 in a spiritualist séance (one organized by Erasmus Darwin and attended by Charles Darwin) refused, finding it "amusing and a source of mockery." For the full anecdote on Lewes's visit to Erasmus Darwin's séance, see Frederick S. Karl, *George Eliot: The Voice of a Century* (New York: Norton, 1995).

With Dr Guppy's Mary Jane, the table becomes sensate wood that symbolically must be honored as the center of the family circle. The table is down to earth and ready to talk. It is as if the table desires to be just one of the girls. But why is it gendered female? Why should a wood table be gendered at all? Guppy is not alarmed at finding himself housed with a "wild animal," who then takes on language and the "quality of intellectuality."[20] Perhaps he elides the categories of animal and woman. Both could only "take on" the quality of intellectuality.

Mary Jane's identity undergoes a process of change. She is found, for instance, even in the course of one evening, evidenced in raps from "behind the sofa" and from the table. Sometimes she is wild and sometimes intellectual: "The chemical emanations which took place, instead of causing the table to run about like a wild animal, took entirely the shape and quality of intellectuality" (310). Mary Jane moves from nonsense to sense and from the preverbal to the verbal. In fact, like a baby, she has a first word. Dr Guppy tells us, "I was present, and must say that the poor table exhibited great want of grammatical education, for it put a dozen of incomprehensible consonants together, worse than a Welsh or Polish name, at last ending with baby" (309).

Shortly thereafter the new drawing room intelligence is christened by Dr Guppy:

> Still, an intelligent being, to be talked to, must have a name, and the house was full of children from school, and country servants. How it was I don't know—having no relative, nor knowing any lady of that name—but I christened the new comer "Mary Jane," and it answered to Mary Jane, and from that time forward Mary Jane has been with us at any time we chose to talk to her, and has even repeatedly called for the alphabet, and given us a very sensible opinion on the subject we were discussing, when we did not think of appealing to her. You may be sure that, on finding a third party so unexpectedly domiciled with us, we asked it every possible question, and we received replies, the sense and accuracy of which pleased and startled us, as clearly proving a distinct and partially superhuman intelligence. (309–10)[21]

It is noteworthy that her name, Mary Jane, comes from no relative or acquaintance; she is a *new*comer and a new force in their home—a third party with whom the Guppys can consult. In this way, she does not replicate a received order but presents her own novel viewpoints.

In fact, Mary Jane is quite forthright in expressing her opinions:

> Mary Jane, making her presential appearance, called for the alphabet, and made a very disparaging remark on the sense of the clergy. I felt rather hurt at such candour; and,

---

20   *Mary Jane; or, Spiritualism Chemically Explained with Spirit Drawings. Also Essays By, and Ideas (Perhaps Erroneous) of, 'A Child at School'* (London: John King, 1863). Further quotes from this work will be cited by page number in the text.

21   Like the communion example, to be "christened" is to have life force consecrated and legitimated.

pushing the alphabet to my reverend friend, requested to talk to Mary Jane; but that young lady not only did not retract her former opinion, but reiterated it, adding a personal and very impolite remark. (340)

At another point, Mary Jane, "the young lady" does not resort to forthright words but to a tantrum: "It appeared immediately as though all the smothered discontents of the day were transferred to the table, which began tilting and stamping with such violence as to frighten my wife" (314). Here, Mary Jane is unruly, not containable, and is in some sense showing the potential to take over the house. In fact, on one occasion the author notes that Mary Jane's raps occur only "after the room was thoroughly, so to say, mediumised" (319). This leads the reader to ask what sort of influence is it to be "mediumised?" If one can be mediumized, the locus for performance comes from without, not from within the body/self. It means that an individual's action is under the influence. It is, most interestingly, to have plural action through a single body and to blend what is inanimate with what is animate.

Mary Jane's exact class and ethnic identities are not clearly fixed. This is evident in yet another rhapsody on her name itself: "What is in a name? It answered, as instantly, always to 'Mary Jane,' as a new servant would, if you told her that, for family reasons, she must answer to the name of Susan" (313). The use of second person address here aligns the author and the reader and differentiates Mary Jane as a servant.[22] In other passages other parts of her identity and status fall into question. For instance, séance visitors "scold her sometimes ... [and] they treat our Mary Jane as a lively mundane spirit, with whom to play cards or dominoes or get drawings from" (352). "Our" Mary Jane, then, is not always an independent spirit but is sometimes more like a lady's maid. In other places it seems the author's friends fear that the name Mary Jane, if revealed "to the public will be unmeaning, and perhaps by some be thought childish" (362).

Certainly, in many regards, even taking into account her status as a piece of furniture, Mary Jane is often the perfect young lady. Dr Guppy wonders why this young lady and not a deceased spirit has come to his house:

> But why the spirits of deceased persons seemed to communicate with him, and why the mediums in Bloomsbury said they were present there to communicate with me, and that they should totally decline to visit me at my own house, and a lively, talkative, musical, and artistical Mary Jane come in their stead, is what I do not understand. (328)

Again, her social attainments and newness are stressed. Mary Jane is not some great-aunt back to make sure the family is still respectable (as Newton Crosland, discussed in Chapter 2, might advocate). This is not to say that Mary Jane does not frequently

---

22   As Carol Mavor notes in *Pleasures Taken: Sexuality and Loss in Victorian Photographs* (Durham, NC: Duke University Press, 1995), Mary Jane is the most common female Victorian servant's name.

uphold Victorian standards of gentility. It is important to keep remembering Mary Jane is not a young woman who is a young lady; she is a table that is a young lady. She performs young lady. Performance is different from being real and often satirizes the "type" portrayed. For instance, Mary Jane makes small presents to the ladies who call on her hostess:

> By-and-bye, Mary Jane asked for the alphabet, and said, "Have patience, and you shall have a flower." The ladies had put two sheets of paper and a pencil on the carpet under the table. Perhaps half-an-hour after, Mary Jane was asked if she had written anything. "Yes." The sheets of paper were found folded up with a flower drawn on each—the one a Tulip, the other a Rose, drawn in that style of Penmanship in which Schoolmasters draw swans, rather roughly done, but quite clear drawings of the flowers. The ladies were highly delighted, thanked Mary Jane, and asked who the drawings were for—and in this, and all subsequent drawings, the same ceremony was observed, Mary Jane answering "No" until the right person was named. (318)

Mary Jane is very much a table schoolgirl here presenting floral offerings to please visitors (see Figure 3.2). In this and in other particulars, Mary Jane is quite the young lady. For instance, she is musical:

> I must not omit the musical talent of Mary Jane. At a séance (out) my wife had held a guitar in her hand under the table, and it had been played on by the good spirits of that domicile, so I could not do less than procure any and every instrument Mary Jane might like to play on; and I purchased an excellent guitar, an accordion, and a child's drum, and borrowed a violin; none answered well except the guitar; the accordion and drum were sounded a little; as for the violin, after Mary Jane had sounded a few discordant notes on it, she undid all the pegs, loosened the strings, broke down the bridge, and wrenched it out of my wife's hand. (311)

Guised in the musical attainments of a young lady, a bit of Mary Jane's power of disruption shows through her violin violence.

Mary Jane is not always reasonable and also is not an independent subjectivity. On one day, for instance, when the maid has been acting up and nothing has gone right and Mrs Guppy has been in a particularly foul mood, the evening's séance does not run smoothly:

> It appeared immediately as though all the smothered discontents of the day were transferred to the table, which began tilting and stamping with such violence as to frighten my wife. W. [a guest] was in his glory, and wanted the table to go up to the ceiling; my wife was frightened, and took off all but her little finger; still the table was outrageous. I wanted to explain to them the phenomenon philosophically, and said … "Let us take all our hands off while I explain." We sat each of us at about a foot from the table, no one touching it; on a sudden the table moved off itself, right up to my wife; and a chair … moved two feet towards her. (314)

Figure 3.2   One of Mary Jane's flower drawings for a sitter
Facsimile courtesy of Watkinson Library, Hartford, CT.

The table is filled with the energy of the medium, Mrs Guppy, and her discontents are picked up and replicated by Mary Jane. Mary Jane, though, is not simply a second self for Mrs Guppy. In fact, Dr Guppy's explanation of Mary Jane's subjectivity is far more complicated than this, and the similes he uses to describe this subjectivity are surprisingly telling. His description rests loosely on the theories of Baron von Reichenbach's concept of *odyll*, or energy that escapes from the medium's fingertips and creates the visiting "spirit."[23]

Who is Mary Jane, really? Dr Guppy offers additional analogies for theorizing the function of the medium. She is also the "mother" of the spirit/table. He defines a medium as follows:

---

[23]   Baron von Reichenbach (1788–1869). See Baron Carl von Reichenbach's *Researches on Magnetism, Electricity, Heat, Light, Crystallization, and Chemical Attraction, in Their Relations to the Vital Force*, trans. William Gregory (London and Edinburgh: Taylor, Walton, and Maberly and Maclachlan and Stewart, 1850). Note Elizabeth Barrett Browning's *Aurora Leigh*: "That od-force of German Reichenbach / Which still from fingertips turn blue." See Elizabeth Barrett Browning, *Aurora Leigh*, 4th edn (London: Chapman and Hall, 1859).

A medium, a thinking being, places her hands on a table, and after a lapse of some minutes, holds conversation with another being, which has been eliminated from her body, as distinct as the child at the breast is from the mother, and exists just as the child, on condition of the supply of nutriment being kept up—and this being is composed of nothing else than the vapours which have emanated from the medium's body; and this being can tell the medium things which her own faculties are unequal to ... The other persons sitting at the table affect the quality of the manifestations, although the Odylic vapours from them are not sufficiently strong to move the table or act intelligently alone ... The female of all animals, as well as the man, is so constituted for the purposes of gestation and lactation as to eliminate more liquids and probably consequently more vapours—that hence more women are mediums than men. (337–8)

The medium is moistly keeping the spirit in presence like a babe at her breast. But the other sitters also affect the "quality of the manifestations." The visiting spirit, then, relies on the medium and sitters and in turn complicates their own singular identities. This raises the question of whether there can be an individual subjectivity for a Victorian spiritualist, and if so, what would that mean? Is subjectivity based on internal or external "reality?" These questions have been posed by Descartes and Hegel; they are old hat after a fashion. However, such inquiries are still relevant, especially with the material at hand, which claims, after all, that these concerns are not philosophical but physical. Daniel Miller, writing on Hegel, notes:

At each stage the subject posits an increasingly complex and particular other, becoming aware of this other as a distance from itself. It then realizes that this apparently alien other is in fact a product of itself, created as a mirror by means of which it might further its own self-awareness. This process of understanding permits the subject to reincorporate the increasingly complex external world it has created, and by so doing to emerge as an increasingly complex subject.[24]

This quotation is consonant with the important theory Mr. Guppy shares, namely, that Mary Jane reflects and is dependent on her sitters, like a baby. At the same time, one infers that the sitters can achieve a greater degree of self-actualization because they are reflected both by the table's smooth surface and its actions. Mary Jane and the sitters have transformed physical ontologies. However, Mary Jane could never become a self-actualized subject through this process. She always remains a subaltern other in the service of the séance. She is a babe at breast, or a servant, or in another surprising turn in her characterization considered next, a runaway slave. Every analogy that Guppy turns to calls on a different politically disenfranchised group.

Dr Guppy draws a direct analogy between the sweat of a runaway slave and the emanations of a medium's body that could cause a table to move:

Certain elements, having undergone a chemical animalisation in the human body, possess the quality of giving the effect of *motion* to inert substances, under certain conditions. Now, the

---

24   Daniel Miller, *Material Culture and Mass Consumption* (New York: Basil Blackwell, 1987), 22–3.

quantity of power so evolved (although, from circumstances hereafter explained, it seldom shows itself) is very great; for, if you consider the case of a negro running away—running fifty miles—and that blood-hounds are set on his track, we see that the elements issuing from his feet attach themselves so firmly to the spots he has trod on, that for hours the hounds find his spur; and that in fifty miles, at a yard a step, he will have made 88,000 steps, and, if his foot covered six inches square, he will have impregnated 44,000 square feet with the emanations from his feet alone, being about forty-four rooms of twenty feet square each. Now it is evident that, if that man had remained in one room all the day, although the emanations would not have been so excessive as during his flight, still they would have filled and permeated that room with these elements. (307–8)

In the case of likening a medium to a runaway slave, the message is somewhat unclear. That is, does Dr Guppy desire some sort of escape for the slave or for the medium? This striking analogy also makes suggestive claims about Mrs Guppy. In the first place, Mary Jane's animation is the result of the emanations of a medium who is implied to be similar to a runaway slave. The analogy seems to hint subtly at the wave of cultural anxiety that followed the practice of mediumship. The terms of this analogy make the séance a site of flight where the medium, in this case Mrs Guppy, might escape domestic social boundaries while simultaneously rarely physically exiting the posited room. In this sense, an alternative public sphere is contained by the walls of domestic space. Flight described as producing a certain quantifiable trace in the emanations left for bloodhounds that has the quality of being able to make other things move, too. In fact, this elusive trace, in the form of the lively Mary Jane, serves to mark a disruption that not even a bloodhound could subdue. The conjunction negro/woman, as two notable representatives of disenfranchised groups in Dr Guppy's analogy, seems ambivalent: Is the excitement that these groups try to get away from their pursuers (ostensibly white men) and can? Or is it that they try to get away and often cannot? Bloodhounds not only chase people who are criminalized such as escapees of slavery but also chase the ubiquitous fox in nineteenth-century accounts. Even authors who are occasionally sympathetic to the fox in tales of the foxhunt, as occurs in Trollope (*The Eustace Diamonds*), ultimately support the beleaguered beast being caught and killed. Mary Jane and Mrs Guppy both may be more like foxes than like people or things.

Unlike the fox in a foxhunt, however, Mrs Guppy is not a singular, lonely creature. There is, instead, a symbiotic relationship between her and her table. Would Mrs Guppy be even more active without Mary Jane soaking up her extra emanations? Because Mrs Guppy is also famous in another séance story for being transported through the London night air from her own home to the top of someone else's séance table, dripping pen and accounts in hand, she is probably just about as animated as possible.[25] Both the medium and the table can be moved by other's wishes and seem to stand as equals. The shock in this juxtaposition of subjectivities is not that a table can walk, talk, and emote, it is that the woman is objectified. In the conjunction of their

---

[25] For an account of this famous mediumistic transportation episode of Mrs Guppy at the house of Messrs Herne and Williams, professional mediums, see Fritz, *Where Are the Dead? Or, Spiritualism Explained* (London: Simpkin, Marshall, 1873), 47–9.

ghostly emanations, Mrs Guppy's and Mary Jane's personhood are both in question. In "rooms of twenty feet square each" comes the undeniable echo that a drawing room has the regulated dimensions of a prison cell—or any other of the marked domestic spaces that contain nineteenth-century subjects of civil inequality.

Beyond the analogy of disenfranchised subjectivities, the essay on Mary Jane presents a confusing melding of scientific postulates, revealing Dr Guppy's attempt to legitimate his spiritualist beliefs by "scientific" explanation. His long essay puts forth a complex theory of the phosphorizing woman. He writes:

> Let any lady go to the South Kensington Museum and see the jar of phosphorus, 1 3/4 lb., being part of a man weighing 154 lb.; and as females have more than men, she will see that she has 2 lb. of phosphorus in her body, daily being added to and eliminated—enough to make 300 boxes of lucifers—in fact, that she is a veritable glow-worm. That we do not see it always, is only because our eyes are made to act by visual and not chemical rays; but it is the chemical rays which make a photograph. If our eyes were so sensitive as to be acted on by the chemical rays, we should be blinded by excess of light. (363)[26]

The author tells the reader that too much phosphorus and the person would be insane, too little and the person would be an imbecile. Phosphorus in this formula is a needed commodity in exact amounts. It is a fascinating image to think of men and women on display, quantifying a standard of sanity that relies on the pounds of phosphorus in their bodies as measured at the South Kensington museum. Does that mean that Dr Guppy's table, too, can pass into a medium of intelligence with the proper amount of phosphorus? In Dr Guppy's view, it seems that it is a chemical infusion that enables intelligence. Subjectivity forges a new reliance on chemistry—it becomes unswervingly scientific and depersonalized. Palpably excited, palpable wood. Insanity, imbecility, a table turned on its head, a turned head—*turning* is the gerund of imposing insanity as well as of *becoming*. To maintain a proper balance, phosphorus is constantly being exchanged—acquired and eliminated. Phosphorus, the most romantic chemical of gloaming glowing, has a profound indirect effect on the furniture—making it silly or, in the case of Mary Jane, intelligent. The issue of subjectivity arises, reminding us of Hegel: "It [the subject] then realizes that this apparently alien other is in fact a product of itself, created as a mirror by means of which it might further its own self-awareness."[27] If others are always products and constructions, why do they need to start out animate—why start out with extra noise and expression that may not adequately reflect the self? Table accounts suggest that Victorians are merely the others of objects and that everyone is just waiting for the proper phosphorous to become an effective individual.

---

[26]   These jars of phosphorus are not currently on display at the V & A.
[27]   Miller, *Material Culture*, 23.

As has been shown, Mary Jane is not a spirit of the deceased but an intellect that reflects the sitters (343). As Dr Guppy's explanation aptly notes, it is chemical rays that create a photograph—and Mary Jane, in Dr Guppy's reasoning, is in evidence to reflect, communicate, and enact the desires of her sitters:

That, owing to the quality and quantity of these vapours given out by certain persons, under certain conditions, they possess a living, acting, and thinking vitality; a vitality, in some cases superior to the being they emanate from; for, if a human being be suddenly and entirely deprived of air, its existence terminates in a very short time—whereas, instances appear to exist where the vitality of this eliminated vapourous being must have existed for a considerable time after the parties from whose bodies it was eliminated have left the room. That the properties of the vapours so eliminated, are power and Intellect ... That the intellect manifested appears to be, in great part, the reflection or embodiment of the minds of the parties present, and by contact with the table giving out vapours, not by any means entirely of the medium, as the medium seems to act rather the part of a steam-boiler, furnishing the materials for the vapours eliminated by the other parties present, of developing that intellectuality which otherwise would not have strength enough to make itself evident. (332)

This argument is developed by Dr Guppy through a stunning set of images. In the first place, Mary Jane is seen as superior to the sitters because she would not immediately fall prey to asphyxiation. She is the result of a stuffy room that is not aired out. Furthermore, it is a stuffy boiler room. The sitters produce steam, and the medium is a steam boiler—Mary Jane is powered by the "steam" of phosphoric vapors. With all of this intellect and power, it is curious that the issue is never raised why the sitters and the medium would not choose simply to express their own opinions and thus eliminate excess phosphorous. Their role, although Mary Jane does still reflect their wishes, becomes dehumanized and mechanistic—with suffocation a metaphorical trope; it seems as if they are in danger of expiring from sheer boredom without the intercession of their superhuman product, Mary Jane. The sitters and Mary Jane forge an equality and are commensurable. In this description of Mary Jane, the reader receives one of the most striking episodes in the account. One learns, at base, that one body never fully equals one subjectivity for these sitters. There is a constant excess or lack that makes a concept of one equals one representation (on which democracy is based) an impossibility.

When Mary Jane first appeared in the drawing room as an animate table, Mrs Guppy tells her husband that the table has turned for her:

"Well," said she, "yesterday evening, Mrs. — declared solemnly and positively that the table moved for her, declaring she was not in joke, so I thought that if it moved for her I did not see why it should not move for me, so I determined to give it a fair trial all alone, and I took the small japanned table and determined to sit steady at it for half-an-hour, and if by that time it did not move, to give it up altogether. Well, in about twenty minutes I felt the table distinctly move, and I got frightened and got up. Recovering myself, however, I again sat down to it, and then it moved in five minutes, and now it moves quite easily in two or three minutes after I put my hands on." (303)

Mary Jane becomes the friend who will come quickly. At first, as we see here, she is in the form of a japanned table. It is intriguing that she should first appear as a "japanned" emissary of the mystical East. The Guppys later try a large rosewood table that moves nearly as easily (304). Again, as it so happens, it is a table made of an exotic wood (this time near Eastern rosewood, not unlike Corelli's near Eastern Chaldeans, who will be discussed in Chapter 4) that does the trick. This change in wood merely underscores the point that Mary Jane is a performer who relies on exchanges, any wood will do.

Mary Jane is ontologically problematic: She performs in culturally diverse woods ("japanned" sometimes, doing "rosewood" at others) and relies on the odyll of promiscuously mixed humans; she is the model of miscegenation. She is not, according to Dr Guppy, beyond the power of science. Guppy writes:

> I have seen a table move, totally alone; and a chair move, totally alone; move, just as you see a leaf carried along by the wind on a turnpike road, and I have reasonable conversations with Mary Jane whenever I please ... So matters went on the fact of the table moving on the one hand and the absurdity of it on the other. A table—wood—the human hand—what relation can they have? ... Puzzling my head with the table—wood—when the words *sensitive plant* flashed across my mind. "True," said I; "a sensitive plant is wood." However, it appeared very clear that something comes out of the human hand, and that something affects a piece of living wood, as the sensitive plant, and of dead wood, as a table ... Here I beg scientific men to note a further remarkable circumstance; namely that from the time the intellectual phenomena [the verbal communication with Mary Jane] took place, the table ceased moving. The chemical emanations which took place, instead of causing the table to run about like a wild animal, took entirely the shape and quality of intellectuality. (309–10)

It is simple to Dr Guppy. There is a continuity, an identity, between the plant, the product, and the owner. The table, like a sensitive plant, feels and reacts. As Guppy says, "So matters went on the fact of the table moving on the one hand and the absurdity of it on the other. A table—wood—the human hand—what relation can they have?" More to the point, the table, wood, and the hand, given Marxist theory, can only exist in relation, having a relation is the only logical option.

Victorian Tables without Contents

Perhaps the reader wonders how these unusual and personified séance tables stacked up against the average Victorian table and if there weren't some sort of suspicion about any and all commodities. Apparently, the average Victorian table was typified by some as being tacky, poorly designed, and ugly. Charles Eastlake, the nineteenth-century arbiter of reform in furnishing design, notes a problem he sees with most tables:

> Among the dining-room appointments, the table is an article of furniture which still stands greatly in need of reform. It is generally made of planks of polished oak or mahogany laid upon an insecure framework of the same material, and supported by four gouty legs,

ornamented by the turner with mouldings which look like inverted cups and saucers piled upon an attic baluster. I call the framework insecure because I am describing what is commonly called a "telescope" table, or one which can be pulled out to twice its usual length, and, by the addition of extra leaves in its middle, accommodates twice the usual number of diners. Such a table cannot be soundly made in the same sense that ordinary furniture is sound. It must depend for its support on some contrivance which is not consistent with the material of which it is made. Few people would like to sit on a chair the legs of which were made to slide in and out, and were fastened at the required height with a pin. There would be a sense of insecurity in the notion eminently unpleasant.[28]

Eastlake is afraid of gouty, domesticated, insecure (and, by extension, movable/ moving/sliding [political]) tables. It is interesting that his description can be read as gendering the table as an insecure matronly woman with gouty legs and decorated with cups and saucers.[29] Or perhaps the comparison now feels expected. Unsound tables: tables that have turned.[30] Tables that accommodate too many sitters. Of this telescoping table (can it also see things at a distance—clairvoyant—like a telescope?), he goes on to write:

> When it is extended it looks weak and untidy at the sides; when it is reduced to its shortest length, the legs appear heavy and ill-proportioned. It is always liable to get out of order, and from the very nature of its construction must be an inartistic object. Why should such a table be made at all? ... When a man builds himself a house on freehold land, he does not intend that it shall only last his lifetime; he bequeaths it in sound condition to posterity. We ought to be ashamed of furniture which is continually being replaced. At all events, we cannot possibly take any interest in such furniture.[31]

A table is an emblematic item of property that can be left to posterity. Sound (sane— note the same language is used to describe what is solid and what has sanity) tables can be left, just like the house, to future generations. A good table is meant to be a

---

[28] Charles Eastlake, *Hints on Household Taste in Furniture, Upholstery, and Other Details* (Boston: J.R. Osgood, 1872), 74–5.

[29] Although gout affects more men than women, it also frequently occurs in postmenopausal women.

[30] Utilizing Eastlake, because he is an exemplary Victorian furniture reformer rather than a typical Victorian consumer, may not at first seem relevant as a way to see into the life of ordinary, inanimate tables and Victorian tastes. Although Eastlake's tastes ran atypically toward the simple (the aesthetic movement) or toward the handmade (medieval and Renaissance-era furniture), he was also tremendously popular with a broad readership in England and America (more widely read than William Morris, for instance). Eastlake was appalled by machine-made, overly elaborate furniture, as represented by these quotations from him. However, he was typically Victorian in desiring furniture that was "in order"; that is, tables that walk and talk would generally be received by most Victorians as ontologically scandalous, if not downright disgraceful. Eastlake preferred graceful furniture that did not get in the way.

[31] Eastlake, *Hints on Household Taste*, 76–7.

still table. Eastlake writes of the ideal table, "It should stand firmly on its legs at each corner. When it is fitted with castors, servants are perpetually pushing it awry."[32] Even common castors are undesirable because they enable dangerous movement. A good table is a still table and not an awry, telescoping movable—or a thrower of tantrums. Eastlake's ideal table was not the Victorian séance table. But the ordinary nineteenth-century tables he does describe suggest a tremendous amount of slippage between the category of "table" and that of Victorian "woman." Their very identities are lessened by their mutually inscribed imperfections.

This chapter on tables showcases two things about Victorian England: First, the lack of civil parity of women and men meant that a woman could be paired/exchanged with any*thing* else; and second, identity in such an unstable climate was always about performance. Mary Jane can be as much or more of a young lady than a young lady can. She embodies a collective performance and ideal. An alternative, unique political state of existence was created by the types of interaction that collective performance fostered. The bonding power of the medium created an extraordinary group identity and a new political space. Further instances and the implications of these types of collective performances are considered next through analyzing Victorian novels about how trance states affected persons and things.

---

[32]   *Ibid.*, 81.

Chapter 4

Rethinking Interiority through Nineteenth-Century Trance Novels

This final chapter addresses a subgenre of the Victorian novel that has not been studied as such, nor named. Beginning in the mid-Victorian decades, a body of fiction focuses its plot lines on the effects that trance states have on young female characters—I call these novels *trance novels*. These works share consistent plot features, such as trance states that evoke scandal, and mediumship, mesmerism, or visions that threaten the institution of marriage. These novels also problematize the fundamental question of how to depict the psychological interiority of a character who can see things beyond the range of the shared social space of the novel while maintaining a discrete focalized personality. In other words, these trance novels feature interiorized characters who have beyond-physical vision and yet usually are not surrogates for the narrator or for an all-encompassing narrative perspective.[1] A focus on trance characters hints at a new kind of narrative omniscience that counters the authority of third-person narration. This at times suggests that the entranced character has a fuller view of the social space of the novel (due to seeing the invisible) than the reader can have. As a result of the categorical dearth of attention to this family of trance novel characters, critics often do not address the type of empowered subjectivity that exists for these characters that fall under the rubric of possessed individualism.[2] Critics have a much

---

[1]   One novel I discuss later in this chapter, Marie Corelli's *Romance of Two Worlds* (1886), features a trance heroine who is also the first-person narrator of the novel. Corelli's heroines are frequently first-person narrators and/or autobiographically modeled on Corelli herself.

[2]   For an insightful analysis of late-century Victorian fiction that treats trance as an element of the gothic trope, see Roger Luckhurst, *The Invention of Telepathy, 1870–1901* (Oxford: Oxford University Press, 2002), especially "Trance Texts: Distant Influence as Gothic Trope," 204–8, and "Remote Control Victorians: The *Beetle* and *Dracula*," 208–13. Luckhurst discusses trance texts that are distinctly gothic with very bad things happening to good protagonists because of mesmerizing characters who have the power to subject innocent characters to "hypnotic criminal suggestion" (207). The late-century fiction Luckhurst calls "trance texts" has some overlapping and some discrete elements from what I call trance novels. On the one hand, the early mesmeric novel I discuss, *Agnes the Possessed*, shows the type of gothic plot Luckhurst describes: Agnes is kidnapped and kept imprisoned in a trance state by a mesmerist until she is rescued. On the other hand, the majority of the trance novels I discuss in this chapter do not follow that type of gothic

fuller vocabulary for discussing how Victorian novels depict autonomous characters' actions and motives within the public and private sphere.

This chapter focuses on understanding the theoretical implications that Victorian mysticism had for the public sphere and identity in literary representations. The periphery of mystical practices, such as actual and fictional séances, challenges the limited concept of public and private spaces. I begin with a working definition of who a medium might be and then move on to show the work of the mystical in a well-known novel of young adulthood, Charlotte Brontë's *Villette* (1853). A further exploration of trance novels follows through T.S. Arthur's mesmeric novel *Agnes the Possessed* (1852). Then two novels about mediumship, *Zillah, the Child Medium* (1857) and *Maud Blount, Medium* (1876), will be considered. Finally, I examine several late-century novels that foreground both powerfully possessed people and objects in an expanded consideration of how these novels figure both West and East through imagining mysticism's cultural centrality. In all of these novels, altered states create a threatening disorder that challenges marriage, the family, lineage, inheritance, and law. Through a consideration of these works, I explore the divide of the public and private spheres and show how these novels' imagination of extra spheres—accessed by astral travel and mystical powers—becomes necessary to a fuller sense of civic participation and idealized concepts of the nation.

Trance Heroines

In the mid-nineteenth century, the cultural practices of mesmerism and spiritualistic mediumship were connected through the common feature of a trance state. The main difference between mesmerism and mediumship resides in what would be considered the cause of a subject undergoing a trance. This constituted a point of disagreement in the mid-Victorian popular press. Mesmerists, such as Dr Zerffi (discussed in Chapter 2), frequently disbelieved and sought to discredit spiritualist mediumship, not because they thought the phenomenon of trance was a fraud but because they thought that mediumship described a misattribution of cause. For a spiritualist, an invisible spirit (the spirit control) is acting on the nervous system of another (the medium). From the standpoint of mesmerism, a trance is caused by the mind of one person (a mesmerist) acting on the central nervous system of another (the mesmerized). Mesmerism's objection to mediumship is that it is an immaterial body (spirit or ectoplasm), rather than a material body, that is described as the agent causing a physical effect on a medium. However, in many particulars, beyond the disagreement about whether an immaterial body can cause a physical effect, mesmerism and mediumship work

---

plotline. In the second half of this chapter, for instance, I consider a number of late-century trance novels that do not follow gothic plotlines that end in murder or mayhem for the entranced but instead resolve gothic crimes and problems through celebrating the detective and transformative powers of trance.

through highly similar mechanisms, such as trance, even though they proclaim different attributions of cause (human or non human). Depictions of mesmerism and of mediumship have a common unsettling effect on personal identity and concepts of social organization.

In the literature of possession, popular practices such as mediumship require thinking beyond conventional views of gender and social organization because often a single body houses more than one personal identity. Promiscuity, denotatively speaking, the mixing of the unlike, such as entranced conversations between the living and the dead, or a body mingling with diverse spirits can be reconsidered as a force that enables a different type of social and self-organization for the possessed. In turn, trance complicates the simple notion of representation when one person no longer equals one person. Many Victorians—particularly women without extensive political rights—were experimenting with the mystical in part because it valued a rare type of sensory organization. Their mystical practices defined the physical body that could channel others as special. They provided a type of somatic capital that, through trance, could produce spirits and visions. Mediumship, for instance, was a sensory state that formed cultural capital through the conduit of a gifted body. Mediumship was, then, an issue of sensibility because it was a skill that could only be performed because of a susceptible body. Characters undergoing trances can pose a threat to logic, order, and social divisions in both their ability to achieve and their preference for imaginary interactions. Subjects who do not care about or exclusively attend to the real world are, in turn, unruly. Trance novels about the possessed depict new, fluid boundaries between real and imaginary, visions of nonstable hierarchical relationship, a new sense and new aesthetic sensibility.

Mediums, through their ability to channel spirits, exercised a unique power. A potential medium needed certain qualities. Dr Samuel Guppy, the hydropathist of George Henry Lewes and the author of *Mary Jane*, discussed in Chapter 3, and the husband of Mrs Guppy, a famous London medium, wrote about what traits predispose someone to mediumship:

> "What sort of person is a medium?"—"Am I a medium?"—"In what does mediumistic power consist?"—"Can I become a medium?"—I will reply to *you* Ma'am ... Have you good taste in dress? And in jewelry? Are you proficient in making all sorts of ladies knik-knaks? Can you ride five-and-twenty miles over hill and dale, and find your way back alone? Have you good eyes? Do you excel in archery? Are you a good pistol shot? Are you excessively nervous; but with a resolution which carries you through in spite of it? Are you jealous, and can't help it? Can you produce at times phosphoric lights at your fingers' ends? If you have all of these qualities, sit down with confidence, and lay your hands flat on a very light table; and in the course of a quarter of an hour you will find a beating sensation in the muscle of your thumb, and at the tips of your fingers, and the table will begin to move.[3]

---

3   *Mary Jane; or, Spiritualism Chemically Explained with Spirit Drawings. Also Essays by and Ideas {Perhaps Erroneous} of, 'A Child at School'* [Samuel Guppy] (London: John King, 1863), 337.

Dr Guppy's definition is different from the more common depiction of the medium, which is often encountered in the vast secondary literature on spiritualism: In these accounts, the medium is usually described as a passive tool for garnering wisdom from beyond the vale.[4] Guppy's definition describes an influential and active subject. The perfect medium had good taste, was creative, had endurance, was good at target games, was nervous and jealous, and produced phosphoric lights. This seems like a list that could only describe rare individuals indeed—unless the reader considers the heroines of Victorian literature. There, the heroine is frequently a jealous archeress or a nervous and creative woman with fantastic endurance. In short, the above-mentioned woman could have been expert horsewoman Lizzie Eustace of Trollope's *The Eustace Diamonds*, nervous Lucy Snowe who courageously overtook the incubus in *Villette*, prize-winning archeress Gwendolen Harleth of *Daniel Deronda*, or one of many members of the broad middle class for whom the Victorian novel heroine stands as an idealized synecdoche.

In trying to delineate what types of people actually became Victorian mediums, we are met with a multitude of choices. There were working-class mediums and spiritualists, such as Alfred Russell Wallace, FRGS, the other discoverer of evolutionary theory; there were professional public mediums, such as the American

---

4   The depiction of the medium as a passive tool is a widely repeated claim in secondary literature. See, for instance, Gauri Viswanathan, "The Ordinary Business of Occultism," *Critical Inquiry* 27 (Autumn 2000), 10, available online at http://infotrac.galegroup.com. In turn, Viswanathan cites Alex Owen, *The Darkened Room: Women, Power and Spiritualism in Late Victorian England* (Philadelphia: University of Pennsylvania Press, 1990) and Helen Sword, "Necrobibliography: Books in the Spirit World," *Modern Language Quarterly* 60:1 (1999). Sword writes, "Mediumship itself remained very much in the province of women, for it offered one of the few means by which women of virtually any social or educational background could earn money, pursue high-profile careers, lay claim to otherworldly insight, and subvert male authority, all while conforming to normative ideals of feminine passivity and receptivity" (90). Roger Luckhurst provides a useful, detailed account of the concept of women's nervous sensitivity in the 1880s and 1890s in *The Invention of Telepathy*, especially in the beginning of Chapter 6, "The Woman Sensitive: Nerves, New Women, and Henry James," 214–19. In discussing late Victorian argument that educating boys and girls together was dangerous, Luckhurst writes about the assumption that supported that position, "Sexual inequality was embedded in biological differentiation: males were active and katabolic, whilst females were passive and anabolic" (215). Luckhurst extends the claim noting, "The medium conformed to the passivity ascribed to the 'anabolic' female; she preserved the race by giving voice to its dead through her sensitive nervous apparatus" (218). Versions of this claim are plenteous in secondary scholarship because there was Victorian rhetoric that figured men as active and women as passive across many domains of social life. Yet frequently in nineteenth-century primary accounts, fiction and nonfiction, mediums are also shown behaving in nonpassive ways. The commonly repeated claim about the passive medium does not capture the full story and cannot account for figures such as Miss Showers, Mrs Guppy, Mary Jane, Zillah, Lucy Snowe, Prince Mihira, Conrad Hertrugge, Lois Waisbrooker, and Harriet Martineau, who are all nonpassive mediumistic types.

Fox sisters; there were theosophists, like Madame Blavatsky; there were private mediums exploring the home circle; then there were the upper-middle-class mediums seeking rehabilitation, such as MP Laurence Oliphant's mother who, along with Laurence, also joined Thomas Lake Harris's cult the New Life for a time. There were also the upper-middle-class participants seeking parlor entertainment: Witness the great scene of mesmerism in Mrs Humphry Ward's best-seller, *Robert Elsmere*.[5]

Lucy Snowe's "Ghosting"

The thematic of trance can be found not only in popular fiction but also within canonical works. A person's special somatic capabilities, qualities defined by Dr Guppy, often appear in very dramatic novels that explore trance states, such as Charlotte Brontë's *Villette* (1853). It shows how clairvoyance contributes to narrative subjectivity within the context of a *bildungsroman*.[6] In *Villette*, Lucy Snowe has a remarkable mediumistic potential, given Dr Guppy's specifications. She has mind-altering bouts of unconsciousness, dreams akin to second sight, hallucinogenic night walks and is convinced she is being haunted by the ghost of a nun. This list of features forms for Lucy a rare list of mediumistic qualifications. The novel itself does not read so very differently from other members of the trance subgenre, such as *Maud Blount* and *Zillah*.

Brontë's Lucy often interacts with the invisible and the virtual instead of favoring the visible and the actual. This constitutes a promiscuity. Her preference for the spectral is evident in everything from the carnivalesque night celebration, theater, and museum (all image and representationally centered, rather than real) to Lucy's (sexual) encounters with the ghostly nun. After the specter of the nun appears to Lucy a few times, she and Lucy finally have a physical encounter:

My head reeled, for by the faint night lamp I saw stretched on my bed the old phantom—the NUN. A cry at this moment might have ruined me. Be the spectacle what it might, I could afford neither consternation, scream, nor swoon. Besides, I was not overcome. Tempered by late incidents, my nerves disdained hysteria. Warm from illuminations, and scourge, I defied spectra. In a moment, without exclamation, I had rushed on the haunted couch; nothing leaped out, or sprung, or stirred; all the movement was mine, so was all the life, the reality, the substance, the force; as my instinct felt. I tore her up—the incubus! I held

---

5   See Harry Clements, *Alfred Russell Wallace: Biologist and Social Reformer* (London: Hutchinson, 1983); Ann Braude, *Radical Spirits: Spiritualism and Women's Rights in Nineteenth-Century America* (Boston: Beacon Press, 1989); and Peter Washington, *Madame Blavatsky's Baboon: A History of the Mystics, Mediums, and Misfits Who Brought Spiritualism to America* (New York: Shocken Books, 1995).

6   Throughout the entire Brontë oeuvre, problems with the paranormal frequently arise: Ghosts show up in Charlotte Brontë's *Jane Eyre* (New York: Harper, 1847) and *Villette* [1853] (New York: Penguin, 1986) and in Emily Brontë's *Wuthering Heights* (New York: Oxford University Press, 1981).

her on high—the goblin! I shook her loose—the mystery! And down she fell—down all around me—down in shreds and fragments—and I trode upon her.[7]

Here we have Lucy's destruction of an ectoplasm. It is highly analogous to the tense and sometimes sexualized encounters described in Victorian accounts between both spirit and medium and mesmerizer and mesmerized.[8] These episodes ask the reader to question who holds the reality and power within the encounter.

Beyond the nun, *Villette* displays a larger pattern in which Lucy is habitually "ghosting" her human acquaintances.[9] Real people frequently become dematerialized for her. For instance, the nun is not the only sexually unavailable female who ends up in her bed. There is a supremely charged moment when the small child Paulina is lured into Lucy's bed.[10] Little Paulina, like the nun, is figured specifically as a ghost, although she is a real girl. The text shares that Paulina "came … instantly, like a small ghost gliding over the carpet" (29). Lucy directly visualizes what she wants and sates her desire through tranquilizing and cherishing the ghost-like child, who is "like a little Odalisque," or harem concubine (24).

But what does it mean when Lucy overpowers that incubus, the nun?[11] Has Lucy forcibly stopped the nun, the romanticized emissary from the spectral ideal realm,

---

7   Brontë, *Villette*, 467. Future reference to this work in the present discussion will be cited in text by page number.

8   See Daniel Pick, *Svengali's Web: The Alien Enchanter in Modern Culture* (New Haven: Yale University Press, 2000).

9   Terry Castle argues in *The Apparitional Lesbian: Female Homosexuality and Modern Culture* (New York: Columbia University Press, 1993) that "it is perhaps not so surprising that at least until around 1900 lesbianism manifests itself in the Western literary imagination primarily as an absence, as chimera or *amor impossibilia*—a kind of love that, by definition, cannot exist (30–31). In analyzing eighteenth-, nineteenth-, and twentieth-century literary examples of female characters, Castle claims that "to 'be a ghost' is to long, unspeakably, after one's own sex" (32). The example of *Villette* shows a distinct and yet related pattern. Lucy Snowe is not necessarily ghostly, but everyone she desires, whether it be children, nuns, or letter writers, is ghostly. Furthermore, in *Villette*, this ghost love is implicitly autoerotic in its somatic spectrality, showing affiliative desires and fruition working beyond the category of the real. Ghosts and humans are frequently described in engaged erotic scenarios in nineteenth-century fiction—thus providing possibilities for a character's predilections that predate a late-nineteenth-century language of homo- and heterosexuality.

10   "I saw the little thing shiver. 'Come to me,' I said, wishing, yet scarcely hoping, that she would comply: for she was a most strange capricious little creature, and especially whimsical with me. She came, however, instantly, like a small ghost gliding over the carpet. I took her in. She was chill: I warmed her in my arms. She trembled nervously; I soothed her. Thus tranquilized and cherished she at last slumbered" (*Villette*, 29).

11   An incubus is an evil spirit that lies on individuals when they sleep and, specifically, one who has sex with sleeping women. Interestingly, in her handwritten fair copy of the novel, held in the manuscript collection of the British Library, the word *incubus* was written in above a crossed-out *recumbent night man*.

from "taking" her? Has she thus impeded the progress of promiscuity? Or has she whetted her appetite for future frottage with the ghostly out of reach? All of Lucy's moments of overcoming and quelling the spectral take place in her enticing bed that seems to serve as a magnet for spectral beings. These encounters, which result in her feeling powerful, narratively develop her sexual desire as being fulfilled not by flesh and blood but by interactions that are at once imaginative and autoerotic, producing a sense of personal effectiveness and dominance for Lucy. It seems that by the ending of *Villette* the object of Lucy's love is out of reach and out of sight. Lucy loves her absent husband, M. Paul, because in his three years away, her happiest, he is a devoted letter writer with no "hollow unreal in him" (489). So it might seem, with her love for him, as if she has banished the lure of the invisible from her desiring heart. However, the reader will recall that she is happiest with him *away*, and it is his letters that she finds so very gratifying. Considering her past fetishistic record with Dr John Bretton's letters, which she reads while sitting on her bed, she perhaps has not fully banished the lure of the imaginary. Her letters from Dr John are highly revered by Lucy as representing a potential love affair. After they have been read by Madame Beck, though, Lucy feels that they are no longer her own and have become like a river that has ceased to flow (290). She buries Dr John's dead letters in the school yard. The penultimate paragraph of the novel seems to establish that Lucy is still tied foremost to the imaginary:

> Here pause: pause at once. There is enough said. Trouble no quiet, kind heart; leave sunny imaginations hope. Let it be theirs to conceive the delight of joy born again fresh out of great terror, the rapture of rescue from peril, the wondrous reprieve from dread, the fruition of return. Let them picture union and a happy succeeding life. (491)

Whatever returns to her from across the sea seems to be the idea of her beloved rather than an actual body.

Lucy is remarkable because not only her primary erotic ties live in the realm of imagination but also her central economic ties are geographically distant. M. Paul, her husband and financer, lives across the sea. She doesn't see him for years; it seems the relationship has never been consummated. Even Lucy's physical world seems unreal. She is away from her native land, England, and in a fictional land, Villette. She is surrounded by a foreign religious economy, marked by Catholicism's tradition of angels, saints, and devils, and by Villette's culture of illusion, such as the night carnival/parade. In short, there is nothing around her that is as solid as the idea in relief of Victorian England. There is nothing centering, grounding, or familiar. It is all illusion, from the ground she walks on to the sea that separates her from her lover and her economic support. Lucy is at a double remove from England's public sphere. She is not held by English law or custom. She is already at an imaginary cultural remove in Villette. Her engagement with the spectral is yet another remove from an analogous construct of the public: Villette. All of Villette's society is presented as suspect, based on surveillance, superstition, and personal and by extension familial interest. In a sense, then, Villette could be any non-English Western social order.[12]

By the double remove of Lucy's mystical engagements, the construction of the public sphere (of any public sphere) as artificial and arbitrary (not to mention estranging) is drawn to the fore. By relegating her desires to the realm of imagination, Lucy remains independent of the public sphere and yet emotionally attached and socially engaged. It is as if Lucy removes herself from the social equation of "woman = ?" discussed in Chapter 3. She no longer has to equal anything specific (such as economically productive governess) because she explores her desires and her community in an extra sphere. It is interesting, in terms of seeing mysticism and liberalism as part of the same Victorian construct, that her marriage at the end of the novel, which comes with funds from an absent husband, continues to enable her to do this.

The character of Lucy is a good example of a new type of single woman portrayed in many Victorian novels. This trance heroine has a fair amount in common with typical nineteenth-century heroines in that she has independent thoughts and is creative. This type of heroine, though, also has some singular features: She is liberated, rather than marginalized, at those points where she lacks connection, respectability, and family. Even this, of course, is not unique to mystical fiction. Jane Eyre, for instance, comes into her selfhood because she is tortured and rejected by her extended family and called wicked before being exiled to the Lowood Institution. In trance novels, however, the heroine has the additional subgenre trait that she can be related to anyone, seen or unseen, living or dead. With this feature, the heroine of the trance novel is affiliated with scandal of promiscuity and its disorder. In the middle of the nineteenth century, this type of heroine seems to be like real women who are agitating for their own unmediated political life or experiencing an alternative social order through their mystical practices. This may be one reason why the fantasy of the trance is so widespread.

Agnes: Possessed by Lawless Desire

Values and order are questioned and unfixed for female characters experiencing the phenomenon of mediumship and/or mesmerism within novels. One of the earliest novels that concerns something akin to mediumship is T.S. Arthur's *Agnes, the Possessed* (1852).[13] It is a tale of mesmerism, which also is a part of a mid-

---

12   It also obviously relies on an anti-French, anti-Catholic politics of representation. Villette is often assumed by Brontë biographers to represent Brussels.

13   T.S. Arthur, *Agnes the Possessed: A Revelation of Mesmerism* (London: J.S. Hodson, 1852). Future references to this work in the present discussion will be cited in text by page number.

century genre of novels that are afraid of the unseen.[14] However, many of the main philosophical concerns that we see in medium novels are foregrounded here. This novel's fear of the invisible extends beyond mesmerism to mediumship and goblins and ghosts—in short, to those works in which the immaterial can have material influence on the real world. For instance, in *Agnes* there are both the idea of communication with another world and the conundrum of what it means if more than one soul is in a single body.

Agnes, the young maiden heroine, is extremely susceptible to mesmeric influence. She is kidnapped by mesmeric showman, Frenchman Monsieur Florien, to ascertain the limits of what can be accomplished through the use of mesmerism and the impact that it has on the subject. I include here a photograph of turn-of-the-century professional Walford Bodie who, as a mesmeric showman, sounds a lot like Monsieur Florien (see Figure 4.1). After a certain experiment with Agnes, Florien and a doctor friend discuss the nature of possession:

> "Depend upon it," said the Doctor, "it is possession and nothing else. The girl's body, now, I am satisfied, is in the entire possession of some spirit, with whom and not with her spirit, you have been conversing."
> This was what fell upon the ear of Agnes, and arrested her attention.
> "That, to me, is inconceivable," returned Florien. "If her body be possessed by another spirit, where is *her* spirit in the mean time? It must be either in or out of her body. If out of her body, where is it? If in her body how can two spirits be in possession of one bodily organism at the same time?" (120–21)

Time and time again the same riddle is played out by other situations of spirit possession. Who possesses the body? What power is there in the possession? How does trance work? Is it evil or good? Of the state of possession itself, Agnes remarks that "it seemed a kind of ecstasy" (26),[15] to which her fiancé replies that he knows not where all of this will lead and that "if one person is to have such entire control over another as mesmerism gives, who knows for what dreadful end it may be used? It seems to me that no one is safe" (27).[16]

---

14 Other early novels on mesmerism include Henry Aitchenbie's *Melchior Gorles. A Tale of Modern Mesmerism* (London: John Camden Hotten, 1867); Baroness Prochazka's *The Abduction; or the Marvels of Mesmerism* (London: William Shoberl, 1850); *Magic and Mesmerism: An Episode of the Eighteenth Century* (London: Saunders and Otley, 1843); and Mrs Isabella F. Romer's *Sturmer: A Tale of Mesmerism* (London: R. Bentley, 1841).

15 Luckhurst writes, "The first offical report on Mesmerism in 1784 had a private addendum, in which women's 'more mobile nerves' and 'more easily excited' imaginations were cited as dangers. It is difficult to misinterpret the source of this anxiety" (206). Through subsequent quotation Luckhurst strongly implies that the danger in question was female orgasm. Agnes certainly seems to undergo this type of pleasure while mesmerized.

16 The antimesmeric bent of *Agnes* did not go undetected by 1850s readers. One book reviewer was very unhappy about the novel's bias against mesmerism. See *The Zoist*, 11 March 1853 (London: Walton and Mitchell, 1853), 57.

Dr. Walford Bodie Mesmerising a Subject.

Figure 4.1   **Walford Bodie mesmerizing a subject**
Illustration from Walford Bodie, *The Bodie Book* (London: Caxton Press, 1905).

The same fear is elucidated by Mr Carter who says:

> Is not the mind of a mesmeric subject controlled by the magnetizer? Is it not, for a time deprived of its own organ of sense, by which it acts in the natural plane of its existence, and forced to see, and hear, and feel, by means of another's sense? In such a state is any one free to choose evil or good? To do right or wrong? No. For a time he is deprived of his self-hood. Is no longer a man, but a machine by which some other mind acts. (43–4)

The danger of Agnes's ecstatic state of clairvoyance seems to be the threat of losing selfhood. The specific fear that a possessed person is one who has lost her selfhood and thus lost social membership and autonomous agency appears as a central concern in almost all trance novels.

Losing a fixed selfhood could impair or challenge Agnes's (or any possessed character's) fixed place within a domestic hegemonic order because if she is possessed, she is no longer a dependable or predictable person. She is also no longer necessarily accountable for her actions. Concerning Agnes, her fiancé, Ralph Percival, draws the following conclusions:

> What troubled him most, was the too evident desire felt by Agnes to be mesmerized ... Such a state he clearly saw to be a disorderly one, and being disorderly, he very naturally inferred that it was governed by evil influences, for none other could reign over disorder. Evil influences, he further saw, always lead to over-action and excess, and tend to destruction. (52)

When characters have a desire for "disorderly" trance states, it seems that the true threat is that the character prefers an alternative, nonvisible social order. Agnes's melodrama ends when her fiancé rescues her from the hands of Florien and they marry. One wonders, though, if her abnormal desires are completely quelled and contained. This novel is as interesting for the spiritual questions it raises as for the insight it gives into Agnes's desiring heart. The fulfillment of desire provided by her "ecstasy" is interpreted here as that which interrupts free will and the order it perpetuates. Disorder and enjoyment are openly described as evil. Mystical desires that can be acheived in an imaginary milieu stand against the interests of order and also are found in novels about mediums.

Zillah and Maud: The Threat of Mediumship to Marriage

Zillah, the Child Medium (1857), and *Maud Blount, Medium* (1872), both center on the mediumship of young, single women; both end in marriage; and both novels present mediumship as antithetical to married life. In *Zillah, the Child Medium*, Zillah, a girl of seven or eight, channels the spirit of her recently deceased mother, also named

Zillah.[17] The novel's true heroine, though, is Zillah's governess, Rachel Olio. Rachel at first does not believe in mediumship, then she finds herself with mediumistic powers; she nearly marries a spiritualist, who turns evil; and she finally marries a clergyman, (in)appropriately named Mr Godwin.[18]

In *Maud Blount, Medium*, Maud is a girl of roughly 18 whose mother is a devoted spiritualist because it brings her in contact with the spirit of her dead husband.[19] In spite of her skepticism, Maud seems to be a true medium, constantly receptive to spirit influences. Her hobby turns to continual pastime once she has married William Campbell, a young pastor in a rural parish. She spends the daytime, while her husband is off making clerical rounds, in continual trances with the spirit of her dead father. William sees Maud's mediumship as the direct cause of the premature birth and death of their first child, a son named after Maud's deceased father. Eventually Maud renounces spiritualism; they have a second child, a daughter named Effie, and all of the professional mediums in the novel are shown to be fakes. Maud's mother also gives up séances and marries the older cleric friend of her son-in-law.

Mediumship in both novels is denigrated and shown to be the domain of the young, single woman, who, once married, can only be marred by the practice. Both authors find mediumship, and possible connection to the mystical, to exist outside of marriage, and both conditions make antithetical claims for the young heroine. Rachel only marries after her young friend Zillah, the medium, dies. Maud cannot mother a living child until she stops being a medium. Marriage, in relief then to these two writers, seems like the Victorian institution to keep a woman in the here and now and not one to allow her to be transhistorically minded.

The idea that mediumship and marriage are opposed is frequently expressed in the nineteenth century. Marlene Tromp, in writing about the mediumship and marriage of Florence Cook, a Victorian medium who channeled spirit control Katie King, notes that once Florence was married to Captain Corner, everyone expected her to give up her mediumship and that her husband was opposed to its continuance.[20] Cook, however, did continue her mediumship. Tromp argues that "spiritualism made social violations of all kinds possible and respectable because it blurred the boundaries between the

---

17 *Zillah, The Child Medium; A Tale of Spiritualism. By the Author of "My Confession; The Story of a Woman's Life,"* etc. (New York: Dix, Edwards, 1857).

18 There is a double pun here. While in the end, "God wins," William Godwin is, of course, a famous Enlightenment atheist and anarchist.

19 *Maud Blount, Medium. A Story of Modern Spiritualism* (London: Tinsley Brothers, 1876). Worldcat (OCLC) lists the author as Charles Maurice Davies (1828–1910). The copy referenced and quoted that I read in the British Library lists no author. Charles Maurice Davies published several nonfiction works in the 1850s to 1870s treating religious life in London (the Anglican Church, the Broad Church, orthodoxy, heterodoxy, etc.), including *Mystic London; or, Phases of Occult Life in the Metropolis* (London: Tinsley Brothers, 1875).

20 Marlene Tromp, "Spirited Sexuality: Sex, Marriage, and Victorian Spiritualism," *Victorian Literature and Culture* (2003), 77.

spiritual and the material," speaking at one point, for instance, of the alleged affair between Florence and William Crookes and the freedom Cook had through the practice of mediumship.[21] Beyond the freedom of mediumship that Tromp points out, I additionally argue that a central threat of a trance state is that mediums have an enlarged and simultaneously changing social setting that devalues all fixed ties and institutionally sponsored relationships. That is, séances provide a dynamic extra sphere that is more seductive than the legal ties of fixed family and public networks.

Maud Blount mentions early on that her mother, the wealthy Mrs Blount, is rather generous in regard to the professional mediums she has visit her home to give séances. A friend says, "You are far too promiscuous in your charity, dear madam."[22] The problem seems to be not how much money she gives away but where it goes. The adjective to describe Mrs Blount is *promiscuous*. In other words, her alms help bring into contact unlike types. Her séances mix class, mix genders, and mix up the fortunes of the quick and the dead—the séance room has its own order, and this order is heedless of the fixed boundaries of Victorian society. At one of these séances, a sitter notes, "I believe this—that in that darkness and silence—possibly in that magnetic contact—the real self comes to the surface" (97). The "real" self, then, is not defined for the spiritualist through the known networks of self—age, race, marital status, class, religion, ethnicity, gender. This is a disruptive state of affairs. Some characters in this novel define spiritualism as "hysteria *plus* the devil"; others note that they live on a "haunted planet"; and in still other places, mediumship is referenced as being like "freemasonry" (64, 59, 37). In other words, it creates a secret society marked by evil, insanity, and haunting—it has its own secret order that is antithetical to day-to-day life. Even the clergyman who eventually marries Mrs Blount is a convert for a time and discovers that "christening a baby ... only meant mesmerizing it" (58). Taking this image and reversing it, if the Victorian sitters at a séance become mesmerized (held in a trancelike state), it is as though they become christened into a new society, in the silence and the dark, and begin to know themselves differently: selves not anchored by conventions.

Just over halfway through the Blount novel, though, the tides inexplicably turn, and the mediums seem to be on the side of family life. For instance, one medium hastens the engagement between Rev. Willie Campbell and Maud—giving them both messages to the effect of "If he asks, she will say yes." This promptly occurs the next day. As Willie tells her, "Then Maud—dear Maud—the spirits have obviated the necessity of a very embarrassing avowal on my part; but I endorse the few most true words they have written. What is your reply?" (95). Another séance sitter notes to the medium, "I don't believe that [he] would have got his proposal out ... if you had not written it down for him on a piece of paper" (157). It is as if the medium, not Willie, has proposed to Maud. Even after her marriage, Maud spends much of

---

[21] Tromp, "Spirited Sexuality," 68, 76–7.

[22] *Maud Blount* 28. Future references to this work in the present discussion will be cited in text by page number.

her time entranced and "married" to the spirit of her dead father, perhaps figuring an endogamous bond as rapture because death is presented as the dissolution of the subject (her father is not a person anymore, but a spirit). Yet, this novel also portrays the evils of spiritualism in commercial public spaces of mediumship, adjudicated by such men as "Frank Squirm, medium." Such places are shut down and turned into Broad-Church publication houses and reading rooms (295). The novel ends with the following moral, given at the dinner table: "We all, male and female, went in more or less for mania in reference to Spiritualism while we were single, and became clothed and in our right mind soon after we were married. Evidently Providence meant people to be married. Eh, wife?" (329).

Zillah also takes place largely outside of married life. Early in *Zillah*, the governess Rachel, taking her lead from Romantic poetry, asks the following inappropriate (as deemed by the angry minister, Mr Godwin, Rachel's second fiancé and future husband) question about Zillah:

> Who was her father?
> Who was her mother?
> Had she a sister?
> Had she a brother?[23]

Zillah is so otherworldly that all of her genealogy comes into question. The effrontery caused by the questions seems to be that it denies Zillah the respectability of a known family tree. Because she could be anyone, she is, instead, no one. In reverse, as well, this questioning calls any and all relationships into question. Through mediumship the most surprising ties can be formed. At any point the mediumistic subject can come into contact with spirits, who, were they people, would have been of a different social rank. This succinctly isolates one central threat of spiritualism: It ignores and dismisses all socioeconomic boundaries. Later when Rachel discovers that young Zillah is not just a somnambulist but a medium, the author notes, "Do what she would, Rachel could not bring herself to mention to any one Zillah's trance powers. She felt it to be almost a duty she owed the child herself; she was unwilling to expose her needlessly to the notoriety that must inevitably follow the disclosure" (119). Rachel's horror in learning Zillah is a medium categorizes being a medium with shameful darkness. She finds it very upsetting. It seems that Zillah's relations can only be known if one can see ghosts: There is no earthly connection for this young orphan. Her relationships are the antithesis of earthly family order.

If Zillah's mystical power is not threatening enough, Rachel discovers that she, too, has mediumistic gifts:

> Her eyes were fixed dreamily on vacuity; yet, to her amazement, every line, every curve of the pen in that unfolded letter became visible. Without looking upon it, she read it as

---

23 *Zillah*, 114. Future reference to this work in the present discussion will be cited in text by page number.

plainly as she afterward perused it by natural sight. At this, she lost courage. She touched her arm, to see if it were real; she went to the little mirror, and closely examined her face, half expecting to find some other than her own. This sudden development of clairvoyant sight, was, to say the least, appalling. (122)

It seems that by association alone, Rachel's own identity becomes destabilized.[24] She can read a letter without reading a letter. She can see it in her mind without holding the paper in her hand. This particular construction of images challenges the truth and the ascendancy of documents. In fact, later on in the novel, the man whom Rachel eventually marries has spent years in jail because of a contested will and the allegation that he has forged this document. If one can read documents in her mind, without the paper and pen as physical effects, then a notary is out of the question. Rachel is appalled because she reads her own ability as absolutely lawless—so much so that it leads her to question if she herself is a real physical presence. It seems that, if she can see *everything* without seeing any *thing*, then she might be anyone or no one at all. Rachel's horror is that of discovering the ghostly nature of her identity, her preordained contingency—what happens, indeed, when the face that greets her in the mirror is not her own? Rachel cannot theorize her own ontology outside of a system governed by law, and this is part of the decentering threat that an extra sphere poses for the public sphere in this novel and more broadly within nineteenth-century literature and culture.

To the Victorian spiritualist believer, mediumship had the power to unfix history and patrilineal descent because mediums frequently preferred spiritual to sexual intercourse and might not reproduce.[25] For example, young Zillah, who in the novel is illegitimate (her parents were not married) can only find her proper place with her dead mother through her own death. Their family order is spiritual and not of this earth. Another instance of this logic occurs when Rachel and Ogilvie, her first fiancé, travel to a spiritualist tent revival. There, they point out a number of dangerous women, those in favor of women's rights, the type of strong woman the novel claims a man is always attracted to but whom he would never want to marry. The novel describes one such "believing medium":

That she was very beautiful, no one would have hesitated to acknowledge, and yet it was a fierce, savage beauty, that made you tremble while you gazed. Her eyes were black, and as piercing in expression as any maniac's, alternately emitting sudden flashes of light that thrilled the beholder with dread, and glittering with the mild, innocent splendor of

---

24 On the topic of mediumship and destabilized identity, see Owen, *The Darkened Room*, particularly Chapter 6, "Medicine, Mediumship, and Mania," 139–67.

25 For one distinct and yet not atypical theory of a preference for spiritual rather than physical evolution and nonprocreative sex, see, as discussed in Chapter 2, Lois Waisbrooker, *The Fountain of Life, or, The Threefold Power of Sex* (1893). Waisbrooker prolifically published (from the late 1860s to 1909) on her anarchist views and was an American sympathetic medium and sex radical.

childhood. She was very large, almost Amazonian in height, but this only added to the pride of her appearance. At a glance, you saw she was one of those women whom men very often admire most—yet never, by any chance, desire to marry. (197–8)

The medium is depicted as being as much savage Amazonian maniac as beautiful woman and child dreamer.[26] The disruptive agency that mediumship fosters is brought to the fore in this quote. The "thrill of dread" provides "the beholder" with the ecstasy of self-cancellation that, because it supplants individual personhood, is the opposite of desire.[27] The thrill of trance and emission of "sudden flashes of light" provide pleasures that are dreadful to the observer because they work beyond individual autonomy. The medium described here also forms a part of a competing genealogy. Clearly, she does not seem likely to reproduce through marriage and motherhood, yet she is of an admirable type—as if she will be promulgated (channeled) by mediumship alone. This also, in turn, suggests that although desire is needed to forge human relationships, spiritual communities that use trance to be possessed by spirits can therefore instead just enjoy rapturous pleasure, without the arduous work of desiring and pursuing other living humans for love, affection, and the perpetuation of inheritance.

Zillah, in contrast to the "believing medium," is anything but Amazonian. To Ogilvie's obvious dislike for young Zillah, Rachel retorts, "Oh, Ogilvie! jealous of a child—a mere puny, loving little girl. Surely I have room for both" (202). Zillah's smallness in the world is accomplished through the use of three diminutive adjectives—*mere*, *puny*, and *little*. Why then, we may ask, is tiny Zillah such a big and threatening problem to Freeland ("free" land) Ogilvie? If power has an imaginary locus, as opposed to in property ownership and law, the threat is clear. Again, as in *Maud Blount*, mediumship, even of the puny and mere, potentially disrupts earthly order by unsettling the category of reality and the ascendancy of legal documents and property.[28]

Mediumship in these examples can be figured as antithetical to social order because it makes subjectivity unstable. In *Zillah* and in *Maud Blount*, mediumship resists order because it functions outside of marriage, without property (and against legal documents), and beyond fixed identity. It replaces family, inheritance, and physical reproduction with a spiritual, invisible community. In short, mediumship and

---

[26] This characterization of the medium is very similar to Zenobia in Hawthorne's *The Blithedale Romance* (1852).

[27] In articulating this point, I am grateful for a series of conversations with Justin Crumbaugh in Spring 2005.

[28] Mediumship's disruption of nineteenth-century legal categories (such as marriage) also occurs in some late-century mediumistic novel plots, such as Annie Thomas [Mrs Pender Cudlip], *No Medium* (London: F. V. White, 1885) and Hamlin Garland, *The Tyranny of the Dark* (London: Harper and Brothers, 1905). The plot, in brief, of these types of novels is that mediums and spirit girls are unmarriageable until their parentage is known and they no longer undergo trances.

its separate civic imaginary locality are described in these novels at best as poorly replicating the hegemonic logic of the public or private spheres. In the realm of mediumship, public and private spheres are peripheral to the extra sphere within the self. Theorizing this frequent reversal of the presumed location of power (given the millions of spiritualists and thousands of mediums in the nineteenth century) means rethinking the utility of placing the model of the public sphere (and/or private sphere) as the central relief for inquiries into the connection between gender, political life, and resistance in the nineteenth century.[29]

In dozens of novels, mediumship creates multiple subjectivities that form an identity within a single body, meaning descriptively that civic plurality, business, congress, exists within a single body that is physical rather than social in nature. Mediumship works through mechanisms of promiscuous community, performance, and polymorphous desire—creating situations of complexly possessed individuals. To consider being possessed as a mode of individualism is to reimagine social structure outside of the public and private spheres: The dissolved identity of the possessed threatens real social order.

For Victorian spiritualists, the nineteenth century presented a liminal space in which person and spirit could have commensurate exchanges. Perhaps the biggest ideological upset, though, was the séance, and with it multiple subjectivity, which produced an alternative history that challenged the written word and the ascendancy of documents. As *Zillah* indicates, alternative imaginary lineage and nonmaterial documents serve to question the efficacy (and possibly the existence) of written law. No longer did one who accepted spiritualism need to refer to the historical past for a sense of tradition or an iteration of law; one could simply ask the ectoplasms at home or read a document clairvoyantly.

The Victorian séance did not simply present itself as an alternative text of "how it is," but rather presented itself as an alternative vision of "how it should be." The past and the present mingled together, defying the finality of death; socioeconomic class boundaries held less sway; political empowerment in its traditional and legal sense was demoted and replaced with membership in an invisible society; person and thing could both become possessed, upholding the possibility of all types of fantastical new social orders, implicitly critiquing the bourgeois individual.

These trance novels did more than hint at an alternative political ideology in which there was an expanded polis and suffrage would become a potentially equalizing force. These new compound subjectivities in the novel placed stress on the entire concept of the public sphere by underscoring the Lockean claim that citizenship can at times be a matter of choice rather than of birth. Trance novels take the precondition of political disenfranchisement into a state of imaginative freedom, making clear, in relief, that movements such as séances serve as a decentralization

---

[29] Viswanathan's article, "The Ordinary Business of Occultism," does an excellent job of considering the power reversals of mediumship in a colonial context.

of power.[30] Trance novels redefined the actor/citizen as well as the scope of possible action.

A political utopia could be achieved through surrendering to the lure of imagination. In these mediumistic and mesmeric examples, it is as if the reader envisions an emerging vital, political woman, wrapped in a whirlwind of engaging sociability. Later in the century, these novels focus less exclusively on female characters who are possessed. They also have plots about possessed men and possessed objects. Reading backward, I attribute this change to a much more widespread sense of political dissatisfaction as civic inequality and disenfranchisement (along lines of gender, class, and race/ethnicity) became more widely acknowledged and thus even more culturally visible in such phenomena as increasingly popular campaigns for universal suffrage, on the one hand, and the virulently racist assumptions of the late century's high imperialism on the other hand.[31] A floodlight (culturally speaking) swings to focus on difference, rather than homogeneity, in reference to race, gender, and religion, as the century progresses.

Late-Century Trance Novels: Moving Trances out of England

Late-century trance novels build off of the generic features of mid-century ones, sharing several traits. To begin with, as it was in earlier examples, trances are opposed to marriage in several examples, such as Julian Hawthorne's *Spectre of the Camera* (1888), Cora Linn Daniel's *The Bronze Buddha* (1899), Emeric Hulme Beaman's *Ozmar the Mystic, Sheyhk Hassan: A Tale of Spiritualism*, and Laurence Oliphant's *Masollam*. Additionally, all focus on a singularly charismatic mystical hero who

---

30 Owen writes about one element of women's political disenfranchisement: "Prior to the passing of the 1882 Married Women's Property Act, for example, married women had no separate identity from that of their husbands. In the words of the old adage, in law 'husband and wife are one person, and the husband is that person.' ... The second half of the century was a period of shifting attitudes, holding out a promise of broader and brighter horizons, but it was also a time of anxiety and uncertainty as the old order began grudgingly to give way to the new" (Owen, *The Darkened Room*, 3–4). In turn, see Lee Holcombe, "Victorian Wives and Property: Reform of the Married Women's Property Law 1857–1882," in Martha Vicinus, ed., *A Widening Sphere: Changing Roles of Victorian Women* (London: Methuen, 1980). Trance novels are one way to examine this uncertain period. They provide a circumnavigation of disenfranchisement by redefining social space within the imaginary.

31 See Robert J.C. Young, *Postcolonialism: An Historical Introduction* (Malden, MA: Blackwell, 2001), 30–41, and Elleke Boehmer, *Colonial and Postcolonial Literature: Migrant Metaphors* (Oxford and New York: Oxford University Press, 1995). Boehmer writes, "In brief, Victorian high imperialism was distinguished by the following factors: geographic magnitude; the mass organization and institutionalization of colonial power, often expressed in forms of aggressive nationalism; and, as the century matured, the formalization of imperialist ideologies, especially those pertaining to race, encouraged in part by the spread of Social Darwinist thought" (31).

generally garners respect versus a reputation for freakishness. This model works well, for example, for Daniel, who is a charismtic "executive self" in *Daniel Deronda*, but not for Gwendolen, who represents the system of bourgeois individualism in the novel. This trait of a respectable mystical protagonist, seen, for instance, in Marie Corelli's *A Romance of Two Worlds* (1886), is a significant departure from the mid-century model of marginalized trance heroines like Agnes, Maud, and Zillah. Late-century trance novels also revel in the conflation of all things Eastern, Near Eastern, and North African, through using such props and settings as sarcophagi, Buddhism, Chaldeans, and Palestine. Another feature of trance novels probably has most to do with the late-century popularity of detective novels. Mystical heroes can aid in crime detection and at times prevention. This crime-solving feature of the mystical individual plays centrally in the plots of *Ozmar the Mystic*, *Spectre of the Camera*, and *Sheyhk Hassan*. Trance novels, both mid- and late century, constitute a genre that employs, questions, reinforces, and problematizes the promiscuous trope of popular mystical practices sometimes called mesmeric or spiritualist and at other times called Buddhist or Muslim. Late-century trance novels use mystical people and mystical places to break down the usual boundaries of social organization, such as families, nations, sexes, or classes, and remake a volatile and temporarily unbound social space.

The interest of these novels lies in the way they play with and challenge conventional notions of power. From a twenty-first-century perspective it is sometimes difficult to imagine power that circulates predominantly in networks rather than mainly in institutions, and it is just such a tension that these novels explore. It is even more off-putting that the networks of power in these novels enable clairvoyance, clairaudience, telepathy, and astral-body travel, working though invisible or semi-visible routes, literally.[32] In this sense, these novels posit that the unknown may be more powerful than the known, that the Eastern and "primitive" may be more advanced than the Western and modern, that love may not require marriage, and that an amorphous box named "other" and containing spiritualism, Buddhism, free love, mesmerism, materialism, spirits, Palestine, India, Egypt, and mediums may be a centrally important network, not a peripheral one.

At base, all these novels also can be seen as romances with lots of idiosyncrasies, gothic elements, haunted places, and love stories. Yet they are not framed by the typical solutions of gothic plots—rescue from the convent; the ghosts turn out to be pirates; the hero will try to kill the monster he creates. In this sense, trance novels keep gothic problematics of inverted order and hidden power in play.[33] There are gothic problems

---

[32] For a fascinating look at the conjunction between mediumistic practices and technology at the turn of the twentieth century, see Pamela Thurschwell, *Literature, Technology and Magical Thinking, 1880–1920* (New York: Cambridge University Press, 2001).

[33] For insightful analysis of the gothic and inverted order see Terry Castle, "The Spectralization of the Other in the Mysteries of Udolpho," in Felicity Nussbaum and Laura Brown, ed., *The New Eighteenth Century: Theory, Politics, English Literature* (New York: Methuen, 1987) and Terry Castle, "Phantasmagoria: Spectral Technology and the Metaphorics of Modern Reverie," *Critical Inquiry* 15:1 (1988): 26–61.

without gothic resolutions. Basically, with late-century trance novels, it is as if Emily St Aubert is stuck in the middle of the castle of Udolpho without any anxiety and without an evil uncle—perhaps an esoteric uncle instead. These trance novels do not so much plot good against evil—which, of course, they will do at times because they are novels—but rather good against other. The point of the gothic genre seems to be that after a time of abnormality and unexplained mysteries, that the normal and the known—the good marriage, the righteous nation, the holy church—will become permanently reinstated. With trance novels, a different trajectory occurs. An abnormal period with unexplained mysteries is followed by abnormality becoming acceptable to the protagonists in the novel. The formerly frightened and incredulous characters become credulous because of their new respect for the invisible and semi-visible, often permeable networks of power. These networks have a decentralizing effect on the concept of a known bourgeois, Western culture and seem to be a direct response to a changing and growing world where the holdings, business, and travel associated with colonialism and imperialism directly define a widening cultural identity in England and the United States.

Marie Corelli's *Romance* and Victorian Women in Outer Space

Bestselling Marie Corelli's first novel, *A Romance of Two Worlds* (1886) imagines the world as part of a bigger place or as a different place than it seems. It offers strange and strangely familiar alternative paradigms of how the world should work at a time of great social change. This novel seeks to conserve a concept of what is natural and godly. It presents an ideology of how things should be by guiding the reader through highly descriptive revelations, fashioned as travel accounts. Its distinct social context and literary status creates a space for viewing a trope with both a thematic and a political content.

Cruikshank's famous cartoon, "The Plum Pudding in Danger," illustrates the cultural anxiety that adheres to conceptualizing the world as a big place that is controlled and administered through competing nation-states. This same anxiety seems further heightened when the competition in question is envisioned as operating between worldly order and God's dominion. One difference that appears in narratives that describe God's world is imagining more than one plum pudding or a plum pudding that is mostly invisible. Some of the common features of this trope of extra-worlds mystical narratives pertain to the definition of God, the nature of space, and the concept of individual identity.

In such plots, God frequently has a special relationship with the protagonist, space and travel are given significant discussion by the narrative, and the protagonist has special bodily powers, sometimes supplied by religious faith or scientific innovation, that enable such things as astral travel and clairvoyance. Late-century trance novels are mystical adventure stories through these plot features. *A Romance of Two Worlds*, as well as a range of other Victorian novels such as Eliot's *Daniel Deronda*, Brontë's *Jane Eyre* and *Villette*, Daniels's *The Bronze Buddha, Zillah the Child Medium*, and Hawthorne's *The Spectre of the Camera*, share these features. In this regard, *Romance* is neither obscure nor exemplary, it just marks one good example of a recognizable trope that occurs across a wide range of Victorian narratives, both canonical and popular. Not only is this trope surprisingly frequent, it also has important implications for how subjectivity is imagined.

The mystical individuals in *Romance of Two Worlds* and other novels like it have both more agency than most and also agency in which their somatic capabilities are harnessed by and thus subordinated to a higher power. As a result, their identities are often described as nonautonomous—sometimes as multiple subjectivities in a single body and sometimes as subjectivities having out-of-body experiences. The structure of these narratives also takes faith out of the domain of belief, doctrine, and institutional affiliation, and places it instead in the realm of lived experience and the empirical realm of first-hand experience.

Corelli's *Romance of Two Worlds* uses elements of Victorian spiritualism and Orientalized mysticism to explore protagonists who contain and perform more than a single subjectivity. Their subjectivities are collective and embodied through process rather than through identity. For the protagonists of *Romance* and of other late Victorian trance novels, gender can only become decipherable through internal subjectivities that plurally work through a singular body.[34] A single gender identity and subjectivity, then, remain unfixed because these types of accounts only imagine identity within a spiritual collective of others, both human and divine. For the women in *Romance*, for instance, identity becomes a question of collectivity and space—both inner and outer; it becomes, in short, a question of empire in which individual identity is replaced by a collective identity. *Romance* focuses on *where* its characters are able to go and the roles they are able to play because of their investment in mystical models of intersubjectivity. In effect, its heroine and the other spiritually special characters in this novel become idealized citizens who have latitude due to their unique somatic capabilities. This narrative also relies on witnessing an alternative mystical reality that leads to and justifies faith in God.

Electricity and Astral Travel: Science and Fiction United

> In brief, this Earth and God's World were like America and Europe before the Atlantic Cable was laid. Now the messages of good-will flash under the waves, heedless of the storms. At one time people mocked at the wild idea that a message could flash in a moment of time from one side of the Atlantic to the other by means of a cable laid under the sea; now that it is an established fact, the world has grown accustomed to it, and has ceased to regard it as a wonder. Granting human electricity to exist, why should not a communication be established, like a sort of spiritual Atlantic cable, between man and the beings of other spheres and other solar systems?[35]

---

[34]   See Judith Butler, *Gender Trouble: Feminism and the Subversion of Identity* (New York: Routledge, Chapman and Hall, 1990), on gender as performance.

[35]   Marie Corelli, *A Romance of Two Worlds* (Chicago: W.B. Conkey, 1886), 200–201. Future reference to this work in the present discussion will be cited in text by page number.

In Corelli's *Romance of Two Worlds*, the reader sees what it means to have an empire of exteriority. After being cured of depression by imbibing many electrical elixirs administered by Heliobas, the Chaldean spiritual electrician, the heroine, fashioned after Marie Corelli herself, travels to outer space to examine life on other planets. Corelli's concept of the new science of electricity becomes the catalyst for transporting her characters to astral destinations.

The heroine of *Romance of Two Worlds* begins drinking electrical beverages and thus preparing for outer space travel while visiting Heliobas at his Parisian residence, called the Hotel Mars. The opulence and modernity of the Hotel Mars lends credence to the electrical path that Heliobas recommends for the heroine. In *Romance*, Chaldeans are an enlightened people who are working for the good of humanity rather than for its downfall and dissolution. The enlightened Heliobas cures the heroine (ostensibly Corelli herself) of her melancholy, which is inhibiting her career as a great pianist. As with other Victorian novels, the Near East is romanticized and seen as integrally tied to mystical power. It also exists, of course, as a threat and/or a gateway to British cultural ascendancy. Corelli's novel affords her heroine space travel to diverse spiritual promised lands on other planets that more fully and naturally enact God's order than England does.

This displacement of history into imaginary and/or mystical sites is inextricable from questions of identity. Corelli places her heroine in utopias (through Chaldean aid) to explain the ways identity may be unfixed. Subjectivity becomes a historically changeable and liberating type of role-playing.[36] It seems that this type of freedom and play hinges on the lack of political representation and direct power women hold in the public sphere. They imagine themselves instead in a society of their own making, partly real perhaps, but also partly imaginary. All that is needed, in a sense, is something like one of Masoch's contracts—made by necessity with one's self, as opposed to a social contract that Locke would describe as being made between individuals. In the realm of imaginary political action, much more is possible and action can be likened directly to role-playing and plural representations of a single circumstance taken simultaneously from different views and angles. This is like Masoch structurally, except, unlike Deleuze's depiction of coldness and cruelty, the reader of *Romance* instead gets a picture of warmth and community, as if the only contract that the heroine has signed is to stay a few nights at a four-star resort in outer space. Here, a religious subjectivity, which showcases an individual who is free from history, threatens Marxist determinism and a recognizable class identity. The interdigitation of the real and the imaginary allows a woman the freedom to seek to be a liberated political subject in terms of her association with an imaginary polis.

Given that Corelli herself chose to become Italian, creating her own ethnicity by changing her name from Minnie Mackay, it is not surprising that one of the most striking features of *Romance* is how racial identity is figured as a precursor

---

36   Compare Gilles Deleuze, *Coldness and Cruelty* in *Masochism* (New York: Zone Books, 1991).

for spiritual enlightenment.[37] The ancient, enlightened people for Corelli, across several of her novels, are the Chaldeans.[38] At the time *Romance* was being written, the British Museum was busily arranging some of its first Babylonian exhibits and translating Babylonian cuneiform inscriptions and books of magic incantations. In general, this segment of the Victorian age was marked by an increasing fascination with prebiblical languages and people. The Near East and northern Africa were sites for imagining enlightened ancient cultures that had direct, nontextual intercourse with divinity. This trope of ancient enlightenment versus Western modernity is based on a common imperialist binary construction.[39]

The necessity of being Chaldean to have commerce with the mystical is confirmed not only by Heliobas, but also by the Chaldean priest, who officiates at the death of Heliobas's sister, Zara. Also Chaldean, of course, Zara dies when her angel lover strikes her with lightning (marking the beginning of her spiritual marriage). The priest is not surprised when this angel electrifies Zara and explains that his belief in the powers of the invisible is a result of his ethnicity. He says, "If I were inclined to be skeptical on spiritual matters, I should not be of the race I am; for I am also Chaldean" (265). It is interesting to note, too, that Chaldeans being considered more spiritually attuned seems to be a prevalent Victorian assumption, and not only Corelli's notion. This perhaps is related to a common belief that the biblical wise men were Chaldean. For instance, consider Elizabeth Barrett Browning's lines in *Aurora Leigh*: "We Chaldeans discern / Still farther than we read. I know your heart, / And shut it like the holy book it is."[40]

Electricity, however, is at the center of Corelli's story. It takes an ancient lack of skepticism (a lack apparently inherent to Chaldeans) to be able to attribute so much power to electricity. Electricity is *styled* as being scientific in this novel while never being discussed in scientific detail. The reader actually learns very little scientific knowledge of electricity from Corelli. What the reader is given is a series of homilies

---

[37] See Theresa Ransom, *The Mysterious Miss Marie Corelli: Queen of Victorian Bestsellers* (Stoud, Gloucestershire: Sutton, 1999).

[38] *Chaldean* is a term that functions like *Oriental* in the second half of the nineteenth century.

[39] See Jaya Mehta, "English Romance; Indian Violence," *Centennial Review* 39:3 (Fall 1995), 611–57, and Viswanathan, "The Ordinary Business of Occultism," for fascinating discussions of this binarism. Mehta's brilliant analysis of Collins's *The Moonstone* discusses, for example, the way in which "the binarisms of eastern mysticism and western rationalism" that construct the novel's "universe are put under pressure at several points" (631). This permeable construction of Western rationalism and Eastern mysticism marks a partial reversal of the pattern I detect as a theme in many late-century trance novels: Namely, rational Eastern mysticism (whether Buddhist, Chaldean, Muslim, or Druze) enables Western protagonists to become educated about metaphysical matters beyond their dense resistance.

[40] Elizabeth Barrett Browning, *Aurora Leigh*, 4th edn, revised (London: Chapman and Hall, 1859), 73.

as to the brilliance of electricity. For instance, as Zara tells the heroine about electricity, we see her explanation for the superior senses of ancient people:

> "You enthusiast!" she said, "it is nothing new. It was well known to the ancient Chaldeans. It was known to Moses and his followers; it was practised in perfection by Christ and His disciples. To modern civilization it may seem a discovery, because the tendency of all so-called progress is to forget the past. The scent of the human savage is extraordinarily keen— keener than that of any animal—he can follow a track unerringly by some odor he is able to detect in the air. Again, he can lay back his ears to the wind and catch a faint, far-off sound with certainty and precision, and tell you what it is. Civilized beings have forgotten all this; they can neither smell nor hear with actual keenness. Just in the same way, they have forgotten the use of the electrical organs they all indubitably possess in large or minute degree." (142)

Electricity is used here as a warrant for the claim that primitive Chaldean civilization is more sophisticated and scientific than the modern age. This is developed through the idiomatically imperialist reference to the "human savage" and the forgetfulness of "civilized beings."[41] The heroine also learns from Heliobas that electricity, through each person's invisible electric ring, controls both love and antipathy. Interestingly, the circumference of each individual's electric ring varies with the individual's capabilities: "Each one of us walks the earth encompassed by an invisible electric ring—wide or narrow according to our capabilities. All these human electric rings are capable of attraction and repulsion." (97) It is, in fact, these great electrical hula hoops that have allowed both Heliobas and Zara to find their spiritual correspondences. Corelli's "scientific" concept of electricity continues to motivate much of the novel's plot, such as electrical shock for Prince Ivan, who is lovelorn for Zara; the repulsion of the heroine when she tries to kiss Zara in her sleep; Zara's death by electricity; and the heroine's outer space travel. Electricity's goals, then, are of life-or-death importance to humans. As Heliobas explains to a dinner guest: "Electricity," he said, "though the most powerful of masters, is the most docile of slaves. It is capable of the smallest as well as of the greatest uses. It can give with equal certainty life or death; in fact it is the key-note of creation" (224). The heroine finds this a reiterated claim as she experiences an out-of-body travel through outer space after she drinks electrical potions. After the heroine has reached a certain state of grace, in fact, electricity becomes hers—and enlightened Chaldeanity becomes a type of transitive identity. Being Chaldean here means being electrical. At one point in the novel, when Prince Ivan asks the heroine if she is "one of them," it is not clear whether he means being electrical or being Chaldean (103). Being Chaldean means being racially superior

---

41   Young writes about late Victorian references to savagery: "The idea of imperialism, and the notion of a civilizing mission presupposed racial superiority, for the fundamental difference between civilization and savagery that justified and required the civilizing mission assumed a basic differentiation between white and non-white races, and this was made in increasingly absolute and derogatory terms" (32–3).

in this novel because of special electrical capabilities, beliefs, and knowledge. It is fashioned in *Romance* as a powerful, electrical ancient civilization that trumps the prosaic and philistine powers of the British Empire.

Heliobas tells the heroine, "At any rate, the greatest force in the universe, electricity, is yours—that is, it has begun to form itself in you—and you have nothing to do but to encourage its growth, just as you would encourage a taste for music or the fine arts" (176). Properly speaking, then, Corelli's electricity is an aesthetic category and a practice that leads to enlightenment. It need only to be encouraged as one nurtures the development of "taste." It becomes a new field for discernment—something one develops, or something one achieves through a state of grace, not something one would scientifically harness—an internal sensibility, not just an external force. In fact, it seems that electricity allows Corelli's metaphysics to become not a discourse but a constitutional capability.

The dramatic culmination of the novel is the heroine's outer space travel. In God's world, social institutions are not needed. In fact, in enlightened outer space, an absence of English social institutions mark the complete supernatural ascendancy of the idealized English social values of true love, liberalism, and belief. The heroine presents comparative sociology in the two worlds in terms of difference rather than analogous construction. She notes:

> The three important differences between the inhabitants of this planet and those who dwell on Earth are these: first, they have no rulers in authority, as each one perfectly governs himself; second, they do not marry as the law of attraction which draws together any two of the opposite sexes, holds them fast in inviolable fidelity; thirdly, there is no creature in all the immensity of this magnificent sphere who has ever doubted, or who will doubt, the existence of the creator. (155–6)

This system, then, lacks what Corelli finds problematic with her own England—namely, government, marriage, and agnostic doubt. Yet as we see, her problems with these English institutions and states of mind portray her conservative outlook.

Far from radical, one reads through Corelli's work an idealized portrait not of expression but of order: "Each one perfectly governs himself." As for marriage, it is unnecessary. No need for legal binding through an institution, if there is an inviolable, scientific, active law of attraction in which no bond can become undone. Finally, there is no agnostic doubt—how could there be in this fixed, naturalized paradigm where subjects fit perfectly into a system that possesses an unquestionable, larger-than-life, electrical logic? The natural law of a precursing natural state that governs these alternate spheres marks an antithesis to British law while romanticizing British social order.

Even if the system is fixed, the subjectivities that it fosters are not. The most striking polysemic moment for the heroine is when she sees, hears, and is touched by Christ. She describes, "At the same moment a number of other faces and forms shone hoveringly out of the Ring; one I noticed like an exquisitely lovely woman, with floating hair and clear, earnest, unfathomable eyes ... upon whose broad brows rested the faint semblance of a crown of thorns" (171).[42] The figure goes on to say, "Have I not dwelt in thy clay, suffered thy sorrows, wept thy tears, died thy deaths? One with my Father, and yet one with thee, I demand thy love, and so through Me shalt thou attain immortal life!" (171). Christ here becomes "like an exquisitely lovely woman."[43] Like so much else in this novel, Christ operates electrically. As Heliobas states, "It can be proved from the statements of the New Testament that in Christ was an Embodied Electric Spirit. From first to last His career was attended by electric phenomena" (203).

The Passion is noted by the faint crown of thorns, but otherwise it is the heroine's passion and Christ's ties of love to God and the heroine that are important. This is a personal connection and acquaintance, not based on faith or a religious belief. Salvation becomes a question of romantic friendship and identification. "Have I not dwelt in thy clay, suffered thy sorrows, wept thy tears, died thy deaths?" Christ has been her—in her clay. Now she is asked to become a part of Christ. Her life in relief becomes a group of episodic affects made of clay, sorrows, tears, and deaths. As an exquisitely lovely woman, Christ demands the heroine's love in return for "immortal life." In this other world, distant from the Earthbound England, residents have space marked by the absence of hegemonic Victorian theology. Freed of English imperatives, Christ no longer need be a man because being a man is not a transplanetary imperative; here, Christ can be a beautiful woman.

Corelli's novel is striking in the way that it reworks the concept of space, making it an imaginary construction only reachable through somatic capability. Space becomes an otherworldly geography that not only enables but necessitates alternative political economies. It seems probable that this construction is borrowed from the domain of newly developing social sciences: from the first archeological attempts in Palestine and in North Africa and from the modernizing sciences of geography and mapmaking.[44]

An element of make-believe is inspired by the emerging fields of archeology and geography that is picked up in popular novels like *Romance*: Anything can be drawn up; and anything can be made up—including new modeling for political subjectivity. During the 1880s, which had produced agitation without result for woman's suffrage,

---

42   Corelli's depiction of Christ as a woman is not so atypical. Depictions of a female Christ had been popular in iconography and spiritual accounts since the Middle Ages and were also popular with other Victorian writers, such as Christina Rossetti and Camilla Crosland.

43   This same-sex electric moment is consistent with positive romantic connections between women, the narrator, and Zara, for instance, elsewhere in the novel. It also biographically relates to Corelli's long-term romantic companionship with her housemate, Bertha Vyver, to whom Corelli left her estate. See Ransom, *The Mysterious Miss Marie Corelli*, 206–7, and Annette R. Federico, *Idol of Suburbia: Marie Corelli and Late-Victorian Literary Culture* (Charlottesville and London: University Press of Virginia, 2000), 174–85.

44   Consider for further detail Kristin Ross's *The Emergence of Social Space* (Minneapolis: University of Minnesota Press, 1988) or Neil Silberman, *Digging for God and Country: Exploration, Archeology, and the Secret Struggle of the Holy Land, 1799–1917* (New York: Knopf, 1982).

perhaps it makes sense that new political realms, free from the limits of gender, established governments, and religion, should be brought into being across a range of narratives. Some trance novels distinctly imagine women's bodies in terms of space travel. Women here are described as colonizers and as colonized. The affiliation between women's bodies and unexplored space marks a typical political tandem during this period, yet one whose implications have not been adequately explored. Perhaps most interesting is the way in which these accounts do not imagine women's civic participation within the public sphere or within a private domestic realm. Instead, their travel, talents, and communities are described as existing in a communal, godly, outer space of extra spheres. Many other late-century trance novels, besides *Romance*, focus exclusively on the Earth and take East and West, not this world and other planets, as the point of comparison for their sociologies.

Keep Moving Out into the Gap: The Conflation of Mystical Buddhism, Islam, and Spiritualism

One turn-of-the-century novel, *The Bronze Buddha: A Mystery*, by Cora Linn Daniels, explores a desire for continuity between East and West, an implied desire in Corelli's *Romance*. It is a late-century example of a fairly common plot into which the mid-century mediumship novel grows. Namely, a mystical man—in this case a young, handsome Buddhist prince named Mihira—comes to the West, specifically New York, in search of the bronze Buddha that has been robbed from an Indian temple decades ago. Through the figure of the Buddha, India's spiritual capital as well as actual wealth in terms of the purported magical financial powers of the bronze Buddha have been stolen. Several Western protagonists, including the heroine, Silvia Romaine, are also interested in recovering the Buddha. Prince Mihira is somewhat clairvoyant and, in fact, mesmerizes his first cousin Silvia to force their marriage. However, the novel ultimately frowns on both the practice of cousins marrying one another and the possibility of miscegenation between the East and West. The wealthy young man and first-person narrator of the novel, Arion Estcourt, who will ultimately become Silvia's husband, figures out that Mihira has mesmerized Silvia during the fraudulent ceremony. He carries Silvia from the forced wedding at the church before she says "yes."[45] Arion's name sounding like Aryan, and Daniels troping him with racially "superior" traits is certainly no coincidence.

This is only one sign of the sharp distinction between and designation of East versus West that this novel maintains. This difference is sustained not only through race but also through religion. In fact, when Mihira has not returned to India with the Buddha in a short period of time, another Brahmin priest heads West to reiterate to Mihira his mission: "Dwell grandly among men and mould them. Read their secrets

---

[45]   *The Bronze Buddha* switches narrative voice repeatedly between some chapters in the first person voice of Arion Estcourt and others in the third person.

with the clairvoyant eye, hear their histories with the clairaudient ear. Find, let it be where it will, the great Buddha, and bring the god back to his own."[46] This ends up as a complicated, novel-length process. The Buddha is actually held by Mihira's wealthy Western father, Silvia's uncle. His father finally unveils the bronze Buddha to both Silvia and Mihira at the same time. It is filled with rare and costly jewels. Silvia and Mihira split the jewels between them. Silvia becomes a philanthropist, and Mihira returns to India with the Buddha and his share of the spoils to introduce a project of economic redevelopment via Colorado farming practices and land privatization to his home region. He has been inspired to do this by learning of his paternal Western racial heritage from his father. Previously Mihira had only known himself to be an orphan left at the monastery while still a baby:

> Then each drop of blood in [Mihira's] body suddenly thrilled with racial traits. Like a new birth, a revolution, a springing to life of strong dormant qualities never before aroused, out of his utter weakness—the yielding almost to death of his other self—grew into full being the profounder, the deeper racial attributes of a patriotic, honest, frank, and generous ancestry. (191)

In addition to his mystical attributes, the sudden taking on of his Western racial self helps actualize the plot. In a baldly imperialist characterization, the "deeper racial attributes" of his father, Henry Dusart, who has made his fortune through inheriting "an old firm, Dusart and Co. importers," (76) enable Mihira to become manly. Even Mihira's father, American Henry Dusart, is described through racial and cultural hybridity by Arion Estcourt:

> How nature ever made an American (for he was an American) to look so thoroughly like a Hindoo I cannot conceive. His mellow, liquid, deep-brown eyes, prominent and full lips, bearded with jet, his straight, well drawn nose, his oriental complexion, his dignified gait and bearing, were so unique in one whom I still saw at once to be my own countryman, that he ... should have been habited in rich colors and a turban! (1–2)

As the novel progresses, it seems that Henry Dusart looks "Hindoo" because he has spent a lot of time in India. Prince Mihira, who appears in the clubs and society of New York City in the "usual dress of an English or American gentleman," has a home in New York in which "the very atmosphere of India seemed to have been transported" (79). "Once so prosaic," the house is "now a dream of splendid opulence" (79). Prince Mihira not only takes after his father and Indian mother (who died in childbirth) but also garners power from his reverence for the wealth-holding, mystically Eastern, bronze Buddha. It is not always clear whether it is the Buddha's valuable contents or the Buddha as deity that is more venerated. When its treasure is discovered, the reader learns: "[There were]

---

46   Cora Linn Daniels, *The Bronze Buddha: A Mystery* (London: Gay and Bird, 1899), 99. Future reference to this work in the present discussion will be referenced in text by page number.

thousands of gems from the body of the image, rolling in lavish profusion to the very sides of the room ... For a few moments they were all beside themselves—It was a sight to stir the coldest bosom" (283–4). Sylvia Romaine is the true inheritor of the Buddha, because she possesses the ancient electrical ring with the image of the bronze Buddha on it, but she gives half the jewels and the shell of the Buddha to Mihira. His money from the sale of the jewels goes toward agricultural development in India. The reader is told that "the traveler to India who does the empire thoroughly will at this late day come across a part of the country which will amaze him" (288). Though it is originally Indian wealth, through the hidden jewels that fund this agriculturally flourishing region, it is also Mihira's American side and Western knowledge that allows for this success of modernization and capitalism to take place. Mystical agency, however, is also left a sizable role in this novel, which ends by noting that:

> another month saw the separation of these devoted friends who had been drawn together by so many unexpected incidents, and knitted in their mutual love by the singular influence of the Bronze Buddha. If there is a soul of things, an invisible, and occult power which pervades the universe and enters into the destinies of human lives, may not the subtle essence of that magnificent creation have moulded these events, which made for the highest good. (294)

At every turn, this novel marries a stereotypical version of Western agency and Eastern mysticism.[47] The tensions created by the battle between agency and the mystical "soul of things" looks very familiar in reference to earlier trance novels, like *Agnes*, *Zillah*, and *Maud Blount*. Marriage, here as in the earlier novels, is placed as an antithesis of mystical trances. Also, property and earthly wealth stand in sharp counterdistinction to mystical properties and esoteric capital. These same tensions between the mystical troped as Eastern and the rational troped as Western get played out in several late-century novels, such as *The Bronze Buddha*.

In these novels, the repeated though nonidentical assumption is that Buddhism always really means something esoteric that may well not even be Buddhist.[48] This

---

[47] Imagining India as particularly in touch with ancient magic also occurs much earlier in the century. See, for instance, *"To Daidmonion," or the Spiritual Medium* (Boston: Gould and Lincoln, 1852).

[48] There are several helpful secondary accounts of Buddhism in the nineteenth-century West. See Susan Thach Dean, "Decadence, Evolution, and Will: Caroline Rhys Davids's "Original Buddhism," in *Women's Theology in Nineteenth-Century Britain: Transfiguring the Faith of Their Fathers*, ed. Julie Melnyk (New York: Garland, 1998); Eve Kosofsky Sedgwick, *Touching Feeling: Affect, Pedagogy, Performativity* (Durham: Duke University Press, 2003), esp. Chapter 5, "Pedagogy of Buddhism"; Philip C. Almond, *The British Discovery of Buddhism* (Cambridge: Cambridge University Press, 1988); Thomas A. Tweed, *The American Encounter with Buddhism, 1844–1912: Victorian Culture and the Limits of Dissent* (Chapel Hill and London: University of North Carolina Press, 2000); and J. Jeffrey Franklin, "The Counter-Invasion of Britain by Buddhism in Marie Corelli's *A Romance of Two Worlds* and H. Rider Haggard's *Ayesha: The Return of She*," *Victorian Literature and Culture* (2003): 19–42.

formula of equating Buddhism and garish mysticism occasionally gets applied to Islam instead.[49] What Buddhism usually ends up equaling is either spiritualism or animate materialism. In *Ozmar the Mystic*, by Emeric Hulme Beaman, for instance, a character unacquainted with Ozmar asks, "But what bearing has the creed of Buddhism upon Ozmar the Mystic?" The reply is none too elucidating:

> "Simply that he is a Buddhist," replied my companion, "a Buddhist of a rather unusual type, moreover. He ... [disclaims] all supernatural powers ... [and] yet [is] able on occasion to achieve results so startling ... as to lead us to question whether ... the wisdom of the East has not far outstripped the researches of the most advanced of our modern scientists."[50]

This potential connection between Buddhism and science was discussed by Victorian buddhologists. For instance, Susan Dean writing about Victorian buddhologist Caroline Rhys Davids, notes that "[David] argued, if Buddhist concepts of the nature of reality 'could be adequately expounded so as to be intelligible to Western philosophy,' ideas might emerge that would be 'not a little sympathetic' to current trends in science."[51] Dean further explains that Davids saw this connection between Western science and Buddhism due to the Buddhist "law of causation" that Davids described as the "'ultimate reality' consist[ing] of 'throbbing energies whirling in ordered rhythm, whether of solar systems or our own hearts and intelligences.'"[52] To put it coarsely, the idea seems to be that because Buddhism has a concept of cosmic causation, this is sympathetic to scientific understandings of the world and its workings because both Buddhism and science posit enormous systems of cause and effect. In late-century trance novels troping Buddhism, everything has a cause; all causes have effects; and many mystical things, like astral travel and clairvoyance, have a reasonable and yet invisible causation that works in some scientifically mystical way. In Buddhist trance novels, this is precisely what the reader is asked to believe and assume. Ozmar's talents strike the reader as amazing and far more sophisticated than modern science, yet they are described as consonant with electrobiology. They include telepathy and the use of the astral body to travel great distances in a few moments. Ozmar, in fact, explains that some modern practices were actually first ancient mystical practices.[53] In speaking of mesmerism, Ozmar says:

---

49   Later in this chapter I consider two such examples of the pseudo-Islamic, S.A. Hillam's novel, *Sheykh Hassan: The Spiritualist. A View of the Supernatural* (London: W.H. Allen, 1888) and Laurence Oliphant's *Masollam* (London: Blackwood, 1886), 3 vols.

50   Emeric Hulme-Beaman, *Ozmar the Mystic* (London: Bliss, Sands, 1896), 17. Future references to this work in the present discussion will be cited in text by page number.

51   Dean, "Decadence, Evolution, and Will," 218. Quotation from Caroline Rhys Davids from Caroline Rhys Davids, ed. *Compendium of Philosophy*, trans. Shwe Zan Aung (London: Pali Text Society, 1910), preface, xvi.

52   *Ibid.*, 218. In turn, Dean quotes from Caroline Rhys Davids, *Buddhism: A Study of the Buddhist Norm* (New York: Holt; London: Williams and Norgate, 1912), 246–7.

53   This claim is also made in Corelli's *A Romance of Two Worlds* in reference to the powers of ancient Chaldeans.

Mesmerism—which is but the modern name for electrobiology, or animal magnetism—is a very ancient practice indeed—and though in the hands of charlatans it is but a foolish means of imposition—yet in the hands of the physician [is powerful] ... In ancient Egypt ... was the practice ... known and employed by the priesthood. (315)

In this explanation and in the way Buddhism is more generally portrayed in this novel and others like it, there is nothing particularly Buddhist about Buddhism that would make it distinct from spiritualism, mesmerism, or from other religions with mystical elements, such as Islam or the imagined religions of ancient Egypt. The same sorts of strange mystical abilities the reader sees in mid-century trance novels appear in late-century mystical novels, frequently under the name of Buddhist.

Another good example of this trend is Julian Hawthorne's (son of Nathaniel Hawthorne) novel, *The Spectre of the Camera or The Professor's Sister* (1888).[54] The protagonist of this novel, Conrad Hertrugge, is a university professor embodied with mystical talent. Briefly, the plot introduces Conrad's 25-year-old stepmother, the widow of Conrad's father, who has evil plots to kill Hildegarde, Conrad's guileless 18-year-old sister. Conrad, in turn, works to mystically thwart his stepmother, protect his sister, and secure the marriage plot between Hildegarde and his former student, Ralph. Ralph explains Conrad's powers to his skeptical friend, the narrator, noting that "Buddhists are all materialist at bottom. What they call spirit is but a refined form of matter. His results are sensational, and have a fascination of their own. But I am afraid they will get him into trouble yet."[55] Indeed, it seems that his results *should* get him into trouble—as they end up veering liberally into the campy and bizarre realm of a certain type of necrophilia. Yet they never do. His outcome in the novel is that of a well-established European scientist. Sadly, though, he is not ultimately able to save Hildegarde from his stepmother's evil machinations. The narrator witnesses Conrad's first remarkably heroic miracle carried out through his astral travel. The narrator separates from the rest of the group on a day hike and ascends a hill to look through a camera obscura, while Conrad is hundreds of miles away. Shocked by what he sees, the narrator remarks:

> How it had come there was more than I could conceive; an instant before, a glare of lightning had shown the place vacant. The next flash had, as it were, brought [Conrad] there—... the effigy cast by the lens had a kind of luminous quality in it, as if it had absorbed some of the electric light which charged the atmosphere. The figure extended his left hand towards Hildegarde ... [towards whom his stepmother had rolled a boulder as Hildegarde stood on a precipice] ... when I looked again for the apparition of Conrad Hertrugge, it had vanished. (87–8)

---

54 Julian Hawthorne expatriated from the United States to London, where he spent his adult life. For an elucidating biography, see Maurice Bassan, *Hawthorne's Son: The Life and Literary Career of Julian Hawthorne* (Columbus: Ohio State University Press, 1970).

55 Julian Hawthorne, *The Spectre of the Camera or, The Professor's Sister. A Romance* (London: Chatto and Windus, 1888), 35. Future reference to this work in the present discussion will be referenced in text by page number.

The narrator is quite flustered by this and considers that "the figure had not appeared to me directly, but through the medium of the lens of the camera; and I had never heard of a hallucination presenting itself in that manner" (92–3).[56] The technology of the camera is used to marshal the truth claims of the miraculous vision—as was done in terms of spirit photography in the 1870s.

Unfortunately, the stepmother's next attempt on Hildegarde's life is more successful. She feeds Hildegarde a pathogen scraped from her suitor's microscope, which makes the girl deathly ill. Much later, Conrad, in fact, has the narrator visit him in his private study to see what a beautiful cadaver his sister makes before her burial. She looks just as fresh as she did on the night of her engagement party to Ralph before she became ill. This rare beauty trait of Hildegarde's, a dewy deathliness, is remarkably persistent. The next time we see her is two years later, when we realize that the tireless Conrad has still been working at his salvific plot. Hildegarde's body has actually remained in Conrad's office all this while. In a scene with distinctly Eastern sarcophagal touches, the reader learns that:

> There was a filling of dried rose leaves within, but these sifted down on either side and revealed—what, of course, I had all along expected to see—the pure, pale, countenance of Hildegarde.
>
> "What do you think?" said Conrad, appealing to me as a sculptor might ask my opinion of his statue. "I can see no change, can you?"
>
> "None!" said I.
>
> And, indeed, after the lapse of these two years, she seemed as fresh and untouched as on the day when she stood beside Ralph as his betrothed wife. The skin seemed soft and pliant; the long eyelashes, resting on the cheeks, needed but a thought to lift them; and the curved line between the lips would melt at a breath. And yet, for two years, no breath had passed them, nor had any life visited the eyes. (214–15)

The reader then discovers the nature of her remarkable state. Although she had appeared dead, Conrad had actually put her in a trance for two years. Her body had been removed from her coffin in the graveyard and secretly returned to Conrad's office. Conrad finally remarks, "You must bear in mind that very little is understood of the real nature of trance" (229). Ralph and Hildegard are able to be married after all, and this has the effect of disinheriting the evil stepmother, and yet they are not set up as a reproducing couple. Hildegarde still has the fatal illness her stepmother gave her and refuses the magnetizing treatments her brother can perform to keep her alive because Ralph has sustained a lethal knife wound in a duel that takes place shortly after the wedding. She feels it right for them not to (again?) be parted by death.

Even in this particularly unusual and more-than-gothic novel plot, some of the staple features of earlier trance novels are maintained, such as that there is an antagonistic relationship between mysticism and the institution of marriage. The

---

56 The truth of photographic images was, of course, of huge discussion and debate at the turn of the century. For a discussion of the mediumship of camera lens, see Chapter 2.

powers of a mystical protagonist also upset the social order of the novel here even more than a murderer can. It is interesting that mystical powers often seem to be in close relation to crime in these novels. In the earlier trance novels, an ability to produce or undergo a trance is potentially criminal, as it is presented, for instance, in *Agnes*. In these later trance novels, sometimes it is still criminal, as in *The Bronze Buddha*'s failed marriage plot between Mihira (mesmerizer) and Silvia (mesmerized), because it is illegal to try to marry one's cousin if one has just mesmerized said cousin. Other times, though, producing trances aids in crime prevention, as is a cornerstone of the plot in *The Spectre of the Camera*. This crime prevention/detection narrative turn is also seen in *Ozmar the Mystic* and to a lesser degree in *Sheykh Hassan*, two other novels that fit in this genre. S.A. Hillam's *Sheykh Hassan: The Spiritualist* (1888) is also noteworthy because it describes crime-solving clairvoyant trance states through the "spiritualism" of Islam.

Pseudo-Islamic Trance Novels and the Charismatic Possessed Individual

Sheykh Hassan is a mystery novel that tells the sad story of Sheykh Hassan, whose mother and whose child, the reader finally learns, have been murdered by his jealous cousin, who has kidnapped his wife, who later dies as well. Hassan is a religious man who studies Islamic mysticism. His practice of Islamic mysticism allows him a vision in which he learns the true identity of the murderer of his family (his wealthy cousin). Unfortunately, although Hassan has the gift of seeing the past and the future, he has no power to rectify the wrongful deaths (though he is tempted by a pseudo-Satan Islamic god in a vision to trade his soul for bringing his family back from the dead). Shortly after his clairvoyant vision reveals his cousin's crime, Hassan is murdered in an unrelated plot line by vengeful men from another tribe who mistake his ethnic identity. This is all witnessed and recorded in the novel by a visiting Western narrator who has gone East to study Islamic mysticism.[57]

Unlike Ozmar, Hassan is not given a heroic capability to right the wrongs of detected crime. I include this brief discussion of *Sheykh Hassan* because it shows yet another trope direction of the trance novel and the fungibility of the terms *spiritualist* and *Muslim*, just as other novels discussed show the exchangeability of the terms *spiritualist* and *Buddhist*. This increasing conflation of all mystical practices in the late-nineteenth-century popular press shows the way Eastern mysticism seeps into the English imagination and the way English mysticism is used to explain the religions of the Near East. This latter trait of spiritualism inflecting a depiction of a Shi'ite tribe can be found in Laurence Oliphant's novel, *Masollam*.

Masollam is a trance novel based on the incredible charismatic force of the mystical individual. This is seen to a degree both with the character of Mihira in *The*

---

57 S.A. Hillam, *Sheykh Hassan: The Spiritualist. A View of the Supernatural* (London: W.H. Allen, 1888).

Bronze Buddha and with Ozmar of *Ozmar the Mystic*. To a somewhat lesser degree it also pertains to Conrad of *The Spectre of the Camera*. These characters are often the ones around whom plots orbit. They also have both the power and authority in the novels to fix serious and difficult problems, like murder and intimidation. Oliphant's *Masollam* (1886) shows a centrally charismatic title character. Philip Henderson, one of Oliphant's biographers, makes the claim that Oliphant based his characterization of Masollam on Thomas Lake Harris, the leader of the New Life, the cult of which Oliphant was a member for several years.[58] Indeed, the physical description of Masollam matches well to spiritualist Harris. Henderson quotes this description from the novel that also can describe Harris: "Like his voice [his eyes] had a near and a far-off expression, which could be adjusted to the required focus like a telescope, growing smaller and smaller as though in an effort to project the sight beyond the limits of natural vision."[59] The novel muses at length about the great personal abilities of Masollam, even though the novel exposes him to be a charlatan who later reforms. He is a man who left the Christian West in his youth to live for a time in Damascus and then the land of the Druses. There he learns Eastern magic—largely presented as mesmerism and clairvoyance—and uses these gifts first for good and then, later, for amassing personal wealth. The third volume of the novel takes place mainly in the Land of the Druses (figured as being in Syria/Palestine).[60] The fact that Masollam as well as the novel's young English lovers are all actually ethnically Druse is interesting. Druze (modern American spelling) is a sect of Shi'ism began in the Egyptian empire under the Ismaili ruler of Egypt al Hakim (996–1021). al-Hakim declared himself an emanation of the divine, and to Druzes he represents intellect. Druzes, a sect that has continually existed from the eleventh century to the present, living in modern-day Syria and in the modern state of Israel, believe that al Hakim is not dead but in hiding.[61] It seems that Oliphant, in his obsession with Harris, has a particularly wild system of substitution going on in this novel through which Harris = Masollam = the hidden al-Hakim (or salvific intellect).

Late in the novel, Masollam attempts to kill his evil wife before repenting of his crimes and again aligning himself with the forces of good. His magnetic qualities, whether for good or for evil, are consistently brought to the fore. Two other characters discussing him note the following:

> "There is no man, I suppose, in the world so much and at the same time so little an individual as he is."
> "That is because there is perhaps no other man in the world so highly developed as he is, whose nervous organization is so keenly sensitive to all the passing emotions of those

[58]   For another discussion of Thomas Lake Harris and the New Life, see Chapter 1.

[59]   Philip Henderson, *Life of Laurence Oliphant* (London: Robert Hale, 1956), 112.

[60]   Laurence Oliphant, *Masollam* (London: Blackwood, 1886), 3 vols. Future reference to this work in the present discussion will be referenced in text by volume and page number.

[61]   See "Druzes," in *The Perennial Dictionary of World Religions*, gen. ed., Keith Crim, assc. eds Roger A. Bullard and Larry D. Shinn (New York: Harper and Row, 1989), 230–31.

with whom he has established an internal *rapport*. For the time that any individual influence is thrown violently upon him, he almost feels himself to be that individual." (1:245)

In this case, as with Mihira from *The Bronze Buddha*, Masollam is both Eastern and Western. Perhaps being both allows him to identify with everyone in the novel. Masollam is a character depicted so that the Western reader can better imagine a non-Western, Druze-mystical subject position and agency through a character who is racially Caucasian. Masollam (which sounds a lot like *Muslim*), having lived both in the Near East and the West, has an enormous intuition, or "internal *rapport*" with others. The dialogue cited is fairly typical of the novel and its esoteric concerns. Masollam is like any or all individuals; he can be good or bad, at once himself or distinctly someone else. His very flexibility means that his ascendancy and power in the novel are never questioned. His flexible personal identity is consistent with the description of a sympathetic medium who can embody another's personality. He is a possessed individual. Unlike in many mediumship accounts, however, in *Masollam* this particular gift is neither questioned nor marginalized. Oliphant is not all seriousness, though, about his characters and their mystical ways. At one point, for instance, the narrator impersonates his readers' likely reactions to the novel:

> "We are tired," they will say, "of this perfectly impossible group of people, with their quickened organic sensitiveness, their highly developed inner faculties, their new moral and immoral consciousness, their invisible influences and spiritual combinations, their charlatanism, their aspirations and so forth. We prefer lifelike descriptions of people we know and see everyday." (2:56–7)

This same statement might indeed express Oliphant's views of visionary types after he left Harris's community, the New Life.[62] Nonetheless, the novel argues that this mystical type does exist and, more important, that it might be the type that can save the world through a new social formation. This assertion has a match in Oliphant's own life. Not only was he a member of the Brotherhood in the New Life, he also was a member of Parliament who had a plan to colonize Palestine with European Jews (I discuss this in greater detail in Chapter 1). The vision *Masollam* promotes for the social significance of possessed people and places is described by a visionary character in the novel named Santalba:

> There are social, theological, and scientific barriers which impede the flow of the new divine life into the human organism in the modern Babylons of the West, which have no existence in the more primitive regions; and it may be that once again, as of old, the scene of its first operation will be in this ancient land of Palestine, within the borders of which you are about to build your new home. (3: 262)

---

[62]   See Henderson, *Life of Laurence Oliphant*, 112.

Not only are visionary characters needed, but so is a primitive region free from social, theological, and scientific barriers: Here such a place is posited, in a typically proto-Zionist way, as Palestine. This free, primitive place would arguably foster more enlightened thinking. The diversity of actual inhabitants and cultures of Palestine are mainly ignored (outside of the Druzes)—imagining instead a Palestine that can be remade as a utopian settlement. Also of note in this quote is the way in which West and East are imagined as distinct and yet as integral to one another in terms of imagining the influx of "new divine life." In another passage in the novel Druzes and English Unitarians are conflated through an equivocated Arabic word *muwahideen*, which means unitarian (as Druzes see their faith as a unitarian belief system). One character explains the Druzes' views of England, saying:

> "They all believe that England contains many numbers of their sect; and you will find, if you travel among them, that one of the first questions you will be asked is, whether there are many Unitarians or Muwahideen in England? … And the reason for this is, that it is by the English Druses that the immediate advent of the Messiah is to be announced." (3: 214–15)

The text further toys with the possibility that this "new divine life," or Messiah, is the English/Druze character Masollam.[63]

Masollam notes his own powers, drawing them in counterdistinction to those of spiritualists, whose spirits "seek to communicate with man by rapping on tables," further saying that "I have passed through both experiences and the difference between a 'medium under control,' and arriving at a permanent condition of free and independent mental association, with a pure intelligence of the upper region, is greater than can be described" (3:27). Masollam, then, is depicted here as the charismatic individual who can communicate with "pure intelligence" through undergoing trances. Oliphant, in writing *Masollam*, uses the trance novel to expand his claims about the mystical hero somewhat arduously (as this novel cannot be described as a page-turner) through the medium of social realism in the form of a 750-page triple-decker about socially minded mystical Druzes.

Conclusion

Although one story about empire is that of a common British culture being carried out into a non-Western world (Matthew Arnold), another story imagines the inroads of

---

63   Masollam is consistently a *roman-a-clef* characterization of cult leader Harris throughout several examples in the novel. Harris did, in fact, declare himself to be divine to his followers. In one personal account, for instance, Harris refers to himself as like Thomas Edison and George Fox because of receiving the open respiration of the divine. See Thomas Lake Harris, *Brotherhood of the New Life: Its Fact, Law, Method, and Purpose* (London: E.W. Allen, 1891), 5.

non-Western culture into the metropole.[64] There is a third and somewhat related story we see in trance novels—namely, the pseudo-Western mapped onto the pseudo-Eastern or the pseudo-Eastern mapped onto the pseudo-Western. The historical inaccuracy of these novels is interesting because they envision the relation between Eastern and Western, visible and invisible, in idealizing ways. At a literal level, trance novels posit that there are outer eyes and inner eyes, physical bodies and astral bodies, minds and souls, an earthly self and a radical other, a spirit from beyond the vale. Allegorically speaking, this is also a West/East, Occident/Orient narrative. There is an heiress; there is a bronze Buddha. There is a daughter with a strange illness; there is Ozmar the mystic. There is a hidden camera; there is a specter. The boundaries between known and unknown, West and East, life and death, real and imaginary, evident and impossible, proof and possibility become fluid. It makes good sense that the genre of trance novels arises in the nineteenth century when the boundaries of the known world were changing and the power of the nation and of its institutions were challenged by the seemingly boundless globe and all of the conditions and forms of colonialism and competing nation-states.

Trance novels provide a unique space to think through the theoretical implications that mystical possession held for the public sphere. When novels feature a trance heroine or hero, the periphery of mystical practices questions the limited concept of public and private space by recentering civic space. Brontë's *Villette*, Arthur's *Agnes the Possessed*, *Zillah, the Child Medium*, *Maud Blount, Medium*, Daniels's *Bronze Buddha*, Hulme-Beaman's *Ozmar*, Hawthorne's *Spectre of the Camera*, Hillam's *Sheykh Hassan*, and Oliphant's *Masollam* all reconfigure society around the civic center of imagined community where seeing, knowing, and experiencing others from a distance in an imaginary extra sphere accessed by one's mystically apt physical body leads to the creation of new societies and solutions to problems in the real world. Though mid-century trance novels argue that altered states create a threatening disorder that challenges marriage, the family, lineage, inheritance, and law, late-century trance novels imagine wild plots of social unification and connection between West and East through entranced heroic protagonists who are cosmopolitan subjects. By the late nineteenth century, mysticism is no longer esoteric; it is instead consistently (if not exclusively) figured as political.

---

[64] See Catherine Hall, "Introduction," in *Cultures of Empire: Colonizers in Britain and the Empire in the Nineteenth and Twentieth Centuries. A Reader* (New York: Routledge, 2000).

Bibliography

Abraham, Lyndy. *A Dictionary of Alchemical Imagery.* New York: Cambridge University Press, 1998.

Aitchenbie, Henry. *Melchior Gorles, A Tale of Modern Mesmerism.* London: John Camden Hotten, 1867.

Allibone, S. Austin. *A Critical Dictionary of English Literature and British and American Authors ... to the Later Half of the Nineteenth Century.* London: J.B. Lippincott, 1908.

Almond, Philip C. *The British Discovery of Buddhism.* Cambridge: Cambridge University Press, 1988.

Anderson, Amanda. "George Eliot and the Jewish Question." *Yale Journal of Criticism* 10.1 (1997): 39–61.

Apraxine, Pierre, Denis Canguilhem, Clement Cheroux, Andreas Fischer, and Sophie Schmit. *The Perfect Medium: Photography and the Occult.* New Haven and London: Yale University Press, 2005.

Armstrong, Nancy. *Desire and Domestic Fiction.* Oxford: Oxford University Press, 1987.

Arnold, Matthew. "Sweetness and Light." In *Culture and Anarchy* ed. with intro. by J. Dover Wilson. Cambridge: Cambridge University Press, 1990.

Arthur, T.S. *Agnes the Possessed: A Revelation of Mesmerism.* London: J.S. Hodson, 1852.

Barrow, Logie. *Independent Spirits: Spiritualism and English Plebeians, 1850–1910.* London: Routledge and Kegan Paul, 1986.

Bassan, Maurice. *Hawthorne's Son: The Life and Literary Career of Julian Hawthorne.* Columbus: Ohio State University Press, 1970.

Berry, Catherine. *Experiences in Spiritualism: A Record of Extraordinary Phenomena Witnessed Through the Most Powerful Mediums, with Some Historical Fragments Relating to Semiramide, Given by the Spirit of an Egyptian Who Lived Contemporary with Her*, 2nd edn, enlarged. London: James Burns, 1876.

Bigland, Eileen. *Marie Corelli. The Woman and the Legend, a Biography.* London: Jarrolds, 1952.

Bodie, Walford. *The Bodie Book.* London: Caxton Press, 1905.

Boehmer, Elleke. *Colonial and Postcolonial Literature: Migrant Metaphors.* Oxford and New York: Oxford University Press, 1995.

Bosanquet, Theodora. *Harriet Martineau.* London: F. Etchells and H. Macdonald, 1927.

Boyarin, Daniel, and Jonathan Boyarin. "Diaspora: Generation and the Ground of Jewish Identity." *Critical Inquiry* 19 (1993): 693–725.

————. *Powers of Diaspora: Two Essays on the Relevance of Jewish Culture.* Minneapolis: University of Minnesota Press, 2002.

Braude, Ann. *Radical Spirits: Spiritualism and Women's Rights in Nineteenth Century America.* Boston: Beacon Press, 1989.

Bray, Charles. *Illusion and Delusion; Or, Modern Pantheism versus Spiritualism.* London: Thomas Scott, 1873.

————. *On Force, Its Mental and Moral Correlates; and on That Which is Supposed to Underlie All Phenomena: with Speculations on Spiritualism and Other Abnormal Conditions of Mind.* London: Longmans, Green, Reader, and Dyer, 1866.

Briggs, Asa. *Victorian Things.* Chicago: University of Chicago Press, 1988.

Brontë, Charlotte. *Jane Eyre.* New York: Harper, 1847.

————. *Villette.* New York: Penguin, 1986.

Brontë, Emily. *Wuthering Heights.* New York: Oxford University Press, 1981.

Brown, Gillian. *Domestic Individualism: Imagining Self in Nineteenth-Century America.* Berkeley: University of California Press, 1990.

Browning, Elizabeth Barrett. *Aurora Leigh*, 4th edn rev. London: Chapman and Hall, 1859.

————. *A Note on William Wordsworth with a Statement of Her Views on Spiritualism.* London: Printed for Private Circulation Only by Richard Clay and Sons, 1919.

Burnoff, Eugène. *Introduction à l'histoire du buddhisme indien,* 2nd edn, with an intro. by Barthélemy Saint-Hilaire. Paris: Maisonneuve, 1876.

Butler, Judith. *Gender Trouble: Feminism and the Subversion of Identity.* New York: Routledge, Chapman and Hall, 1990.

Caron, James. "The Rhetoric of Magic in *Daniel Deronda.*" *Studies in the Novel* 15:1 (Spring 1983): 1–9.

Castle, Terry. *The Apparitional Lesbian: Female Homosexuality and Modern Culture.* New York: Columbia University Press, 1993.

————. "Phantasmagoria: Spectral Technology and the Metaphorics of Modern Reverie." *Critical Inquiry* 15:1 (1988): 26–61.

————. "The Spectralization of the Other in the *Mysteries of Udolpho.*" *The New Eighteenth Century: Theory, Politics, English Literature.* Felicity Nussbaum and Laura Brown, eds. New York: Methuen, 1987.

Clements, Harry. *Alfred Russell Wallace: Biologist and Social Reformer*, foreword by Richard Clements. London: Hutchinson, 1983.

Comte, Auguste. *The Positive Philosophy of Auguste Comte Freely Trans. and Condensed by Harriet Martineau.* London: J. Chapman, 1853.

Conder, Claude Reignier. *Tent Work in Palestine: A Record of Discovery and Adventure. 2 vols.* London: Richard Bentley and Son, 1878.

Coombs, Katherine. *The Miniature in England.* London: Victoria and Albert Publications, 1998.

Corelli, Marie. *A Romance of Two Worlds.* Chicago: W.B. Conkey, 1886.

————. *The Sorrows of Satan.* Philadelphia: Lippincott, 1895.

————. "The Plain Truth of the Stratford-on-Avon Controversy, concerning the fully-intended demolition of old houses in Henley Street and the changes proposed to be effected to the national ground of Shakespeare's birthplace." 1903.

————. *The Opinions Freely Expressed on Certain Phases of Modern Social Life and Conduct.* London: R. Constable, 1905.

————. *Woman or Suffragette? A Question of National Choice.* London, 1907.

————. *Is All Well with England?* London: Jarrolds, 1917.

Cottom, Daniel. "On the Dignity of Tables." *Critical Inquiry* 14 (Summer 1988): 765–83.

————. *Abyss of Reason.* Oxford: Oxford University Press, 1991.

Crary, Jonathan. *Techniques of the Observer, On Vision and Modernity in the Nineteenth Century.* Cambridge: MIT Press, 1990.

Crim, Keith, ed. *The Perennial Dictionary of World Religions* (associate eds Roger A. Bullard and Larry D. Shinn). New York: Harper and Row, 1989.

Crosland, Mrs Newton [Camilla Toulmin]. *Light in the Valley. My Experiences of Spiritualism.* London: Routledge, 1857.

————. *The Island of the Rainbow. A Fairy Tale. And Other Fancies.* London: Routledge, 1866.

————. *Memorable Women: The Story of Their Lives.* New York: G.P. Putnam and Sons, 1868.

————. *Stories of London Re-Told for Youthful Readers.* London: W.H. Allen, 1880.

————. *Landmarks of a Literary Life: 1820–1892.* New York: Charles Scribner, 1893.

Crosland, Newton. *Apparitions: A New Theory.* London: Effingham Wilson, 1856.

————. *The Eltham Tragedy. Revued by C.* London, 1871.

————. *Apparitions: An Essay Explanatory of Old Facts and a New Theory; to Which Are Added Sketches and Adventures.* London, 1873.

————. *Pith: Essays and Sketches, Grave and Gay: With Some Verses and Illustrations.* London, 1881.

————. *The New Principia; or, The Astronomy of the Future.* London, 1883.

————. *Transcendental Vagaries; Being a Review and an Analysis of "The Perfect Way; or, the Finding of Christ."* London: E.W. Allen, 1890.

Crowe, Catherine. *The Night Side of Nature: Or, Ghosts and Ghost Seers, Vols. 1 and 2.* London: T.C. Newby, 1848.

Crowell, Eugene. *Spiritualism and Insanity.* Boston: Dolby and Rich, 1877.

Daniels, Cora Linn. *The Bronze Buddha: A Mystery.* London: Gay and Bird, 1899.

Darrah, William C. *Cartes de Visite in Nineteenth-Century Photography.* Gettysburg, PA: W.C. Darrah, 1981.

Darwin, Charles. *On the Origin of the Species by Means of Natural Selection.* London: Murray, 1859; reprinted in *The Essential Darwin*, eds. Robert Jastrow and Kenneth Korey. Boston: Little, Brown, 1984.

Davids, Caroline Rhys, ed. *Compendium of Philosophy*, trans. Shwe Zan Aung. London: Pali Text Society, 1910.

————. *Buddhism: A Study of the Buddhist Norm.* New York: Holt; London: Williams and Norgate, 1912.

Davies, Charles Maurice. *Mystic London; or, Phases of Occult Life in the Metropolis.* London: Tinsley Brothers, 1875.

D.C. [De Morgan, Mrs Sophia]. *From Matter to Spirit. The Result of Ten Years Experience in Spirit Manifestations. Intended as a Guide to Enquirers.* London: Longman, Roberts, and Green, 1863.

Dean, Susan Thach. "Decadence, Evolution, and Will: Caroline Rhys Davids's "Original Buddhism." *Women's Theology in Nineteenth-Century Britain: Transfiguring the Faith of Their Fathers*, ed. Julie Melnyk. New York: Garland, 1998: 209–31.

DeGrazia, Edward. *Censorship Landmarks.* New York: R.R. Bowker, 1969.

Deleuze, Gilles, *Coldness and Cruelty* in *Masochism.* New York: Zone Books, 1991.

D'Emilio, John and Estelle B. Freedman. *Intimate Matters: A History of Sexuality in America.* New York: Harper and Row, 1988.

Derrida, Jacques. *Spectres of Marx, the State of the Debt, the Work of Mourning, and the New International*, trans. Peggy Kamuf, intro. by Bernd Magnus and Stephen Cullenberg. New York and London: Routledge, 1994.

Dickens, Charles. *Our Mutual Friend.* New York: J. Bradburn, 1864.

————. *Bleak House.* New York: Viking Penguin, 1997.

————. *Great Expectations.* New York: Tor Doherty, 1998.

Doyle, Arthur Conan. *The Case for Spirit Photography.* New York: George H. Doran, 1923.

Eastlake, Charles. *Hints on Household Taste in Furniture, Upholstery, and Other Details.* Boston: J.R. Osgood, 1872.

Eliot, George. *The Lifted Veil.* New York: Harper, 1878.

————. *The Mill on the Floss.* New York: Washington Square Press, 1956.

————. *Daniel Deronda.* New York: Penguin Books, 1986.

————. *Middlemarch*, ed. B. Giltonback. Boston: Norton, 1979.

Engels, Friedrich, and Karl Marx. *The Communist Manifesto* [1848]. New York: Penguin Putman, 1998.

Federico, Annette R. *Idol of Suburbia: Marie Corelli and Late-Victorian Literary Culture.* Charlottesville: University Press of Virginia, 2000.

Flourens, Pierre. *Recherches experimentales sur les proprietes et les fonctions du systeme nerveus dans les animaux vertebres.* Paris: Crevot, 1824.

Frankel, Edward. "Corpuscular Optics and the Wave Theory of Light: The Science and Politics of a Revolution in Physics." *Social Studies of Science* 6 (1976): 141–84.

Franklin, J. Jeffrey. "The Counter-Invasion of Britain by Buddhism in Marie Corelli's *A Romance of Two Worlds* and H. Rider Haggard's *Ayesha: The Return of She.*" *Victorian Literature and Culture* (2003): 19–42.

Frazer, J.G. *The Golden Bough: A Study in Comparative Religion.* London: Macmillan, 1890.

Fritz. *Where Are the Dead? Or, Spiritualism Explained.* London: Simpkin, Marshall, 1873.

Gabriel, Mary. *Notorious Victoria.* Chapel Hill, NC: Algonquin Books, 1998.

Gagnier, Regenia. *The Insatiability of Human Wants: Economics and Aesthetics in Market Society.* Chicago: University of Chicago Press, 2000.

Galton, Francis. *Hereditary Genius.* London: Macmillan, 1869.

————. *Memories of My Life.* London: Methuen, 1908.

————. *Essays in Eugenics.* London: Eugenics Education Society, 1909.

Garland, Hamlin. *The Tyranny of the Dark.* London: Harper and Brothers, 1905.

Gates, Sarah. "'A Difference in Native Language': Gender, Genre, and Realism in *Daniel Deronda.*" *English Literary History* 68:3 (2001): 699–724.

Guppy, Samuel. *Mary Jane; or, Spiritualism Chemically Explained with Spirit Drawings. Also Essays By and Ideas {Perhaps Erroneous} of, 'A Child at School.'* London: John King, 1863.

Hacaen, Henri, and G. Lanteri-Laura. *Evolutions des connaissances et des doctrines sur les localisations cerebrales.* Paris, 1977.

Haight, Gordon, ed. *The George Eliot Letters.* 9 vols. New Haven: Yale University Press, 1978.

Hall, Catherine, ed. *Cultures of Empire: Colonizers in Britain and the Empire in the Nineteenth and Twentieth Centuries. A Reader.* New York: Routledge, 2000.

Hall, Spencer T. *Mesmeric Experiences.* London: H. Bailliere, 1845.

Hallote, Rachel. *Bible, Map, and Spade: The American Palestine Exploration Society, Frederick Jones Bliss, and the Forgotten Story of Early American Biblical Archaeology.* Piscatawy, NJ: Gorgias Press, 2006.

Hardy, Robert Spence. *The Legends and Theories of Buddhists, compared with history and science: with introductory notices of the life and system of Gotama Buddha.* London: William and Norgate, 1866.

Hardy, Thomas. *Jude, the Obscure.* New York: Harper and Brothers, 1903.

Harris, Thomas Lake. *Modern Spiritualism. Its Truths and Its Errors; A Sermon Preached at the Marleybone Institute, Edwards Street Portman Square, London, Sabbath Morning, January 15, 1860.* New York: New Church Publishing, 1860.

————. *The Mission of the New Church, and How It Is to Be Accomplished.* Glasgow and London: James Fowler and Fred Pitman, 1868.

————. *Star-Flowers, A Poem of the Woman's Mystery.* Fountaingrove, 1887.

————. *Brotherhood of the New Life: Its Fact, Law, Method, and Purpose.* London: E.W. Allen, 1891.

Hawthorne, Julian. *The Spectre of the Camera or, The Professor's Sister. A Romance.* London: Chatto and Windus, 1888.

Hawthorne, Nathaniel. *The Blithedale Romance.* Oxford: Oxford World Classics, 1998.

Henderson, Philip. *Life of Laurence Oliphant.* London: Robert Hale, 1956.

Hillam, S.A. *Sheykh Hassan: The Spiritualist. A View of the Supernatural.* London: W.H. Allen, 1888.

Hirsch, Robert. *Seizing the Light, a History of Photography.* Boston: McGraw-Hill, 2000.

Holcombe, Lee. "Victorian Wives and Property: Reform of the Married Women's Property Law 1857–1882." In *A Widening Sphere: Changing Roles of Victorian Women,* ed. Martha Vicinus. London: Methuen, 1980.

Houghton, Georgiana. *Chronicles of the Photographs of Spiritual Beings and Phenomena Invisible to the Material Eye: Interblended with Personal Narratives.* London: E.W. Allen 1882.

Howitt, Anna Mary (afterward Watts). *The Pioneers of the Spiritual Reformation. Life and Works of Dr. Justinus Kerner. William Howitt and his Work for Spiritualism. Biographical Sketches.* London: Psychological Press Association, 1883.

Hugo, Victor. *Hermani: A Tragedy,* trans. and pub. Camilla Crosland. London: G. Bell and Sons, 1887.

Hulme-Beaman, Emeric. *Ozmar the Mystic.* London: Bliss, Sands, 1896.

Irwin, Jane. *George Eliot's Daniel Deronda Notebooks.* Cambridge and New York: Cambridge University Press, 1996.

Jolly, Martyn. *Faces of the Living Dead: The Belief in Spirit Photography.* London: The British Library, 2006.

Judd, Denis. *Empire: The British Imperial Experience, 1765 to the Present.* New York: Basic Books, 1997.

Karl, Frederick R. *George Eliot: The Voice of a Century.* New York and London: W.W. Norton and Company, 1995.

Kelves, Daniel J. *In the Name of Eugenics.* New York: Knopf, 1985.

Kent, Susan Kingsley. *Sex and Suffrage in Britain, 1860–1914.* Princeton, NJ: Princeton University Press, 1987.

Kidwell, Claudia Brush, with Nancy Rexford, "Foreword." *Dressed for the Photographer, Ordinary Americans and Fashion, 1840–1900.* Kent, OH: Kent State University Press, 1995.

Kitson, Alfred. *Spiritualism for the Young. Designed for the Use of Lyceums, and the Children of Spiritualists in General Who Have No Lyceums at Which They Can Attend.* Keighley: S. Billows, 1889.

Koeppen, Carl Friedrich. *Die Religion des Buddha und ihre Engstehung.* 2 vols. Berlin: Ferninand Schneider, 1857–1859.

Lawrence, Edward. *Spiritualism Among Civilized and Savage Races: A Study in Anthropology.* London: A. & C. Black, 1921.

Lee, Edwin. *Report upon the Phenomena of Clairvoyance or Lucid Somnambulism, (from personal observation.) With Additional Remarks.* London: John Churchill, 1843.

Levine, George. "Eliot's Hypothesis of Reality." *Nineteenth-Century Fiction* 35:1 (1980): 1–28.

LeWarne, Charles Pierce. *Utopias of Puget Sound, 1885–1915.* Seattle: University of Washington Press, 1975.

Lewes, George Henry. *Problems of Life and Mind.* London: Trubner, 1874.

Locke, John. *Two Treatises of Government.* London and Vermont: Everyman, 1998.

London, Bette. *Writing Double: Women's Literary Partnerships*. Ithaca, NY: Cornell University Press, 1999.

Luckhurst, Roger. *The Invention of Telepathy, 1870–1901*. Oxford: Oxford University Press, 2002.

Macpherson, C.B. *The Political Theory of Possessive Individualism: Hobbes to Locke*. Oxford: Clarendon Press, 1962.

Magic and Mesmerism: An Episode of the Eighteenth Century. London: Saunders and Otley, 1843.

Malin, James C. *A Concern about Humanity: Notes on Reform, 1872–1912, at the National and Kansas Levels of Thought*. Lawrence: Regents Press of Kansas, 1964.

Marryat, Florence. *Gup: Sketches of Anglo Indian Life and Character*. London: R. Bentley, 1868.

————. *There Is No Death*. London: Kegan Paul, Trench, Trubner, Ltd, 1891.

————. *The Spirit World*. Leipzig: Bernhard Tauchnitz, 1894.

Marsh, Margaret S. *Anarchist Women, 1870–1920*. Philadelphia: Temple University Press, 1981.

Martineau, Harriet. *Illustrations of Political Economy, of Poor Laws, and Paupers, and of Taxation*. London: Charles Fox, 1832–1834.

————. *Selected Letters*, ed. Valerie Sanders. New York: Oxford University Press, 1990.

Martineau, Harriet, with Henry G. Atkinson. *Letters on the Laws of Man's Nature*. London: J. Chapman, 1851.

Marx, Karl. *Capital, Vol. 1*. New York: E.P. Dutton, 1939.

Matlock, Jann. "Ghostly Politics." *Diacritics* 30:3 (2000): 53–71.

Maude Blount, Medium. A Story of Modern Spiritualism. [Davies, Charles Maurice]. London: Tinsley Brothers, 1876.

Mavor, Carol. *Pleasures Taken: Sexuality and Loss in Victorian Photographs*. Durham: Duke University Press, 1995.

Mehta, Jaya. "English Romance; Indian Violence." *Centennial Review* 39:3 (Fall 1995): 611–57.

Meyer, Susan. "'Safely to Their Own Borders': Proto-Zionism, Feminism, and Nationalism in Daniel Deronda." *English Literary History* 60:3 (1993): 733–58.

Mill, John Stuart. *On Liberty*. Chicago: Henry Regner, 1955.

Miller, Daniel. *Material Culture and Mass Consumption*. New York: Basil Blackwell, 1987.

More, Thomas. *Utopia*, trans. Ralphe Robynson. Boston, Lincolnshire: R. Roberts, 1878.

Muller, Johannes. *Uber die phantastischen Gesichterscheinungen*. Coblentz, 1826.

————. *Zur vergleichenden Physiologie des Gesichtsinnes des Menshen und Thiere*. Leipzig, 1826.

Myers, Frederic, and William Henry. *Human Personality and Its Survival of Bodily Death in Two Volumes.* London, New York, and Bombay: Longmans, Green, 1903.

Noakes, Richard. "Spiritualism, Science and the Supernatural in Mid-Victorian Britain." In *The Victorian Supernatural*, eds Nicola Bown, Carolyn Burdett, and Pamela Thurschwell. Cambridge: Cambridge University Press, 2004: 23–43.

Oliphant, Laurence. *Land of Gilead with Excursions in the Lebanon.* New York: Appleton, 1881.

————. *Massolam.* 3 vols. London: Blackwood, 1886.

Oppenheim, Janet. *The Other World: Spiritualism and Psychical Research in England, 1850–1914.* Cambridge: Cambridge University Press, 1985.

Owen, Alex. *The Darkened Room: Women, Power and Spiritualism in Late Victorian England.* Philadelphia: University of Pennsylvania Press, 1990.

Pichanick, Valerie Kossew. *Harriet Martineau and Her Work, 1802–1876.* Ann Arbor: University of Michigan Press, 1980.

Pick, Daniel. *Svengali's Web: The Alien Enchanter in Modern Culture.* New Haven: Yale University Press, 2000.

Powell, J.H. *Mediumship: Its Laws and Conditions; with Brief Instructions for the Formation of Spirit-Circles.* London: Author, n.d.

Putzell-Korab, Sarah M. "The Role of the Prophet: The Rationality of Daniel Deronda's Idealist Mission." *Nineteenth-Century Fiction* 37:2 (1982): 170–87.

Ragussis, Michael. *Figures of Conversion: "The Jewish Question" and English National Identity.* Durham: Duke University Press, 1995.

Ransom, Theresa. *The Mysterious Miss Marie Corelli: Queen of Victorian Bestsellers.* Stoud, Gloucestershire: Sutton, 1999.

Reichenbach, Carl von, Baron. *Researches on Magnetism, Electricity, Heat, Light, Crystallization, and Chemical Attraction, in Their Relations to the Vital Force*, trans. by William Gregory. London: Taylor, Walton, and Maberly, and Edinburgh: Maclachlan and Stewart, 1850.

Richet, Charles. *Thirty Years of Psychical Research.* New York: Macmillan, 1923.

Rinn, Joseph F. *Searchlight on Psychical Research. A Record of Sixty Years' Work— Interwoven with an Intimate Biographical Sketch of Houdini.* London: Rider, 1954.

Robbins, Bruce, and Pheng Cheah, eds. *Cosmopolitics: Thinking and Feeling beyond the Nation.* Minneapolis: University of Minnesota Press, 1998.

Roden, Frederick S. "The Kiss of the Soul: The Mystical Theology of Christina Rossetti's Devotional Prose." In *Women's Theology in Nineteenth-Century Britain*, ed. Julie Melnyk. New York: Garland Publishing, 1998: 37–55.

Romer, Mrs Isabella C. *Sturmer: A Tale of Mesmerism.* London: R. Bentley, 1841.

Ross, Kristin. *The Emergence of Social Space.* Minneapolis: University of Minnesota Press, 1988.

Rossetti, Christina. *Annus Domini: A Prayer for Each Day of the Year, Founded on the Text of the Holy Scripture.* Oxford: James Parker, 1874.

————. *Poems and Prose*, ed. Jan Marsh. London: Everyman, 1994.

Royle, Nicolas. *Telepathy and Literature: Essays on the Reading Mind.* Oxford: Basil Blackwell, 1991.

Ruskin, John. "The Queen's Garden," In *Sesame and Lilies.* New York: Thomas Y. Crowell, 1889.

Said, Edward W. "Zionism from the Standpoint of Its Victims" [1979]. Reprinted in *Dangerous Liaisons: Gender, Nation, and Postcolonial Perspectives,* eds Anne McClintock, Aamir Mufti, and Ella Shohat. Minneapolis: University of Minnesota Press, 1997.

Samson, G.W. *"To Daimonion," or the Spiritual Medium.* Boston: Gould and Lincoln, 1852.

Schneider, Herbert Wallace, and George Lawton. *A Prophet and a Pilgrim.* New York: Columbia University Press, 1942.

Searcher after truth, pseudo. *The Rappers: or, The Mysteries, Fallacies, and Absurdities of Spirit-Rapping, Table-Tipping, and Entrancement.* New York: H. Long and Brother, 1854.

Sears, Hal D. *The Sex Radicals: Free Love in High Victorian America.* Lawrence: Regents Press of Kansas, 1977.

Sedgwick, Eve Kosofsky. *Touching Feeling: Affect, Pedagogy, Performativity.* Durham: Duke University Press, 2003.

Shelley, Percy Bysshe. "The Sensitive Plant," in *The Complete Poems of Percy Bysshe Shelley.* New York: Modern Library, 1994: 627–34.

Silberman, Neil Asher. *Digging for God and Country: Exploration, Archeology, and the Secret Struggle for the Holy Land. 1799–1917.* New York: Knopf, 1982.

Silliman, R.H. "Fresnel and the Emergence of Physics as a Discipline," *Historical Studies in the Physical Sciences* 4 (1974): 137–62.

Spencer, Herbert. *The Study of Sociology.* New York: Appleton, 1875.

Spinoza, Benedictus de. *Chief Works,* tran. R.H.M. Elwes, rev. edn London: Bell, 1900–1903.

Stapleton, Julia, ed. *Liberalism, Democracy and the State in Britain: Five Essays 1862–1891.* Bristol: Thoemmes Press, 1997.

Swedenborg, Emanuel. *The Spiritual Diary of Emanuel Swedenborg,* trans. George Bush, ed. Samuel Beswick. Boston: Henry H. and J.W. Carter, 1877.

————. *Heaven, and Its Wonders, and Hell; from Things Heard and Seen,* trans. John C. Ager. Westchester: Swedenborg Foundation, 1995.

Sword, Helen. "Necrobibliography: Books in the Spirit World." *Modern Language Quarterly* 60:1 (March 1999): 85–112.

Taylor, M.W. *Men versus the State: Herbert Spencer and Late Victorian Individualism.* Oxford: Clarendon Press, 1992.

Thomas, Annie [Mrs Pender Cudlip]. *No Medium.* London: F.V. White, 1885.

Thurschwell, Pamela. "George Eliot's Prophecies: Coercive Second Sight and Everyday Thought Reading." In *The Victorian Supernatural,* eds Nicola Bown, Carolyn Burdett, and Pamela Thurschwell. Cambridge: Cambridge University Press, 2004: 87–105.

————. *Literature, Technology and Magical Thinking, 1880–1920.* Cambridge: Cambridge University Press, 2001.

Traill, H.D., ed. *Social England, A Record of the Progress of the People in Religion, Laws, Learning, Arts, Industry, Commerce, Science, Literature, and Manners, from the Earliest Times to the Present Day.* Vol. 1, 11, 1909.

Trollope, Anthony. *The Eustace Diamonds.* Garden City, NY: Doubleday, 1951.

Tromp, Marlene. "Spirited Sexuality: Sex, Marriage, and Victorian Spiritualism." *Victorian Literature and Culture* (2003): 67–81.

Tucker, Robert C., ed. *Marx-Engels Reader*, 2nd edn. New York: Norton, 1978.

Turner, Paul. *English Literature, 1832–1890, Excluding the Novel.* Oxford: Clarendon Press, 1989.

Tweed, Thomas A. *The American Encounter with Buddhism, 1844–1912: Victorian Culture & the Limits of Dissent.* Chapel Hill: University of North Carolina Press, 2000.

Vera Vincent, or the Testimony of T.M. Simkiss of Wolverhampton, to the Truth of Spiritualism. Wolverhampton: E. Roden, 1869.

Viswanathan, Gauri. *Outside the Fold: Conversion, Modernity and Belief.* Princeton: Princeton University Press, 1998.

————. "The Ordinary Business of Occultism." *Critical Inquiry* 27 (Autumn 2000): 1–20.

Waisbrooker, Lois. *Suffrage for Women: The Reasons Why.* St Louis: Clayton and Babington, 1868.

————. *Alice Vail: A Story for the Times.* Boston, 1869.

————. *Helen Harlow's Vow.* Boston, 1870. University of Michigan Graduate Serials/Microfilm, microfilm.

————. *Mayweed Blossoms.* Boston, 1871. University of Michigan Graduate Serials/Microfilm, microfilm.

————. *Nothing Like It, or Steps to the Kingdom.* Boston, 1875. University of Michigan Graduate Serials/Microfilm, microfilm.

————. *Sex Revolution*, intro. Pam McAllister. Philadelphia: New Society, 1985.

————. *The Fountain of Life, or, The Threefold Power of Sex.* Topeka, KS: Independent Publishing, 1893.

————. *Anything More, My Lord.* N.p., 1895.

————. *My Century Plant.* Topeka, KS: Independent Publishing, 1896.

————. *A Woman's Source of Power.* N.p., 1902. University of Michigan Special Collections, microfilm.

————. *Bible Truth Bursting Its Shell That It May Express Its Larger Meaning.* N.p., n.d. [Chicago, Center Research for Libraries: CRL A–10613, Cat. C].

————. *Clothed with the Sun.* N.p., n.d.

————. *From Generation to Regeneration; The Sex Question and the Money Powers; and the Tree of Life between Two Thieves: Three Pamphlets on the Occult Forces of Sex.* N.p., 1891, University of Michigan Special Collections Library, microfilm.

————. *Foundation Principles.* Clinton, Iowa: n.p., n.d. University of Michigan Special Collections, microfilm.

Ward, Mrs Humphry [Mary Arnold Ward]. *Robert Elsmere.* London, New York: Macmillan, 1888.

Washington, Peter. *Madame Blavatsky's Baboon: A History of the Mystics, Mediums, and Misfits Who Brought Spiritualism to America.* New York: Shocken Books, 1995.

Watson, George, ed. *The New Cambridge Bibliography of English Literature*, Vol. 3. Cambridge: Cambridge University Press, 1969.

Watson, Sydney. *The Lure of a Soul (Bewitched by Spiritualism).* London: William Nicholson and Sons, 1915.

Webb, R.K. *Harriet Martineau: A Radical Victorian.* New York: Columbia University Press, 1960.

Welton, Thomas. *Fascination; or the Art of Electro-Biology, Mesmerism, and Clairvoyance, Familiarly Explained, With Cases for Reference.* London: Job Caudwell, 1865.

Winter, Alison. *Mesmerized: The Powers of Mind in Victorian Britain.* Chicago: University of Chicago Press, 1998.

Wintle, Justin, ed. *Makers of Nineteenth Century Culture, 1800–1914.* London: Routledge and Kegan Paul, 1982.

Young, Robert J.C. *Postcolonialism: An Historical Introduction.* Malden, MA: Blackwell, 2001.

Zerffi, G.G. *Spiritualism and Animal Magnetism. A Treatise on Dreams, Second Sight, Somnambulism, Magnetic Sleep, Spiritual Manifestations, Hallucinations, and Spectral Visions.* London: Robert Hardwicke, 1871.

Zillah, the Child Medium: A Tale of Spiritualism: By the Author of 'My Confession: The Story of a Woman's Life,' etc. New York: Dix, Edwards, 1857.

Zoist 11 (March 1853). London: Walton and Mitchell, 1853.

Zoist: A Journal of Cerebral Physiology & Mesmerism and Their Applications to Human Welfare. 12 (April 1854–January 1855). London: Hippolyte Bailliere, 1855.

Index